THE AMERICAN

Diaries

OF RICHARD COBDEN

Portrait of Cobden by Lowes Dickinson

T H E
American Diaries
O F
RICHARD
COBDEN

EDITED, WITH AN INTRODUCTION

AND NOTES, BY

ELIZABETH HOON CAWLEY

GREENWOOD PRESS, PUBLISHERS
NEW YORK

TO MY HUSBAND

ROBERT RALSTON CAWLEY

PREFACE

$\mathcal{G}_N$ 1835 and 1859 Richard Cobden visited the United States. On each of these trips he kept a diary of his activities and of his impressions of American life. These diaries, which remained in the possession of the Cobden family until they were acquired by the British Museum in 1934, have never been published. It is the purpose of this book to make them available.

Cobden belonged to a period in the earlier part of which there existed considerable prejudice against America, a prejudice fostered partly by unfair accounts of various European travelers who were inclined to behold the raw new world with some amusement and some contempt. Cobden, on the other hand, was one of those rare travelers who interpret people and conditions in terms of their own native standards or with reference to parallel classes and conditions elsewhere with which alone they can be compared. His reactions were those of an unprejudiced, yet critical and discerning mind, intent upon seeking the truth. A keen observer, Cobden took care in gathering his facts and drawing proper conclusions. Such judgments were tempered by a generosity of spirit which cordially recognized and warmly appreciated the best in American institutions and society. Penetrating below superficial irregularities in behavior, which were the matters too often emphasized by other travelers in the early decades of the nineteenth century, Cobden valued the intrinsic worth of America as he found it expressed in its democratic government, its educational opportunities, its social equality, its phenomenal material prosperity, and its limitless promise of growth, development, and progress. A man of liberal sympathies, he understood the spirit of the people—their courage in carving out the frontiers of their land and society, "their aspirations toward humane institutions and right living," and their faith in their future.

Cobden did not write the diaries for publication. The records were for his own personal use, and he expresses himself candidly. As he was not obliged to appeal to popular taste or quick sales, his estimates are therefore honest. However abrupt in style—and this is especially true of the notation form of the 1835 diary—the entries at least record uncalculated first impressions. They are trustworthy glimpses of Americans and their ways, as observed by an intelligent, fair-minded, genial person. Of the two descriptions of the United States, the one for 1859, recording the longer visit and composed after many years of wide experience in national affairs, is the more important. The journal of 1835 possesses marked interest for its own sake, but its chief value lies in a comparison with the later account, which shows the vast changes that had taken place in America during the intervening twenty-four years.

Notable changes had also taken place in the life of Cobden himself; and from this second consideration as well the diaries are of significance. When the journal of 1835 was written, Cobden was thirty-one, a relatively unknown business man. Even at this date, however, he was showing evidences of many of his later interests. The diary records familiarity with the new world and impressions of certain elements in it which during the next quarter of a century were to influence greatly some of his attitudes toward governmental policy and social conditions in England. The journal of 1859, at the hand of the mature and distinguished English statesman, reveals something of the development of the man. Cobden's remarks make even clearer the reasons why he took so favorable a position toward America during the middle and last years of his life, and explain in particular why he, among others, played so prominent a part in behalf of England's neutrality during the American Civil War. Since relatively few of Cobden's private papers have been published, the diaries may help to make possible a clearer understanding of the kind of man Cobden was. Although the diaries themselves do not furnish a great deal of new or striking information, they constitute additional source material of a kind to aid in a more accurate interpretation of American life and of Cobden himself.

Finally, the diaries may serve purposes not generally included among the more orthodox ones offered in explanation of the reproducing of historical documents. Cobden, true first to his own country, was a true friend of America; and at this time when the two great English-speaking peoples are drawn more closely together than ever, there is value in reading his estimate of the new world. Some of Dawson's words of a generation ago are even more apt today: "Independently of its influence on contemporary thought, nearly everything he said about America and the Americans still has interest for its own sake, and much of it is particularly opportune at the present time, when the two nations are thrown upon one another as never before, and stand before the decision whether they shall face together and accomplish for the world, as they alone can, a work of peace and civilization which otherwise may remain long unfulfilled."[1] Furthermore, perusal of the journals forces a constant awareness of many of the alterations which have taken place in the national character during the last one hundred years. While some thoughtful Americans may be distressed at certain evidences of moral decline, they may be heartened by the tested strength of many of their social, economic, and political institutions, founded on a democratic government and way of life.

Both of the journals are in the manuscript division of the British Museum, together with the vast bulk of Cobden correspondence and other Cobden items. The diary of 1835, listed as Additional Manuscripts 43807, is contained in part

[1] William H. Dawson, *Richard Cobden and Foreign Policy*, London, 1926, pp. 229-230.

in a small, green, leatherbound notebook, marked under 43807 as A, and in part in loose sheets filed in two envelopes which are catalogued as 43807 B. At the end of the journal, on the last of these separate papers, are Cobden's descriptions of some of his fellow passengers of the return voyage, sketches which are not without a certain literary charm. The later diary of 1859 is known as Additional Manuscripts 43808. It likewise begins in a somewhat larger, plum-colored notebook, listed as A, and is continued on loose sheets, catalogued as B.

Apart from the opening memoranda in the diary of 1835, both diaries were written in ink. In the earlier account Cobden obviously altered a word here and there with pencil, alterations which have since been traced in ink, probably by another person. Cobden generally recorded his observations in a neat hand, particularly in the first journal where the writing is so small at times as to render it somewhat difficult reading. His script for the most part is legible. Occasionally where doubt has arisen as to the intended spelling of a word, I have used question marks, but such cases are relatively few. The diaries are here published exactly as they stand in the original. Nothing has been omitted. Cobden's spelling and capitalization have been retained throughout. (In order not to clutter the text with *sic*, Cobden's misspellings have been allowed to stand without so noting them.[2]) Punctuation and even sentence spacing in as far as practicable, remain the same. The only changes made in preparing the diaries for publication have been the deletion of punctuation under superior letters and the setting of the dates of the entries on

---

[2] In most instances where Cobden misspells a name, it will be found correctly spelled nearby, in the text or in a footnote. The only exceptions to this are the words: Bradocks, Merrimark, Robbins, Brittania, Sarratoga, Van Rensa(e)ller, Ottowa, Montmorenci.

The common words which he misspells (sometimes in a lone case by a slip of the pen, at other times, repeatedly) are: taciturity, flower (for flour), use (for us), employd, returing, volums, agreable, hymed, lightening, awakend, compliment (for complement), exhiliration, trowsers, visiter, smaking, elligible, chace, anedote, sowing (for sewing), continues (for continuous), births (for berths), irresistable.

the left-hand side (where Cobden himself often placed them) and italicizing them in order that they may be noted more readily.

The purpose of the Introduction is two-fold: to interpret the diaries, and to indicate briefly what Cobden thought of America at the times of his visits there and during the years between, as revealed for the most part from his unpublished correspondence. Because such allusions in his printed speeches and publications are available elsewhere, they have not been included in this study. What America thought of Cobden and the whole story of his relations with her particularly during the Civil War, after his last journey there, are separate investigations which cannot be undertaken here. Notes in identification mainly of persons Cobden met have been kept as short as possible since their purpose is not that of historical sketches but rather to help make the diaries more intelligible. In several instances the comparative unimportance of the person referred to did not justify notes; in a number of cases Cobden himself includes enough information to "place" the person; and in a few other instances it was not deemed necessary to identify persons who are well known. More, however, of this last category have been included than might normally be, since English readers cannot be expected to be familiar with numerous figures of nineteenth-century American history.

The preparation of this edition has been aided by many friends. The late Mrs. Cobden Unwin, Cobden's last surviving daughter, kindly granted me permission to reproduce the diaries and to supplement them with pertinent sections from the unpublished correspondence. She was also helpful in acquainting me with Cobden in her entertaining reminiscences from time to time. Professor Hugh Hale Bellot of the University of London generously mentioned the existence of the journals in the British Museum and suggested their publication; the late Professor Arthur P. Newton, also of the University of London, made valuable suggestions affecting the treatment; and Professors Robert G. Albion of Harvard and Paul W. Gates of Cornell kindly gave me some very useful information, the latter loaning me the map of the Illinois Central Railroad which is reprinted in this volume. I am greatly indebted to Mr. Datus Smith, Director of the Princeton University Press, for his cooperation in so faithful a reproduction of the original texts and to Miss Harriet Anderson for her care in the editorial work. In addition, I should like to express my appreciation to the following institutions: to The American Philosophical Society for its grant which made possible the completion of the project; to the Cobden Club, represented by Mr. Francis W. Hirst, for the privilege of staying at Dunford House (Cobden's old home at Midhurst, Sussex) and of using its library and other facilities; and to the British Museum for the courteous assistance of its officials at all times. Finally, I am deeply grateful to my husband for his inspiring helpfulness and loyal support throughout the course of the work, and to my small daughter for her infinite understanding and patience.

ELIZABETH HOON CAWLEY

Princeton, New Jersey
May 27, 1952

CONTENTS

ILLUSTRATIONS

INTRODUCTION
TO THE AMERICAN
Diaries
OF RICHARD COBDEN

"*Sir James Clark asked me my opinion as to the policy of giving letters in place of narrative— In my judgment the most interesting form of biography is that of autobiography— & next to that is the plan of allowing the subject to speak for himself through letters or conversations— The reader will generally make his own criticisms & reflections, with little aid from the compiler.*" Cobden to George Combe, November 25, 1848, Additional Manuscripts 43653, Part 5.

I · RICHARD COBDEN

*". . . His name will be cherished here as in England.
History will be for him more than Westminster Abbey."*
Charles Sumner to John Bright, April 18, 1865, *Memoir
and Letters of Charles Sumner,* edited by Edwin L.
Pierce, IV, 239.

*R*ICHARD COBDEN has been variously condemned by his
opponents as a bourgeois politician, an unsound economist, a misguided internationalist, a visionary idealist. To
ardent admirers, on the other hand, Cobden has been an
apostle credited with an economic system by which prosperity might be automatically achieved, and endowed with a
philosophy of internationalism by which all peoples might
henceforth live together in Utopia. Such ideas, in perhaps less
exaggerated form, have only too often effectively obscured
the real Richard Cobden.

Actually, "the greatest English statesman of the nineteenth
century of those who never held ministerial office"[1] he devoted his life to the advancement of social progress, national
prosperity, and international goodwill. Toward these ends
he worked for education and political and financial reform,
fought for free trade, and labored for peace. He was far in
advance of his times in his enthusiastic support of many of
those fundamental policies which undergird international
cooperation. His understanding of the basic principles of
interstate relations, his informed and unprejudiced attitude
toward other nations, and his wholehearted sympathy with
humanity at large render him a position unique among the
statesmen of his age. Though at times he may have been limited in political vision and mistaken in some of his economic

[1] See Ian Bowen, *Cobden,* London, 1935, p. 9. Cobden was offered but declined cabinet appointment.

and political theories and in his means for achieving his ends, his ideas were basically sound and his highest ideals were those which thoughtful men of today recognize as vital to a civilized world order.

Richard Cobden was born the son of a farmer in the hamlet of Heyshott, Sussex, in 1804. During his early years his father became steadily poorer and finally when Richard was twelve, the family of eleven children had to be divided among relatives. Richard was sent by an uncle to a poor school in Yorkshire, where he suffered for some years in a drab, grim environment. From this disagreeable life he went to work for his uncle in London, there to learn the mysteries of the cloth trade, as a clerk in the London office and later as a salesman on the road. With ambition fired by travel, he and two friends in 1828 established their own business selling calicoes for Manchester manufacturers. So successful were the young partners that three years later they set up their own calico-printing factory not far from Manchester. By the time Richard was twenty-eight, he was the head of a business so prosperous that it became possible for him to turn his attention to other issues which had begun to interest him greatly.

During these years, to keenness of mind, sound practical thinking, imagination, and optimism was constantly added a fund of knowledge gleaned through self-directed study of Latin, French, and mathematics, and the reading of history, literature, political writings, and newspapers. Travel in England, France, and Switzerland led him to think along broad lines, examining his own society—its sources of weakness and power—and studying other nations with reference to it, more particularly the United States. Some of the beliefs which were later to become his guiding principles found expression in his first significant pamphlet, *England, Ireland, and America*, published in 1835, and in a pamphlet on Russia printed shortly after. In 1835, gratifying a long-standing wish, Cobden visited the United States. The journey revealed to him the real and potential strength of America and inspired him with an unbounded faith in her future. In addition it marked the beginning of that period of his life which was to be devoted to public affairs. A trip to Egypt and Eastern Europe in 1836-1837 and to Germany the year after acquainted him with the peoples of those countries and their problems. In the meantime he engaged in active public service: these years witnessed his defeat as a candidate for Parliament; but they also witnessed his efforts to institute national elementary education, his municipal work in behalf of the incorporation of Manchester and the establishment of the Manchester Athenaeum, and his success in enlarging the Anti-Corn Law Association in Manchester into the great Anti-Corn Law League to effect total repeal of the Corn Laws.

England at this time was living under a burdensome system of protective tariffs. Exorbitant taxes on food and industry kept up a high cost of living for the masses and at the same time closed foreign markets to English manufactures. The result was destitution throughout the country caused by high prices, low wages, and unemployment. Cobden early perceived that the Corn Laws constituted "the keystone of the arch of protection."[2] To abolish these duties, thereby alleviating distress, weakening the hold of the powerful landed interests, and liberating trade, he and his coworkers fought for eight years. Cobden's election to Parliament in 1841, and John Bright's support of the cause and his subsequent election to Parliament, strengthened their hands. Cobden soon became the leader of the movement, organizing appeals directly to the people, himself engaging in numerous public meetings up and down the land, and contending for repeal in convincing parliamentary debate. In 1846 the duties were abolished, with the provision that in three years the ports would be opened entirely. The repeal of the Corn Laws

[2] Francis W. Hirst, *The Repeal of the Corn Laws*, issued by The Cobden Club, Dunford House, Midhurst, 1946.

signified the end of the old mercantile order and inaugurated the great era of Free Trade under which Britain achieved a new prosperity. It was a significant milestone in the long history of political and economic reform.[3]

The end of the Corn Law agitation found Cobden in extreme financial embarrassment. He had married some years earlier, and by this time had assumed the responsibilities of a family of four. During the struggle he had sacrificed business affairs to what he conceived to be his first duty; and the resultant ruin overwhelmed him. His fortunes were saved, fittingly enough, by a large sum of money raised by popular subscription and presented to him as a symbol of the esteem in which his services were held. His business, however, was not all that suffered; the long fight had taken its toll upon health as well, and Cobden found it advisable to go with his wife to the Continent for a respite of over a year. The honor which he was accorded on this trip by rulers and statesmen of the principal European countries, upon whom he constantly urged his policy of free trade, was a tribute to an eminent man and a notable achievement.

Upon his return to England, Cobden took his seat in Parliament for the West Riding, which he held for the next ten years. During the earlier part of that period he devoted himself to the enthusiastic support of many domestic reforms. He made numerous speeches both in and out of Parliament in behalf of free, universal, elementary education, acting at the head of the National Public School Association for a time. Wishing to secure a wider, more democratic, and informed participation in government, he supported the proposals for the abolition of the "taxes on knowledge," particularly of the newspaper tax, and the institution of a penny postage, and, with some reservations, favored the causes of electoral reform, secret voting, and the short duration of Parliament. He labored hardest, however, in the pursuit of improved international relations and peace. He helped or-

[3] *Ibid.*

ganize or took a prominent part in most of the international peace congresses held during these years, and at one time largely directed the activities of the National Peace Society. He pressed ceaselessly for disarmament, which would not only improve foreign relations but at the same time effect a reduction in domestic expenditure. He pleaded for arbitration, and had the satisfaction of seeing an arbitration clause included in the treaty at the end of the Crimean War. A consistent opponent of the government's foreign policy, he protested against highhanded dealings with weak states, denounced intervention in foreign disputes, and opposed the Chinese and Crimean Wars. Three pamphlets written during this time, and shortly after, attacked these tendencies. Perhaps more than any other man at this period, Cobden realized the importance of cultivating friendly relations with the United States. Through his knowledge of the country and through meetings and correspondence with his American friends, he did everything in his power to assist them in ways of diplomacy and to interpret that nation to his own people.

Meantime, in his opposition to the Crimean War Cobden had become unpopular with his countrymen, caught up as they were by the war spirit of the times. Though he carried a vote of censure against Palmerston's government in connection with the Chinese War in 1857, at the national election in the autumn of that year he was defeated, and many of his friends with him. This political set-back was one of several blows that fell heavily on Cobden at this time. The year before he had lost his fifteen-year-old son, the only boy among his five children; and a short time later, his close friend, John Bright, experienced a serious physical and mental breakdown. Financial troubles added their burden. Land investments near Manchester had proved unprofitable; and constant calls on an extensive investment in Illinois Central Railroad stock were placing him in straitened circumstances. After two years of retirement, he determined to make his second trip to America, drawn by his interest in the country and by his anxiety as to the exact condition of the Illinois affairs. On this visit his dreams of the progress of the United States were more than fulfilled, and his mind was put at rest on the state of the railroad.

When Cobden returned to England, he was surprised to find that he had been elected to Parliament for Rochdale. Moreover, the policy of the preceding ministry had been so discredited that there was awaiting him an offer from Palmerston of the position of President of the Board of Trade, with a seat in the Cabinet. Consistency in political conduct, fear of having to compromise on basic principles, and the belief that his greatest services could be rendered outside the Cabinet obliged Cobden to refuse the honor, despite the encouragement of his friends. It was perhaps well that he saw so clearly, for it was not only outside the Cabinet but outside Parliament as well that he executed his second great piece of work, the Anglo-French Commercial Treaty of 1860.

Before this time France had a tariff system which enforced not only high protection but prohibition as well. Could French markets be opened to more British exports and her duties reduced, with a reciprocal reduction of British duties on French goods, not only would the trade and industry of both nations be expanded but diplomatic relations, which had been strained, might be greatly improved. In 1859-1860 Cobden, as Britain's representative, together with the responsible French statesmen, negotiated the treaty which committed Britain to free trade and reduced prohibitive French tariffs to reasonable rates. Impressed by the results, the chief European governments, over the next decade, broke down long-standing trade barriers[4] to effect the greatest freedom of trade that the new commercial era had ever known. In recognition of his success, Cobden was offered a baronetcy or a privy-counselorship, both of which he declined.

[4] Arthur Louis Dunham, *The Anglo-French Treaty of Commerce of 1860 and the Progress of the Industrial Revolution in France*, Ann Arbor, 1930, pp. 141-142.

The last few years of Cobden's life found him still in Parliament, an even more bitter opponent of Palmerston's foreign policy. Those were the years of the American Civil War; and Cobden may be ranked as one of those most influential in preserving British neutrality despite widespread pro-South sympathy and several crises which threatened to embroil the two nations in hostilities. Through constant correspondence, Cobden informed his American friends, more particularly Sumner, Chairman of the Foreign Relations Committee, and through him Lincoln, of the state of British opinion and advised them on procedure. At the same time, he sought to enlighten his countrymen and cabinet ministers on the implications of the war and the dangers inherent in Britain's policy toward America. In connection with these efforts he continued to urge disarmament and the reform of maritime law. Cobden did not live to witness the complete triumph of the North. Although in poor health, in March of 1865 he undertook the arduous trip from Midhurst to London in bitter weather to participate in a Parliamentary debate on a plan of Canadian fortification[5] which would strain relations with the United States once again. He was stricken with acute bronchitis and died on April second.

Whatever may be said of Cobden, no statesman of his time gave himself more unselfishly to the welfare of his fellowmen. He did not stop with national boundaries, but extended his efforts to include the interests of humanity as a whole. The significant ends of practically all of his domestic labors were a real internationalism and peace. He believed that free trade would promote good will among peoples, that it would foster common interests which would draw the nations together. Although he somewhat over-estimated the pacific influence of individual material interests and economic intercourse on international relations,[6] his principles were essen-

[5] Cobden was stricken before he could engage in the debate.

[6] William Cunningham, *Richard Cobden and Adam Smith*, London, 1904, p. 12; also pp. 11-13, 14, 17, 19, 20; John A. Hobson, *Richard Cobden The International Man*, London, 1918, pp. 401, 406, also 400-404.

tially right. In addition, non-intervention, non-imperialism, reform of maritime law, arbitration, and disarmament were all parts of that broader internationalism and peace which Cobden visualized and which today remain one of the world's noblest ideals. As has been fittingly remarked, Cobden's life was "a thorough consecration of great powers and opportunities to the service of mankind."

II · THE DIARY OF 1835

"Who can foresee the future power & greatness of that Country if its moral growth should only be commensurate with its material progress." Cobden to Henry Ashworth, July 13, 1857, Additional Manuscripts 43648, Part 2.

C OBDEN was thirty-one when he made his first trip to America. For some time he had been interested in the new nation. He had read much about it and had even chosen to consider it in his first important published work,[1] in which he analyzed the resources of America's strength and declared her England's model and rival. One of his brothers, Henry, was in America at this time, and his experiences there had heightened Cobden's interest. Further, in trips to France and Switzerland Cobden had already tasted foreign travel and liked it. Possessed as he was of unbounded vitality, earnest mental eagerness, and an adventurous spirit, it was therefore a natural thing for him, though comparatively unusual for the times, that he should decide upon a trip to America for a much needed holiday.

The journey in point of time was short. Cobden left Manchester for Liverpool on May 1, 1835, and disembarked at Liverpool on August 16, having spent only the period from June 7 to July 16 actually in America. Even so, he covered an almost unbelievable amount of territory. His route took him by way of New York, Philadelphia, Baltimore, Washington, west to Pittsburgh, north to Youngstown, Conneaut, and Buffalo, east through Utica and Albany to Boston, and back to New York by way of Providence; and in addition there were several side-trips to nearby points of interest. By his

---

[1] *England, Ireland, and America,* 1835. It is not certain whether the pamphlet had been completed at the time of the trip. That it had already been projected is clear from Cobden's memorandum in the back of the diary to send a copy of it to an American friend.

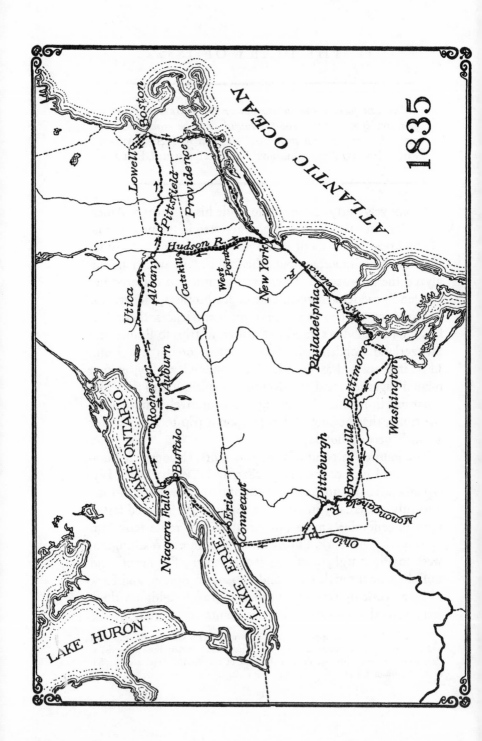

own estimate, Cobden covered 9,036 miles in three and a half months.[2]

When transportation depended almost entirely on sailing-ship, stagecoach, and boat, and only rarely on steam-trains, which were woefully inefficient, Cobden's journey became something of an achievement. Most of his stops during his travels in the States were for one night only; many a time after a long day of travel he drew into a town in late afternoon or evening, saw what he could of the place—even managing a theatre occasionally—and left early the next morning, sometimes before dawn. In a few instances he traveled all night in the coach. Apart from New York, the only places where Cobden spent more than one day or night were Niagara Falls, Albany, a Catskill resort, and Boston. Cobden's reactions on his first trip to America were essentially those of a tourist; he wanted to see as much as could be seen in a limited period of time. His observations, therefore, are frequently surface impressions, though more penetrating and more accurate than those of the average English tourist, because of the interpretations of his brother and some of his friends and his own good judgment.

Cobden was fortunate in having the company of his brother Henry throughout most of the tour. Henry welcomed him to New York, drove him into the country north of the city on his first day there, accompanied him to various places when they returned to New York, and saw him off on the *Britannia* when he sailed for England. Friends helped to make pleasant his stay in several centers. Warren, his fellow-passenger on the *Britannia*, extended warm hospitality in Boston. Entertainment by the Hardys and Burtsells in New York consisted of dinners and teas, an excursion on Long Island, and visits to important municipal institutions and other places of note. Both Hardy and Burtsell were among those who saw him to his ship when he departed. He met

---

[2] The calculation is probably not far wrong; the excessive figure of 3,500 miles for the distance between New York and Liverpool applied to the passage of a sailing-vessel.

many other Americans personally through calls which he made on them; of these, Cassidy of Albany, Prince of Lowell, and Leslie of Westpoint were especially kind to him.[3] The companionship and often very real friendship which he enjoyed with some of his fellow travelers are a tribute to Cobden. In New York he is to be found in the company of his fellow passengers, Hunt (of both voyages) and Grover (of the return trip), and of Waite (captain of the *Britannia*). Dawson of Brownsville, Pennsylvania, and Graham of Pittsburgh were with him on coach and boat respectively and showed him around their towns on arrival. He spent part of his days at Niagara with Cunningham and Church. Warren of Boston has been mentioned. But his association during his days in Boston with Wilsone of Glasgow was the most pleasant. Cobden found in him "more amiability of heart than almost any other man of equal knowledge & talent that I have had the enjoyment of associating with."

The diary is marked by a freshness and buoyancy. With his natural, youthful enthusiasms, the traveler found everything to his interest. As might be expected, his comments on the ladies are vivid. On his first day in New York he was "struck with the pallid & unhealthy complexion of the American ladies who are too thin for my taste   the females generally are *petite* but elegant – deficient in bust & *bustle.* . . ." The Boston women he thought "decidedly prettier than those of New York but still deficient in *preface* & *postcript.*" At breakfast at Westpoint he saw "the only truly handsome girl I have met in America." Enquiring of the landlord of the hotel, he found "this lovely creature to be the daughter of an *English* gentleman. . . ." With that disillusionment the comments on girls end. It is a young man who enjoys beauty and good times who considers "N. Yk the pleasantest situation in the U. States & perhaps in the world in respect to the

---

[3] Among those mentioned in addition are: Lee, Vietor, Robins, Watt, Dixon, and Steele in New York; Brown, Oldfield, and Miss Lemmon in Baltimore; Morfit in Washington; the Horners in Albany; Lowell in Boston; the Lymans in Nahant.

surrounding attractions & facilities for making excursions of health or pleasure." A certain charming naiveté is evident occasionally. Here was a person very serious in his thirty-first birthday resolution "to break myself of an old and ridiculous habit of biting my lips and cheeks in which I have been for twenty years foolishly accustomed [?] to indulge when in cogitating moods. . . ." Now and then Cobden appears to experience embarrassment in meetings with individual Americans. Although, like many travelers of the period, he was impressed with the patriotic egotism among the people, in a few instances he seems personally to have been somewhat uncomfortable in the presence of some of these strangers. In Boston he delivered cards of introduction to several people who "all impress me with the belief in the universality of egotism in this nation – Mr Lowell a warm hearted man though with a cold shake of the hand"; Mr. Thomas Dixon of New York he did "not consider to be too warmly polite."

The diary reveals a young gentleman of some culture. Cobden takes pleasure in conversation with intelligent men; he shows an interest in and knowledge of some contemporary writers, even making an excursion to the scene of *Rip Van Winkle*; he takes care to secure names of important books to buy; he attends the theatre in various cities; he shows discrimination in his comments on art and architecture; he is constantly comparing and contrasting American scenes with their counterparts in Europe. He writes clearly; in a few instances his descriptive passages achieve vivid expression. Of these, his character sketches of fellow passengers on the *Britannia* are among the best. Sensitivity and exuberance of spirit are evident throughout. Perhaps they find their most picturesque expression in his observations on Niagara Falls, which made Cobden "thank God that has bestowed on me health time & means for reaching this spot & the spirit to kindle at the spectacle before me!" It is a person of intense feeling who finds a terrifying thunderstorm "a more sublime sight than I ever before saw."

Independent of mind, unprejudiced, critical and discerning, Cobden usually appraises a situation clearly and analyzes it fairly. Of high personal integrity and fine sensibilities, equable and amiable, he shows swift insight into human nature, sympathy with it, and balanced judgments. Resourcefulness, tolerance, humor, and a fine generosity of spirit are abundantly indicated in his comments on individuals and on features of American society. Long, tiring days, poor accommodations, and crude company were taken in his stride. (It was not until Cobden waited for his coach three hours in the middle of the night at Youngstown that he confesses "[I] lose my temper for the first time in America in consequence!") It was an idealistic young man who found the model Auburn state prison "the most interesting sight after Niagara that I have been shewn in America," and who, on arrival in Pennsylvania, feelingly exclaimed, "Thank God I am no longer in the country of slaves." It is a young man fully aware of his responsibilities in the world who, upon visiting an elementary school in New York, vows, "I hereby dedicate myself to the task of promoting the cause of infant schools in England where they may become an instrument for ameliorating the fate of the children working in the factories whose case I fear is beyond the reach of all other remedies."

In many places the diary bears evidence of Cobden's interest in several of those matters which were later to concern him greatly. The practical manufacturer and economist are reflected in his lengthy descriptions of factory conditions. There are detailed notes on hours, wages, workers, and methods of working, and observations on coal mining and related phases of industry. He is constantly comparing labor conditions as he found them with those which he knew in England, invariably to the advantage of the American establishment. He admired the advance along mechanical lines which conserved labor. He was much impressed with the greater future for laborers which equal opportunity and education offered. His economic bent extended itself to an interest in land values and in American emigration into the west, more particularly into Illinois. Doubtless his knowledge of that country and the conditions of its settlement, gleaned through various discussions with traveling companions, influenced him at a later time to buy Illinois railroad stock, an investment which so seriously affected his fortunes as to draw him again to America after twenty-four years. The effectiveness of the New York schools and of the democratic system of education in general stimulated his great interest in that subject; and from his vow he never wholly departed in his efforts to extend in England an educational system modeled on that of the States. Even the opening memorandum of the diary, which refers to the expense of the Gibraltar fortification, sounds the keynote of much of his activity over the next thirty years—disarmament. More immediately, a trip to Spain, Egypt, and the Near East in 1836-1837 was undoubtedly influenced by the recommendation of a Mediterranean trip, recorded in the beginning of the diary.

This, in brief, was the Cobden who undertook the trip of 1835. The conditions under which the journey was made were, on the whole, typical of those which most foreign tourists encountered. June and July brought their usual severe heat; and the Englishman suffered from it. Occasionally storms caused inconvenience. Sailing conditions were characteristic, Cobden's return voyage including "all the dismals of a summer passage, – heat & calms the greatest, & the latter the most intolerable of all. . . ."

If calms delayed him by sea, bad roads, irregular stage schedules, and unperfected railroads delayed him by land. His entries furnish a striking comment on traveling conditions in the States more than a century ago. ". . . the road all the way from Washington to Frederick is execrable & the dexterity with which the drivers carry a coach & four horses over roads that for ruggedness & occasional steepness surpass our Derbyshire cross-roads would be enough to make our

English *jehus* marvel could they behold it." Somewhere between Youngstown and Brookfield the roads were so bad, the passengers were "obliged to walk part of the way." Arriving that evening in Conneaut on Lake Erie, Cobden had "been forty hours in travelling by mail 110 miles."

Stage schedules, sometimes complicated by his own lack of time, proved a hardship. As an extreme example, in going from Washington to Brownsville, Cobden apparently traveled almost continuously from eleven o'clock on a Saturday morning to four o'clock the following Monday afternoon, except for one three-hour wait and short stops. Continuing his journey the next morning by steamboat, he arrived in Pittsburgh some time that day, and left the following morning at four for the forty-hour ride just mentioned, which included only brief stops and the irritating three-hour wait at night in Youngstown. Several times he was obliged to travel all night, as has been noted above, and at other times he reached his destination too late to secure satisfactory lodging.

It was well that Cobden's experiences on early American railroads were limited to a few short rides in the east. The first railroad had been begun within the previous decade; and the little progress that had been made consisted in a few, short, unconnected, local lines which were far from dependable. Several of Cobden's trips by rail must have proved thoroughly disillusioning. Perhaps that part of the journey from Boston to Providence was the worst of these. First, the train was delayed, then Cobden had to get out and walk, and, finally, the carriage caught fire! Cobden concluded, "The Yankees are too much in a hurry to finish things properly before they 'go ahead.'"

Boat transportation was another story. The steamboat had developed in speed and size to a point which impressed the Englishman. One boat was the "largest & handsomest Steamer I have yet seen"; another was a "fast vessel" which went "at a velocity of fifteen miles an hour over & above the three miles an hour of stream"; still another was two hundred and forty feet long!

The spaciousness of many of the boats was one indication of the prodigious numbers of people traveling. The crowds constantly excited Cobden's interest. After noting the many travelers, Cobden was of the opinion in Buffalo, where hotels were crowded, "that there is as much travelling in the States as in all Europe." Despite the fact that enormous hotels were being constructed to accommodate such numbers of travelers, capacity did not keep pace with demand. More than once Cobden encountered unorthodox sleeping arrangements. His first night in Boston was the most disagreeable. Finding the Tremont House full, he complained that he was forced to "go to an inferior place & am nearly devoured by the bugs." The long tables at which everyone ate at the same time were for Cobden, as for other Europeans, a strange experience. He was surprised at these crowds, but more amazed at their behavior: at one dinner "a crowded table which was wholly vacated in 20 minutes   think of sixty persons at an *English* watering place dining & leaving the table in 20 min!"

A certain disregard of generally accepted principles of conduct and indulgence in questionable habits annoyed Cobden as they did other refined people, American and foreign alike. Particularly loathsome was the ubiquitous spitting— Cobden's "one only consolation every one must have spit himself to death before I again visit America." Eavesdropping, Cobden found "a propensity in this country"; and he met his "first specimen of inquisitiveness on landing." The one single characteristic which impressed him more than any other was "the patriotism of the American character exhibited constantly in the praise of the country."[4] Cobden saw so much of this that one can well understand his reaction to the singing of "America" at a Boston Fourth of July cele-

---

[4] In a letter to his brother Frederick, Cobden has much to say about this matter of self-glorification, and his skillful way of handling it with good humor. See John Morley, *The Life of Richard Cobden*, London, 1881, I, 32-34.

bration, – "how the egotism of this people speaks in the use of the pronouns *I* & *my* & *me* in this little composition."

As an Englishman, however, Cobden was well treated. Probably his experience on a boat to Pittsburgh was fairly characteristic: "Extreme civility of all the passengers on board to us when we were known to be English." He could "believe the Americans feel an instinctive attachment & even respect for *'the old Country'* which nothing can obliterate." His comments on many of his traveling companions are extremely complimentary. He found people fundamentally considerate and generally well-behaved: "have never seen an instance of rudeness or of even boisterous familiarity between two citizens since I have been in the States – same respect as ever paid to the ladies." Moreover, they were good-natured. "I have always observed that the Americans are glad to partake in fun & good humor – & they bear raillery well though they are not clever in retorting it."

Casual conversations with fellow travelers seem to have turned for the most part on industrial activity, social conditions, slavery, and "as usual on land investments & internal improvements." Cobden observed "a remarkable alertness on the part of all Americans on the subject of investments in land by which owing to the sudden construction of a railway or by means of a canal project at a particular point vast profits have been realized." In an Ohio coach he found "as in every other company, the slavery blot viewed as an indelible stain upon & a curse to the country – an intelligent old gentleman would prefer the debt of Great Britain to the colored population of the United States – all agree in the hopelessness of any remedy as hitherto proposed." As for politics, Cobden, like Dickens, remarked that politics were rarely discussed in public conveyances.

Cobden's observations as he traveled through the country range from a passing remark to an elaborate description of some point of interest. His most important notes are those dealing with economic matters, the nature of which has been indicated above. But the entire diary is a running commentary on the social scene. His swift impressions of America's chief cities are colorful. Rapid expansion, high prices of land, and superior stores fascinated him in New York. Philadelphia was "a tame & uninteresting Town from the water – but with more appearance of maturity & stability than New York." After visiting New York and Philadelphia, Cobden could say that "Baltimore is the handsomest place I have yet seen – here are the finest monuments – the prettiest girls and the cleanest City in the Union." As for the Capital, Cobden's statement, "Approach to Washington not very remarkable," probably summarized the general impression that the city made. Pittsburgh was bustling and was "probably one day destined to be the largest [city] in America." Buffalo was "a thriving place . . . the principal street superior to any thing in Pittsburgh." Albany, which Cobden saw before Boston, "looks more like an English Town than any place I have seen." "Boston [was] like an English city – the people like the English, & the surrounding towns & counties I find are named after the English places." It was "the only place almost in America where a class of retired people living on their incomes can be found – & the society is accordingly more like that of England than elsewhere in America."

Cobden found his admiration of the nation justified. "My estimate of American character has improved, contrary to my expectations, by this visit," he wrote to his brother Frederick. "Great as was my previous esteem for the qualities of this people, I find myself in love with their intelligence, their sincerity, and the decorous self-respect that actuates all classes. The very genius of activity seems to have found its fit abode in the souls of this restless and energetic race."[5] The resourcefulness and vigor of the Americans appealed to him strongly. He was impressed with their ingenuity and inventive ability which found expression in numerous time and

[5] *Ibid.*, 1, 39, Cobden to Frederick Cobden, July 5, 1835.

labor-saving devices.[6] Many of their institutions represented ideals of social improvement well in advance of Britain. The physical features of the country were magnificent.

... No one has yet done justice to the splendid scenery of America. [Cobden wrote to his brother.] Her lakes, rivers, forests and above all her cataracts are peculiarly her own, and when I think of their superiority to all that we own in the Old World, and, still more, when I recollect that by a mysterious ordinance of their Creator, these were hid from 'learned ken' till modern times, I fell into the fanciful belief that the Western continent was brought forth at a second birth, and intended by nature as a more perfect specimen of her handiwork.[7]

The country itself possessed unlimited possibilities in national wealth. Time and again Cobden breaks into exclamations at its promise. Upon entering New York harbor for the first time he notes, "What beauty will this inner bay of New York present centuries hence when wealth & commerce shall have done their utmost to embellish this scene!" On his trip on Lake Erie he mused, "what could have been the feelings of those first explorers of this continent who after traversing five hundred miles of uninterrupted forests found themselves on the shore of this fresh water ocean! – what a sublime idea would it convey of the magnitude of that continent which contained within its bounds such a lake, and what food for the imagination in the unknown regions beyond it!" Upon passing over the last summit of the Alleghenies and looking out upon the Mississippi valley, his enthusiasm became fervor, "here will one day center the civilization, the wealth, the power of the entire world." Summing up his observations near the end of his tour, Cobden wrote to his brother:

My journey may be called a real *pleasure* trip, for without an exception or interruption of any kind, I have enjoyed every minute of the too, too short time allowed me for seeing this truly magnificent country. . . . You know I predicted when leaving England for this continent, that I should not find it sufficiently

<hr>

[6] *Ibid.*, I, 39-40.   [7] *Ibid.*, I, 38.

to my taste to relish a sojourn here for life. My feelings in this respect are quite altered. I know of no reasonable ground for an aversion to this country, and none but unreasonable minds could fail to be as happy here as in England, provided friendly attachments did not draw them to the Old country.[8]

These and other statements, both in the diary and in letters to his brother in England, testify vividly to Cobden's enthusiasm over America as he had found it and over its potential greatness. Part of a letter which Cobden wrote to his friend Henry Ashworth, upon the latter's return from a visit to America in 1857, expresses Cobden's feelings about America at the time of his first visit and over twenty years later:[9]

It would indeed give me very great pleasure to have a long chat with you & to hear your account of the U States as they now present themselves to a stranger. – It is only 22 years since I was there, & then I did not find a completed railroad in the interior of the Country. The impression made on me was that the *natural* advantages of that Continent as compared with Europe had not been sufficiently appreciated. The vast sweep of the Country, & its noble lakes & rivers struck me as so superior in magnitude that I sometimes thought of Europe as a mere experiment in world-making on a small scale, whilst the American continent had been reserved for the crowning triumph of creation. – Looking moreover as a political economist at the productive resources of the United States that Country seems equally destined to surpass the old world in population & wealth. – Almost every year they are giving birth to a new State which in extent of rich soil & mineral deposits might compare successfully with one of the kingdoms of Europe. Who can foresee the future power & greatness of that Country if its moral growth should only be commensurate with its material progress. –

[8] *Ibid.*, 1, 38, 40. Cobden rather preferred Washington as a residence, though he also considered Baltimore a possibility.

[9] Add. MSS. 43648, Part 2, Cobden to Ashworth, July 13, 1857. Cobden continued: "On this latter point I am sorry to observe that your report is not altogether favorable. – I am afraid we cannot say much for ourselves in this respect. – As a nation I think we are less 'up' morally to our political & economical elevation than we ever were. – It is true that we have made greater progress in wealth & prosperity during the present generation than at any former period of our history. – The result has been to draw out our less amiable qualities & develop our mere animal propensities instead of leading us to the more active cultivation of our intellectual & moral powers."

III · THE INTERVENING YEARS
1835-1859

"If we force a war on the 20 millions of the Free States *in this their great agony* [the Civil War] *– and there can be no war unless we force it – it will be remembered against us to all future generations.– In the life time of my youngest child, I doubt not those* Free States *will contain 100 millions of prosperous people.– Perhaps it is only one who, like myself, has visited, twice, that region, at an interval of 20 years, that can fully appreciate its solid & rapid progress."* Cobden to Gladstone (when Gladstone was Chancellor of the Exchequer), December 11, 1861, Additional Manuscripts 44136, Gladstone Papers, LI, folios 146-154.

$\mathcal{T}$ HE record of Cobden's interest in America during the twenty-four years between his first and second trips there is a clear indication of what that country was fast coming to mean to him. The whole story of Cobden's regard for the United States, his relations with individual Americans, the ways in which he was influenced by various features of that nation and its society, his support of America's position during periods of strain, more particularly during her Civil War, and his friendship at all times for her would make an elaborate book in itself, only parts of which have been touched upon to some extent by various writers. Examination of the unpublished Cobden papers in the Additional Manuscripts in the British Museum yielded numerous passages showing Cobden's attitude toward America after his first visit there. Although in some instances such passages parallel Cobden's public statements which are to be found in his pamphlets and speeches, since much of the material remains unpublished, brief reference to a few of the more interesting quotations may be justified, more particularly to several of those which refer directly or indirectly to Cobden's stay in America.[1]

The journey of 1835 had inspired Cobden with a profound conviction of the inherent greatness of America. During the next two and a half decades he kept himself closely informed of her progress. As he told George Parkes in 1861, "I have however twice visited the United States after an interval of 25 years, & have given pretty constant attention to its affairs."[2] He read extensively on American matters. He corresponded with Americans; sought them out when they were abroad, and entertained them; and over the greater part of the period, he knew personally the several American ministers to St. James.[3] "Everything I read about the States interests me," he wrote to one friend. Proved right in a disagreement over the cost of the American government, he asserted to another, "I

[1] The Cobden letters quoted or cited throughout the remainder of the Introduction and the Notes, most of which have never been published or used, are in the Additional Manuscripts of the British Museum.

Occasionally in reference to these letters, discrepancy will be found with the bundle number now used. A considerable part of this research was done in 1939; and some changes in the British Museum numbering have been made since then. (For example, a letter from Cobden to Bright of March 25, 1861, was formerly contained in Add. MSS. 43649; it is now in 43651.) Since the letters are still roughly sorted into bundles and remain unbound, with the probability of further changes being made before they are given permanent folio numbers, and since to reexamine the reference numbers for every letter used would involve altogether reexamination of hundreds of letters, the original references of the 1939 research have been retained where used. In the vast majority of instances, they still apply. Individual letters, however, can be found by resorting to the bundle which contains the desired addressee and chronologically selecting the letter of specific date.

In rare instances where the phrase "typed copy" appears in brackets, it does not refer to a copy of the Additional Manuscript cited; rather is the letter itself a typed copy found in the Additional Manuscripts of an original letter probably still retained in private hands.

[2] Add. MSS. 43660 [Part 1], Cobden to Parkes, November 3, 1861.

[3] Cobden had a high opinion of the American envoys. Deploring the "incapacity" of the British minister at Washington, Cobden stated in a letter to Henry Richard, June 1, 1856: "We know who the ministers from the United States to England are, for they send us their most eminent men. – Mr Dallas has been Vice President of the Union – Mr Buchanan has been Foreign Secretary, Mr Bancroft was their first historian, Mr Abbott Lawrence the head of their manufacturing interest, & Mr Everett their most accomplished scholar. These are the men who are sent by America to represent her in England." *Ibid.* 43658, Part 8.

know what I am about in reference to American matters."[4] Writing to Sir Edward Watkin in 1852 he declared, "I have long had my notions about what was coming from the West, and recorded my prophecy on my return from America in 1835. People in England are determined to shut their eyes as long as they can, but they will be startled out of their wilful blindness some day by some gigantic facts proving the indisputable superiority of that country in all that constitutes the power, wealth, and real greatness of a people."[5]

The American system of education was the single achievement which perhaps most impressed Cobden; and upon his return from America, education became the first major social problem in England to which he bent his efforts. Writing to William Tait two years after his visit to the States, he said: "If you travel in that Country every man of whatever shade of politics will avow that his hopes of the permanancy of sound democratic self-government, free from anarchy on the one hand & tyranny on the other, are based entirely upon the great & increasing knowledge of the masses: – education – education – education is the motto of every enlightened democrat in America."[6] Though Cobden's work in behalf of universal education at public expense, begun in Manchester after his return from America, was interrupted by the pressure of the Corn Law fight, it was far from forgotten. Declaring in 1846 after the Corn Law repeal that "education is the only public matter upon which I should be disposed to put on my armour for another 'seven years war',"[7] Cobden increased his earlier efforts. In 1850 he was devoting his great powers to the struggle. He summed up his aspiration in

[4] *Ibid.* 43658, Part 8, Cobden to Richard, November 18, 1853.

[5] Sir Edward W. Watkin, *Alderman Cobden of Manchester*, London, 1891, p. 164. To Sturge Cobden wrote in 1857, "There is hardly an Englishman who does not think it is our mission to regulate the affairs of the whole world. – It is only since another community of Englishmen across the Atlantic have begun to give us a taste of our own quality that John Bull feels the slightest doubt of his omnipotence." Add. MSS. 43722, Bdl. 2, Part 5, Cobden to Sturge, April 15, 1857.

[6] Add. MSS. 43660, Part 2, Cobden to Tait, May 5, 1837.

[7] *Ibid.* 43653, Part 6, Cobden to James Simpson, July 4, 1846 [copy].

a speech at the National Public Schools' Association in Manchester in the autumn of that year:

> You must secure a law which, as in the case of the New England States, as in the State of Massachusetts, for instance, compels every locality or parish to furnish a school and the means of education to the whole of the people, and furnish not merely a building such as our orders in council are now aiming at . . . but to furnish a master under proper control, and the means of giving instruction to the great body of the people in all parts of the country.[8]

The main obstacle to success, by splitting the "reformers," was the religious problem. One section, represented by Cobden, wanted schools as in America to provide purely secular education, leaving religious instruction to the churches. The other "Dissenter" wing, publicized by Baines, insisted on religious teaching as an important part of the curriculum.[9] Despairing of reconciling the two, Cobden finally declared in a letter to George Combe, November 9, 1850: "I shall now go straight at the mark, & shall neither give nor take quarter – I have made up my mind to go for the Massachusetts system as nearly as we can get it."[10] Cobden worked hard. Although immediate hopes of legislation came to nought in 1852,[11] a year later he was still hopeful of "what might be accomplished if something like the American plan were carried out in all the parishes of the kingdom!"[12] He enlisted support of all kinds. He gained Sturge's favorable consideration of the Manchester secular system of education in 1850,[13]

---

[8] Mrs. Salis Schwabe, *Reminiscences of Richard Cobden*, London, 1895, p. 145.

[9] For an excellent short account of Cobden's work, see Simon Maccoby, *English Radicalism, 1832-1852*, London, 1935, pp. 328-330.

[10] Add. MSS. 43653, Part 5, Cobden to Combe, November 9, 1850.

[11] Maccoby, *English Radicalism, 1832-1852*, p. 330.

[12] Add. MSS. 43653, Part 2, Cobden to Combe, December 6, 1853.

[13] *Ibid.* 43722, Bdl. 1, Part 5, Cobden to Sturge, November 2, 1850. See Cobden's letters to Sturge later, in which, while approving of Richard as an editor of the *Star*, he wonders about the wisdom of Richard's selection since Richard favored the Baines group and the *Star* would probably oppose that position. *Ibid.* 43722, Bdl. 2, Part 3, Cobden to Sturge, July 21, 1856; July 25, 1856; *ibid.* 43722, Bdl. 2, Part 4, Cobden to Sturge, November 24, 1856; November 28, 1856.

though Sturge apparently supported the Dissenter view for some time.[14] Early in 1854 Cobden was scolding Bright: "You must take sides on the Education question. – You can't take a neutral part – or a lukewarm attitude. – Is not the time come to declare for the New England system?"[15] During these years Cobden was pointing to the values of the American system of secular education, at the same time that he was showing the greater vitality of religion there than in England.[16] One of his most effective methods was to ask Americans to describe their system in public meetings. His letter to Daniel Gilman, requesting Gilman to address a meeting on general education in Manchester early in 1854, is of interest both in illustrating Cobden's tactics and in indicating the root of the trouble:

> Our difficulty is the religious question. Show the meeting how you reconcile the rights of conscience on religious matters and the demands of society for secular instruction. Give us some statistics of what you are doing in the States, and *shame* us out of our intolerance and supineness. Tell the meeting strongly that you consider in America that all you possess that is most precious in social development and political freedom you owe solely, under Providence, to your system of education.[17]

The national education scheme was defeated in 1856.[18] Separation of the religious and secular elements in education remained the stumbling block. The realization of Cobden's ideal of free universal elementary and secondary education was not to be approached in England for nearly one hundred years.

The effectiveness of the American press, developed essentially for the people, free from burdensome taxes and therefore available to the masses, also strongly appealed to

[14] Maccoby, *English Radicalism, 1832-1852*, p. 328n, and *English Radicalism, 1853-1886*, London, 1938, p. 55.
[15] Add. MSS. 43650, Cobden to Bright, January 9 [?], 1854.
[16] Maccoby, *English Radicalism, 1832-1852*, p. 330.
[17] Add MSS. 43678, Part 2, Cobden to Gilman, January 13, 1854 [typed copy].
[18] Maccoby, *English Radicalism, 1853-1886*, p. 54.

Cobden. The year after his first trip to America he was writing Tait, "We want a new set of papers that will advocate the solid & material interests of the masses – in a word we want an American press & we shall have it by & by."[19] Restrictions that hobbled the press in England and kept it from a wide circulation which might have been a means of increasing an intelligent public opinion among the working classes and thereby of furthering reform, were the "Taxes on Knowledge,"[20] especially the newspaper stamp, which caused many papers to sell at a price far beyond the capacity of most people to pay. For years Cobden worked with others to abolish the penny stamp. Writing to Sturge on the matter in 1851, he said, "We shall never remove great public questions beyond the control of cliques & coteries of political jobbers until the press be as free here as in America."[21] To Bright, he stated that a penny newspaper press "would do more to educate the millions than all the schoolmasters in the land. – Only think how busy every rural hamlet would now be in spelling & decyphering the *published* letters from the 'diggins,' if the press were as free in this Country as in the United States, & consequently as cheap."[22]

The newspaper stamp was abolished in 1855. But long before that Cobden was anticipating the great advantages to the cause of peace and reform that would come with the establishment of a penny newspaper. "We can do nothing until we have a daily paper in London. – What is wanted is one representing the *humanities* – peace, temperance, antislavery etc – in fact a *New York Tribune*, but avoiding its many errors & with sound views on Free trade, which that paper has not. – & it should go for *free trade in land*."[23] During the months that followed, Cobden with several others of

[19] Add. MSS. 43660, Part 2, Cobden to Tait, August 23, 1836.
[20] These were the penny stamp, the Advertisement Duty, and the Paper Excise.
[21] *Ibid.* 43659, Part 4, Cobden to Sturge, January 15, 1851.
[22] *Ibid.* 43649, Cobden to Bright, September 7 [?], 1852.
[23] *Ibid.* 43722, Bdl. 2, Part 1, Cobden to Sturge, February 16, 1855. For an earlier reference, see also *ibid.* 43722, Bdl. 2, Part 1, Cobden to Sturge, April 24, 1854.

the radical "Peace Party" established the first penny press in London in the interests of peace and reform (the *Morning Star* and the *Evening Star*), and "fathered" it through its early troubled days.[24] In making his plans for putting the paper on its feet, the practical Cobden was influenced by the financial success of the New York papers and by the encouragement which he got from Horace Greeley, editor of the *New York Daily Tribune*.[25] Writing to Sturge he reported:

Bright myself & others have had frequent conversations & consultations about a cheap daily paper. We have met Horace Greeley of New York who is now in London, & heard all he can tell us, & we have been in communication with a person who is trying to establish a penny paper. – The result of it all is that I am convinced of the practicability of making such a paper pay. – Greeley says he has not the least doubt about it, & says it would be a good investment of Capital – that the copyright of one of the penny papers in New York [the Herald] is worth £100,000.[26]

Cobden was also encouraged by Bennett of the *New York Herald*. He informed Paulton in 1856 that, "Gordon Bennett of the *New York Herald* told me in a note I had from him last autumn that his paper pays him 80,000 dollars a year profit, & Horace Greely of the Tribune, & he both agreed that the finest opening in the world for a literary venture was in the penny press of London. . . ."[27] "Why [he inquired of Combe] should not 1^d papers pay here as well as in America."[28] Finally, after the paper was well launched,

[24] See Cobden's many letters of 1855 and 1856 to Sturge in *ibid*. 43722, Bdl. 2. By October 31, 1856, Cobden was able to state that the circulation of the *Star* and that of the Manchester daily (both peace organs) far exceeded that of any other paper except the *Times. Ibid*. 43722. Bdl. 2, Part 4, Cobden to Sturge, October 31, 1856. It was Cobden who suggested the name *Star* for the paper. *Ibid*. 43650, Cobden to Bright, January 14, 1856.

[25] Cobden, however, was not interested in the financial end of it for himself, for he consistently refused to put any money in the paper.

[26] *Ibid*. 43722, Bdl. 2, Part 2, Cobden to Sturge, July 28, 1855. For other references to Greeley, see *ibid*. 43659, Part 8, Cobden to Sturge, August 8, 1855 [copy]; *ibid*. 43653, Part 3, Cobden to Combe, November 22, 1855; *ibid*. 43722. Bdl. 2, Part 3, Cobden to Sturge, June 5, 1856.

[27] *Ibid*. 43662, Part 1, Cobden to Paulton [July 15, 1856].

[28] *Ibid*. 43653, Part 3, Cobden to Combe, November 22, 1855.

he was still pointing to the American example. In a letter to Richard of the *Star*, in 1857, he said, "The longer I think of it the more I am convinced that the penny papers in this Country will have to take their model from the United States before they can have equal success – I mean as to the arrangement & plan of dealing with original topics."[29] And the American "pennies" remained models of journalism.

Cobden respected other features of American society. The strength of religion, particularly in New England, stirred him. "Why, I have been there, and I have seen a chain put across the street in a large town in the New England States, to prevent traffic from interfering with religious worship. . . . Every thing in the New England States betokens a deference of religion – every outward and visible symptom."[30] Cobden believed in America's political system. In connection with the middle and lower classes in England, he wrote to Combe, "Look at our race in America – Was there ever in the history of the world a better government than that which plebian Englishmen have organized without crown, coronets or mitres in the New England states, & New York? Take the interior of Massachusetts or of New York, I mean such towns as Northampton, Canandaigen, Utica, Auburn, etc, can such intelligence, civilization, & moral & material well-doing be elsewhere found? Can any thing be compared with it unless indeed it be in the Cantons of Geneva or Vaud, in *democratic* Switzerland?"[31]

But it was America's policy of non-intervention in Europe's turmoils, of small armament expenditure, and of peace in general which Cobden wanted Britain to emulate. Through such a policy, American money and energies were being directed toward internal improvements and reforms, achieving as a result an enviable prosperity which was fast making her a formidable rival. Time and again Cobden called at-

[29] *Ibid.* 43658, Part 4, Cobden to Richard, May 15, 1857.
[30] Schwabe, *Reminiscences of Richard Cobden*, pp. 139-140.
[31] Add. MSS. 43653, Part 4, Cobden to Combe, July 17, 1848.

tention to the great advantages which accrued to America from peaceful pursuits. For example, in 1850 he declared to Bright:

By the way, how little do these *routine statesmen*, who make the old crazy courts of Europe the field of their intrigues, seem to understand what is coming upon us from the West! – I am astonished & almost bewildered at what is going on in the United States – I always thought that the progress of that Country would some day astonish the old world, but I had hardly expected such a potent development of all the elements of wealth & power, & population, as is now going on – In ocean steam navigation, which they only took in hand a year ago, they bid fair to beat us both in size & quality of vessels as completely as they have in sailing ships. – And in the face of the immense array of steam ships of from 2 to 3000 tons each now built or building in America, it is folly to look at the military marines of Europe as the test of naval supremacy – The dominion of the seas will pass to the United States as certainly within 20 years by the overwhelming superiority of their mercantile tonnage as it did from Holland to us. – I am glad the Americans are setting the example of a reduction of their war navy – The only line of battle ship they had afloat last year is now laid up, & unless a war should break out, I don't expect they will commission another. – The late debates in Congress upon the Navy Estimates went strongly for reduction. . . .[32]

Again, during the Crimean War in 1855, Cobden writing to Bright asserted in opposition to a further arms expenditure in Britain, "What an impulse we shall give to her [America's] already formidable rivalry. Whilst all our great establishments such as Whitworth etc are being devoted to purposes of war the Americans are giving all their energies to manufactures & ship building, perfecting their already admirable system of education, & effecting social reforms in temperance etc which amt [amount] to a moral revolution in the habits of the people."[33] Earlier, he had said, "Tested by the education of the people, the use of the printing press, the electric telegraph, railroads, & steamers, they [the Americans]

[32] *Ibid.* 43649, Cobden to Bright, October 18, 1850.
[33] *Ibid.* 43652, Part 7, Cobden to Bright, 6/7/55. See also *ibid.* 43650, Cobden to Bright, September 17, 1855; January 15, 1856.

have won the race. – And the worst of it is that we as a people ignore their mighty progress."[34] Cobden deplored Britain's colonial system which involved dangers to peace and vast expenditure in defending and governing far-flung regions. Here again, he insisted, Britain suffered by comparison with America. Typically, he told his constituents on April 11, 1849: "We have five colonial governors and a governor in our North American colonies, with salaries amounting to £17,000 a year, while the United States, with thirty governors, paid only £14,300; our colonies having a population of 2,000,000, and the United States 20,000,000."[35]

Cobden, perhaps more than any other man, realized the great importance of cordial relations with the United States, fast gaining in social advance and economic power. In 1852, thanking Sir Edward Watkin for a copy of his book relating to America, Cobden wrote that he [Watkin] could not "have done a wiser and more patriotic service than to make the people of this country better acquainted with what is going on in the United States."[36] Continuing in another letter Cobden said, "You talk of my going to America, and then coming back to tell the people here what is going on beyond the Atlantic. I have never missed an opportunity of trying to awaken the emulation and even the fears of my countrymen, by quoting the example of the United States. But the only result is, that I am pretty freely charged with seeking

[34] *Ibid.* 43651, Part 3, Cobden to Bright, September 2, 1851.
During the Crimean War Cobden wrote to Bright: "And what a barbarous fellow the Czar after all that he has reckoned upon his armies, & forgotten or never been able to comprehend the much greater element of *force* which lies concealed in industry, railroads, & navigation. – There is America with half his population, & a territory nearly as great; let a two months notice be given that a descent would be made on a point of the United States, & if necessary two millions of armed men would by means of their railroads be on the spot to smother such an army as Lord Raglan's with the smoke of their cigars!" *Ibid.* 43650, October 1, 1854.
[35] This is quoted by Maccoby, *English Radicalism, 1832-1852*, p. 359. The preceding part of Maccoby's note is equally vivid: "The last appointment made by the United States was a Governor of California, with a salary of £600; our last appointment was the Governor of Labuan, with £2,000 a year."
[36] Watkin, *Alderman Cobden of Manchester*, pp. 164-165.

to establish a republican government here. To shut our eyes to what is going on there is almost as sage a proceeding as that of the ostrich when he puts his head under a sand-heap. However, whether we will or no, we shall hear of the doings of the Americans."[37]

Cobden spoke truly: he employed every means to awaken England to the significance of the New World, working not only through personal associations, speeches, and letters but through the *Star*, organ of the peace interests. He was constantly giving material to the paper, making suggestions for its procedure at a given time, and offering helpful criticism. So he is to be found, on one occasion during a period of strained relations with the United States, reprimanding Hamilton of the *Star* for not giving more American news, "I am obliged to look to the Times for news on a topic of critical interest, & affecting a Country which it should be the aim of the Star to bring into greater prominence & importance by making it better known in this Country."[38] In times of difficulty between the two nations Cobden helped organize sentiment charitable towards America. Thus in 1855 and 1856 he opposed Britain's plan to increase her fleet off the American coast as a threat to the United States because of the rumor that the United States was building privateers for use against England. He furthermore urged arbitration of Central American affairs—one source of trouble in the period—and support of the American proposal for exempting private property from seizure at sea.[39] His greatest efforts in behalf of accord between the two nations, however, came during the Civil War, after his second trip to America.

[37] *Ibid.*, pp. 166-167.

[38] Add. MSS. 43658, Part 2, Cobden to Richard, Jy [July ?] 23, 1856. See also an undated post-script of a letter from Cobden to Sturge, *ibid.* 43722, Bdl. 2, Part 4.

[39] For example, he wrote to Sturge: "By the way your peace society must back the American government in its proposal to exempt private property at sea from capture in case of war. This is a most important proposition. . . ." *Ibid.* 43722, Bdl. 2, Part 4, Cobden to Sturge, September 4, 1856.

From this discussion it must not be assumed that Cobden was blind to American shortcomings. He disapproved of her tariff, her indebtedness, her system of slavery, her conduct towards Texas and Mexico, to name some of the most important. Apropos of slavery he told Sturge: "You know I am opposed to intervention even in anti slavery matters, but certainly I do not wonder at your society being tempted to try to shame the people of the U States out of their present course."[40] Nearly four years later, however, Cobden, in referring to the revolting conditions of the Turkish slave trade, cautioned Sturge, "It seems to me that as this is the slave trade which *we* virtually perpetuate in Europe we are open to the charge of hypocrisy if we go for grievances to America – without noticing evils of a worse kind nearer home for which we are responsible."[41] Though Cobden was glad to perceive that America proceeded along the paths of peace for the most part, he was watchful of any tendencies in the opposite direction. "I am more jealous of *their* falling into the marauding & conquering propensities of the old world than any thing besides."[42] At rare times he was disillusioned with America, but this was always temporary. For instance, in a letter to Sturge in 1851 he wrote:

I observe in to days papers that Generals Scott & Cass are spoken of as candidates for the next presidency. The first is the Conqueror of Mexico, the second the bellicose enemy of England – Now, I repeat to you what I have said before – the danger to peace principles is to be feared from the Americans following the warlike spirit of the old world – If they can't earn for themselves the title of a *new world* in their principles of peace as opposed to the antiquated & exhausted war systems of Europe & Asia, then they fail in their pretended mission as civilizers & improvers of mankind & they throw us back almost indefinitely in our hopes of a great moral progress.–[43]

[40] *Ibid.* 43722, Bdl. 1, Part 5, Cobden to Sturge, November 2, 1850.
[41] *Ibid.* 43722, Bdl. 2, Part 1, Cobden to Sturge, July 28, 1854.
[42] *Ibid.* 43658, Part 2, Cobden to Richard, March 23, 1852.
[43] *Ibid.* 43722, Bdl. 1, Part 6, Cobden to Sturge, April 15, 1851.

During the Crimean War at a time when Cobden disliked a specific American policy, he told Sturge:

As respects the mediation of America, I don't think it would be accepted by England even if offered by the Government of that Country. – Nor do I think it would have much moral weight with the public. – For right or wrong, we have the impression here that the U.S. government is not a whit less disposed than ourselves to break the peace where it can do so with advantage – and where the party attacked is not able to offer a very dangerous resistance. – It is to be lamented that so much of the old leaven is to be found in a Country which had every motive for pursuing a different & nobler course – one which might have invested her with an irresistable moral influence over the destinies of the old world. –[44]

But such feelings were most exceptional with Cobden. He expressed the momentary disappointment of a father when a model child has misbehaved.

From time to time when requested to influence American opinion in connection with some of these features of American policy or society of which he disapproved, Cobden declared that intervention in the affairs of a foreign country was contrary to his principles. Writing to Sturge in connection with the anti-slavery movement, he said, "I am besides as you are aware exceedingly averse to taking any part in agitating upon the evils prevailing in other Countries, for I feel that we have more to do here than can be accomplished in my time; & besides I am of opinion that interference from abroad is not favorable to the progress of reform in any Country, where public opinion requires to be acted upon, as in the case of America."[45] In connection with Richard's (of the *Star*) denunciation of the attack on Sumner in 1856, Cobden advised: "But I would avoid *on principle* going into the question of their 'domestic institutions.' – I have always acted on the rule that *non intervention* should be observed morally

[44] *Ibid.* 43722, Bdl. 2, Part 2, Cobden to Sturge, May 17, 1855.
[45] *Ibid.* 43659, Part 5, Cobden to Sturge, July 16, 1851.

as well as materially."⁴⁶ Until the Civil War, Cobden's efforts on behalf of friendly relations between the two countries, apart from correspondence with personal friends, were largely confined to the influence which he exerted in England.

⁴⁶ *Ibid.* 43658, Part 3, Cobden to Richard, June 18, 1856.

"I have been twice throughout the North & West, at an interval of 24 years.– And I maintain that nobody who has not twice visited the States can comprehend the vitality, force, & velocity of progress of that people, & their inborn aptitude for self-government." Cobden to George Parkes, December 4, 1861, Additional Manuscripts 43660, Part 1.

*A*FTER Cobden's first trip to America, he had been eager to return. A letter to Edward Watkin shows that he had given it some thought at least as early as 1852. "I should like to go once more to America, if only to see Niagara again. But I am a bad sailor, and should dread the turmoil of public meetings when I arrived there."[1] Four years later, he was recommending to John Bright a trip to the Continent and then to America as the best way of regaining mental and physical health: "To pass a fortnight within sight of the spray of Niagara would renovate you more than all the cold water places in England."[2] Early in 1859 Cobden's dream of such a trip was realized. On January 29 he wrote to Bright: "They say I am going to America, but I really can hardly realize it yet. – However I will tell you when I see you in Town in about 10 days."[3]

Perhaps the necessity of some revitalizing change of scene played its part in influencing Cobden himself in favor of such a journey in 1859, for during these years, it will be recalled, misfortune had befallen him. In 1856 he had lost his only son, from which bereavement his wife had suffered a nervous collapse which made her completely dependent on

[1] Watkin, *Alderman Cobden of Manchester*, p. 165.
[2] Add. MSS. 43652, Part 2, Cobden to Bright, March 8, 1856. Later that year (October 24) Cobden suggested Egypt to Bright, and still later (October 30), Italy. *Ibid.* 43650.
[3] *Ibid.* 43650, Part 6, Cobden to Bright, January 29, 1859.

Cobden and incapacitated her over a long period. At approximately the same time his closest friend, John Bright, had experienced a mental breakdown which had caused Cobden deep anxiety. His brother Frederick for many years had lived in his home and looked after domestic affairs, making possible Cobden's nation-wide labors; Frederick had become seriously ill in 1857 and died the following year. In 1857 Cobden had been politically defeated; and the war hysteria of the country with its consequent scrapping of liberal reform had weighed heavily upon him. From 1857 on, financial losses in his Illinois Central Railroad investments had been severe.

It was this last personal problem which caused Cobden to undertake the journey to America in 1859. A desire to investigate Illinois railroad conditions for himself and for his colleagues was his chief motive for the trip; but his vital interest in America, from the time of his first visit there and over the succeeding years, encouraged him in his decision. Writing to Henry Ashworth, February 3, 1859, Cobden said, "You will be surprised if I tell you that I am about to pay a visit to the United States. Personal interests have brought me to the determination – though I have a strong desire on other grounds to see that Country after an interval of 24 years to witness its great progress, & to judge of its prospects for the future."[4] That dual reason, particularly his interest in the republic, is expressed in a similar, colorful letter to George Parkes, two days later:

I am going to the United States. – Some friends & colleagues who have a common interest in an investment in Illinois, with which half England nearly has been fascinated, have been long urging me to go, but I have only just resolved to make the plunge, & have booked myself for the 12th – wishing to be at Washington before the close of the short session. – My mind has been partly bribed to this step by the desire I feel to take another peep at that people before I go hence, & judge for myself as to the progress moral & material they have made during the quarter of a century

⁴ *Ibid.* 43647, Part 5, Cobden to Ashworth, February 3, 1859.

that has elapsed since I was there. – When it was formerly the fashion, as it is now again, to throw dirt at the Americans, I remember old Cobbett, who had done his best in his early days to foster this prejudice, suddenly turned about, &, as was his wont, assailed with unmitigated black guardism those who were taking his side & repeating his arguments. – "Let us see what this hellish thing a Republic really is," roared the Register, & then followed a condensed & graphic summary of the rapid growth of that people in commerce, wealth, education, & morality, & having knocked down his opponents with a huge array of facts & statistics he wound up with the exclamation 'this is the hellish republic you are so frightened about!'. – Now I wish to see the hellish government that Bright is accused of wanting to import into England. – [5]

To Bright on the same day he wrote, "I have actually taken my berth for the 12th, & so, if I am spared, in a few months I shall be able to tell you what this 'hellish' thing they call a Republic is really like (to quote old Cobbett)."[6]

It is possible that Illinois affairs alone would not have taken Cobden on the trip had he not been possessed with such an intense interest in America. Other reliable men had been sent to America by British investors, to investigate for them the condition of the Illinois Central Railroad; it was not, therefore, really necessary for Cobden to go. Had he been in Parliament, it is doubtful if he would have gone. On the other hand, it is even more probable that his interest in the States would not alone have been sufficient to send him there at this time. As he wrote to Ashworth, "Personal interests have brought me to the determination." And from this and another letter there is an indication that Cobden was to

[5] Cobden continues: "My wife will take the children to Paris & reside with an old friend of ours from Manchester, Mrs. Woolley, who takes in boarders. – This will give Katie an opportunity of having good music masters, & all of them will learn French correctly without trouble. – I think the complete change, & throwing her on her own resources will also be of service to my wife. – I shall not be many months absent. – We shall let our house, if we find a customer to our mind, for the summer & autumn. – But I shall not let any 'fast' people into possession. – Now have you any commands for the other side? I must see you before I go." *Ibid.* 43660 [Part 1], Cobden to Parkes, February 5, 1859.

[6] *Ibid.* 43650, Part 6, Cobden to Bright, February 5, 1859.

do more than merely investigate railroad matters; he was to advise and, if possible, act. "There is nothing, I must tell you, in my investment in that Country to cause alarm or render my visit suddenly necessary. – I have gradually yielded to some of my colleagues & friends wishes to go out with a view of infusing some new blood into the management of our affairs."[7] To another friend he added, "All that I have to try to do is to infuse new blood into the Board, & transfer the management from New York to Chicago where the work is to be done."[8]

Why should Cobden have been prevailed upon to make the trip at this time? The answer to this question involves a short survey of his association with Illinois Central affairs.

Cobden and the Illinois Central Railroad

The Illinois Central Railroad was chartered in 1851 to a group of American eastern capitalists who received a federal land-grant of two and one-half million acres and the right to build the railroad in return for a promise to finance the construction of a railroad within a given number of years and to grant to the State a certain percentage of the gross proceeds of operation. To set the enterprise on its feet, a limited amount of capital was immediately secured through

[7] He continues: "But having decided to go this spring, I am starting speedily with the view of getting to Washington before the close of the short session of Congress as I wish to see how the politicians compare with animals of the same species at home. –

Now [since Ashworth had visited America two years earlier] if you have any advice about hotels, or visiting private houses, or any thing else calculated to be of use, pray drop me a letter. – I don't think of going much into the slave states but shall principally confine myself to the North-east & West. – Is New Orleans very well worth seeing? – Did you go to Gilpins house at Philadelphia to stay? He invited me to visit him." (*Ibid.* 43647, Part 5, Cobden to Ashworth, February 3, 1859.)

In response to Ashworth's answer, Cobden wrote him February 7 indicating that he would visit Gilpin, expressing appreciation of Ashworth's offer of letters of introduction, many of which, however, his short stay would preclude his using, and regretting that his hurried departure prevented his seeing Ashworth before he left. *Ibid.* 43647, Part 5, Cobden to Ashworth, February 7, 1859.

[8] *Ibid.* 43722, Bdl. 2, Part 7, Cobden to Sturge, February 3, 1859.

stock assessment and bond sales (mainly to the promoters), and through a temporary "carrying" of Illinois Central bonds by another interested railroad. This, however, was far from adequate to finance construction costs, and a loan was determined upon. With two million acres of the land-grant as security, the promoters decided to place on sale Illinois Central bonds and to seek a market for them in England. After unsuccessful negotiations with the Barings and the Rothschilds of London, the Illinois Central representatives in England induced a British syndicate, headed by Devaux and Company, which had made money in French railroads, to purchase bonds to the amount of £1,000,000. Each purchaser of a $1,000 bond was permitted the privilege of subscribing to five shares of stock, with "every probability" that no calls upon the stock would be necessary. This money, which was paid immediately, made possible the beginnings of construction and constituted a fairly sound basis of credit. To continue construction after this loan had been exhausted, American capitalists were encouraged to buy securities.[9]

1852 and 1853 were good years, but 1854 was another story. Tremendous expansion in business and the Crimean War caused a scarcity of capital for investment; Illinois Central bonds dropped rapidly. Their decline was aggravated by the defalcation of Robert Schuyler (who until the year before had been president of the Illinois Central) in connection with the New York and New Haven Railroad of which he was president. The day Schuyler's fraud became known, a Wall Street panic began. Confidence in Illinois Central se-

---

[9] This short, detailed survey of the history of the Illinois Central could not have been written but for the excellent study by Gates. His pages have been followed closely in those succeeding paragraphs which deal specifically with the history of the railroad. See Paul Wallace Gates, *The Illinois Central Railroad and its Colonization Work, Harvard Economic Studies,* XLII, Cambridge, 1934. For the above paragraph in the text, see pp. 67-74.

Corliss' book on the Illinois Central supplements Gates' account with some colorful detail, and contains some good pictures of several Illinois Central men mentioned by Cobden. See Carlton J. Corliss, *Main Line of Mid-America, The Story of the Illinois Central,* New York, 1950.

curities was shaken; the bottom virtually fell out of its bonds and stocks.[10]

Such a moment was welcomed by a large number of British investors who, convinced of the soundness of the investment with so valuable a land-grant as security, seized upon the low bonds and stock and bought in to such an extent that the price of bonds advanced greatly. From this time on, heavy subscriptions to Illinois Central securities by foreign investors increased until in the 'sixties they had actually gained control of the railroad;[11] and from this earlier period on they took an added interest and part in its affairs.

Cobden was one of the most prominent of the group of British investors, which included such eminent men as William Gladstone, Charles Paget, William Moffatt, and Sir Joseph Paxton. Though his friends (including William H. Osborn, President of the Illinois Central Railroad[12]) tried to discourage him, Cobden invested heavily in Illinois Central stock which was subject to calls and which held little hope of immediate returns. For this purpose, he used a substantial part of that vast sum of nearly $400,000 which had been given him in appreciation of his successful anti-corn law services.[13] For a person in need of income and with no capital to draw upon, the investment was not a wise one.[14] It is the more surprising that he should have invested so deeply, inasmuch as throughout its first decade, the Illinois Central was regarded as a speculative project; and its stocks and bonds were accorded a lower value than those of the best railroads. Furthermore, confidence of the State and the

[10] See Corliss, *Main Line of Mid-America*, p. 38; Gates, *The Illinois Central Railroad*, pp. 75-76; and Howard Gray Brownson, *History of the Illinois Central Railroad to 1870*, University of Illinois, *Studies in the Social Sciences*, IV, 3, 4, Urbana, 1915, pp. 123-124.

[11] See Gates, *The Illinois Central Railroad*, p. 76; Leland Hamilton Jenks, *The Migration of British Capital To 1875*, New York, 1927, p. 169; Corliss, *Main Line of Mid-America*, p. 97.

[12] For a good description of Osborn, see *ibid.*, pp. 38-39.

[13] Gates, *The Illinois Central Railroad*, pp. 80, 81.

[14] Morley, *Life of Richard Cobden*, II, 223.

people in the management was sometimes lacking.[15] Gates asserts that "unquestionably this [the Illinois Central] was a speculative investment, and only the desire for large profits could have induced Cobden to take the risk."[16]

It is clear that Cobden later was aware of the chances he was taking.[17] But he believed his faith in the railroad justified by the valuable land-grant accorded to the Company. On his journey through the States in 1835 he had heard at first hand glowing reports from traveling companions about the fertility of this region of the country. From one of them he had even received a bit of the precious Illinois soil. Undoubtedly this early experience had made a deep impression on him. His mistake lay in his placing too much confidence in the *potential* value of the railroad, without estimating sufficiently the practical difficulties involved in financing the line through these early hazardous years. Nor could he have anticipated the course of nature which was so vitally to affect the fortunes of the railroad.

Meanwhile, although it had been understood that calls would not be made on the stock, the poor conditions of 1854 and 1855 and the low income returned on bond sales made calls and short-term loans necessary. Accordingly, two calls of $5.00 were made in 1854 and a third late in 1855. In 1856, however, stocks and bonds went up, partly because of the great increase in land sales; and the high value of securities continued until the early part of 1857, making further calls unnecessary.[18] The future for the railroad looked bright. Ashworth reported to Cobden from America in May of 1857 that a Philadelphia merchant, McAlister, had said, "that the Rway is good and is likely to improve rather than otherwise. –. . . he said that Illinois was very likely to become one

---

[15] Gates, *The Illinois Central Railroad*, pp. 74-75.

[16] *Ibid.*, p. 81.

[17] See his letter to Moffatt in 1858 as quoted by Morley, *Life of Richard Cobden*, II, 222-223.

[18] For this discussion, see Gates, *The Illinois Central Railroad*, pp. 78-79; also Corliss, *Main Line of Mid-America*, p. 92.

of the most important States of the Union." The attraction of Illinois land for immediate agricultural profits "had given favour to Illinois territory and would as he conceived sustain the prosperity of the Rway." But in this same letter were warnings of the crash which was to come. Another railroad man had told Ashworth that he thought the value of Illinois Central investments had been pushed to the limit. Furthermore, "Macalister remarked of *all* the American Rways, that they are carrying at very *low rates* – advertizing against one another and competing for business, and that they are allowing their floating debts to accumulate whilst they are paying off their money receipts to swell their dividends – From appearances and from the knowledge he had of one or two Concerns which had as much as £500,000 of unfunded debts, he was apprehensive that another year would bring upon some of them a severe crash & confusion."[19]

Nor was McAlister the only person who had his misgivings. President Osborn himself apprehended the dangers in the situation. The earlier calls on stock before Osborn was made president had been so unpopular with the shareholders that the directors had resorted almost entirely to the sale of bonds and short-term loans for the building of the line. Osborn realized that finances were far from sound, and he therefore decided upon more calls; but the British shareholders opposed him, and he was obliged to withhold the assessments. The Illinois Central was unprepared for the depression of 1857 which followed, bringing in its wake shrinkage of credit, industrial inactivity, and low prices. The Company suffered a serious drop in land values and collections and a great loss in traffic revenue. At the same time it was confronted with demands for payment on a large amount of short-term bills and notes. Without money to meet these demands, the only course was temporary assignment of the railroad to a special committee of assignees. This served to send securities to a new low. Conditions were now the most

[19] Add. MSS. 43647, Ashworth to Cobden, May 19, 1857.

critical they had been. A call of $10.00 was made for September 1857; and this was followed by several more calls.[20]

The British investors were alarmed. Many of them had purchased bonds in the belief that the stock would never be assessed. For a man who owned much stock and had little cash on hand, even a small call could prove hard;[21] several calls might plunge him into desperate straits. Such was the case with a number of the British holders. They were likely to feel no better about it after hearing rumors to the effect that certain American investors had taken credit on their calls.[22] Furthermore, their suspicions of Osborn's management had been aroused unfairly by an American faction which opposed Osborn and sought to discredit him with the English shareholders in order that he might be removed.[23]

In view of these matters, the English investors organized "protective committees" which dispatched various representatives to the States to investigate affairs. Sir James Caird, Joseph Fisher, and a number of other eminent persons were among those sent. These investigators found little serious fault with the management of the railroad.[24] Although there were doubts, the English shareholders apparently did not challenge the integrity of the Company. Cobden wrote to Sturge shortly before his departure for America: "I have nothing to do in the way of accounts. – *They* have been overhauled by some of the ablest of our accountants, by Wm Smith among the rest who wound up the Bank of Manchester & is now Secretary to the Victoria Dock. – No flaw was detected." Cobden himself trusted the management:

As a rule I am by no means inclined to the opinion that the Americans are less honorable in the management of joint-stock

[20] For this discussion I am indebted to Gates, *The Illinois Central Railroad*, pp. 79, 79-80, 256. See also Corliss, *Main Line of Mid-America*, pp. 93, 94.

[21] See *ibid.*, p. 92, and Gates, *The Illinois Central Railroad*, p. 80.

[22] Add. MSS. 43663, Part 5, Cobden to Gilpin, April 10, 1859.

[23] See Gates, *The Illinois Central Railroad*, p. 78.

[24] For an account of the British investigators, see *ibid*, p. 80; also Corliss, *Main Line of Mid-America*, p. 97.

affairs than we English who think pretty well of ourselves. – There are some hundred joint stock banks in New York & Boston & the neighborhood. – They have passed through a trying ordeal but I have heard of nothing so bad as the management of banks in London Liverpool Glasgow & Newcastle. – Their railroads are now just about in the same state of confusion from overdoing the thing that we were in in 1847 but I hear of nothing so bad as the exhibition which Hudson & Co then made. – Taking care to compare class with class & [*sic*] I don't think the Americans are worse than ourselves. – The mistake is in our generally comparing our middle class with their entire population. – [25]

During these months Cobden found himself in a critical circumstance. Having tied up practically all of his fortune in Manchester and Illinois Central investments, he was unable to make the payments on his calls which amounted to thousands of dollars; and only the financial assistance of his friends saved him. Thomasson in particular aided him with handsome sums, from which he accepted no return. Some of the names were never known to Cobden. Bright, for example, says years later in his diary that [Charles] Paget, M.P., and the Speaker of the Commons (Evelyn Denison) had each advanced £1,000 to assist Cobden in payment of calls on the Illinois Central shares, Cobden never knowing of the act of the Speaker.[26]

Despite his extreme financial embarrassment, Cobden's confidence in the investment in September 1857 was unshaken:

... If a trifle could be snatched from the fire it would help to pay the heavy calls falling on some of us. – I do not change in the slightest degree my opinion in consequence of the fall in the Illinois. – That the stock will go up again to its former level I have no doubt. It is not as a *railroad* investment that I regard so favorably this undertaking, but its value in my eyes depends on the landed estate, which is the noblest domain ever transferred

[25] Add. MSS. 43722, Bdl. 2, Part 7, Cobden to Sturge, February 3, 1859.
[26] *The Diaries of John Bright*, edited by R. A. J. Walling, London, 1930, p. 292. Both sums were canceled to Thomasson. See Morley, *Life of Richard Cobden*, II, 223-224.

in one conveyance. – Nothing but an earthquake or some other Convulsion of nature can impair the value of 2,600,000 acres of the richest soil in the world, situated in the midst of the most industrious & intelligent population. – The Wall St "bulls" & "bears" will make no durable impression on such a property.[27]

Though he was essentially right, "convulsions" of nature in the following three years did further decrease the value of the land-tract and therefore of the railroad. A number of crop failures, from 1857 to 1859, "caused by unseasonable rains and early frosts," took the money out of land for a time.[28] Early in the spring of 1858 Cobden was still hopeful. Writing to Sir Joshua Walmsley he reported:

The Illinois are under a cloud. – But I saw a letter from Osborn the President to Moffatt dated April 2 in which he says there are slight signs of improvement   The land sales fell almost to nothing – January they were $66,488 – Feby $28,288 – but in March they improved to $98,000, & the correspondence of the Land Office is increasing showing signs of greater business coming. – There is no doubt that, *for those who can hold on*, the future is all that it ever was. – But the *call* has terribly plagued me – coming with other matters. – [29]

In the remaining months of 1858, however, the Illinois farmers met further disaster. Gates states that 1858 was considered by the Illinois Central Land Commissioner as the "gloomiest that ever settled upon Illinois." Immigration was practically halted; and the land sales and collections on land sold decreased sharply.[30] After the disasters of that final year, even the sanguine Cobden was dismayed. In behalf of his British colleagues and his own fortune, he determined to see the conditions which prevailed.

Arriving in America, Cobden lost no time. His first morning in the States he talked with one of the men most closely connected with the incorporation of the Illinois Central,

[27] Add. MSS. 43663, Part 1, Cobden to Walmsley, September 18, 1857 [copy].
[28] Gates, *The Illinois Central Railroad*, pp. 256-257.
[29] Add. MSS. 43664, Part 7, Cobden to Walmsley, April 21, 1858.
[30] Gates, *The Illinois Central Railroad*, p. 257.

Franklin Haven; the second day he was with Osborn; and the third day he attended an Illinois Central board meeting in New York. So his activities continued. His investigation was thorough. He took a prominent part in a board and in a committee meeting in New York, pouring oil upon the waters by getting the directors to expunge some passages from the annual report which would antagonize the British investors. In Chicago he was present at the annual meeting and spent the remainder of the day talking with the officers of the company.

The personnel of the Illinois Central he studied well. Officers, directors, investors, interested parties, British agents, and local Illinois farmers and emigration leaders were examined. He traveled west to Illinois and over the Illinois Central line with President Osborn, and was also accompanied on the latter trip by George B. McClellan, vice-president of the company. In Chicago he was entertained by Ambrose Burnside,[31] the treasurer, and spent some time in the Land Office with him and with Colonel John W. Foster, who was Land Commissioner. In Washington he talked with Robert J. Walker, who had tried to secure the first English loan. With various people, he discussed the efficiency of the officers.

Of as great importance to Cobden for the purposes of his investigation were the directors and other prominent investors. He came to know personally the reputation of the New York Board of Directors. In various places he met or was entertained by many of the men closely identified with or interested in the Illinois Central, among whom were Sturges, Haven, Grinnell, Wiley, Hewitt, Burch, Wood, Newberry, Hart (Canadian), Joy, and Forbes, the last two destined to be known as eminent railroad men. He made a special point of questioning Hewitt of New York and Chouteau of St. Louis, both of whom were involved in a credit on calls. Others, interested for one reason or another in the

---

[31] McClellan and Burnside were later of Civil War fame.

railroad, whose opinions and advice he sought, included such men as McAlister, head of the Philadelphia land company with holdings in Illinois, Ashbell Welsh, the engineer and consolidator of the New Jersey railroads, Erastus Corning, president of the New York Central system, and James Brown, prominent investor in several railroad companies. Cobden consulted still other capitalists who were familiar with economic conditions and some of whom were good possibilities as investors.

He gained additional points of view by discussing Illinois affairs with Sam G. Ward, the American correspondent of the Barings, who entertained considerable hostility toward the Illinois Central, and possibly with Joseph Fisher,[32] the investigator sent over by the British shareholders. Men prominent in the history of the railroad whom Cobden met in Illinois included William B. Burns, head of the Vermont Emigrant Association which settled Rutland, Ovid Miner, an important traveling agent, instrumental in organizing certain settlements, Michael Sullivant and Curtis, large-scale farmers, and M. L. Dunlap, a farmer and farm periodical editor who advertised the work of the railroad and supported Osborn's policies.

Cobden was pleased with what he learned. Concerning the officers of the company, he reported: "In common with every body who has visited Illinois, I have been well satisfied with the character of all the employes both in the Land Office, & on the Line." As for McClellan, who practically managed the railroad at the Illinois end, Cobden added to another's high estimate of the man that he had "found him ingenuous & modest yet full of energy."[33] Burnside, the treasurer, did not equal McClellan intellectually, but Cobden was impressed with "his high *moral* qualities" and thought

[32] The Fisher whom Cobden visited in Philadelphia may have been Joseph, or conceivably Joshua Francis Fisher. See p. 173 and n.

[33] Add. MSS. 43663, Part 2, Cobden to Sale, March 26, 1859. For Jefferson Davis' opinion of McClellan, see *infra*, p. 153.

him "as truthful & honorable a man as could be found."[34] Cobden does not specifically commit himself on this trip in his feelings about Osborn, either in the diary or in the letters which he wrote from America. Several entries in the diary record other people's unfavorable opinions of him; but Cobden did not hold him at fault. "There are two sides to the question of Osborns indemnity,"[35] he asserted. The fact that he made no serious effort to alter the management is a tribute to Osborn. Two years later, however, Cobden still deplored the strength of the New York influence. Writing to C. S. Ellis, he stated:

. . . It has been suggested that if Caird, & another person of equally good standing but well acquainted with *railway* matters, could be appointed as European Directors with the understanding that they should spend a couple of months in the autumn of each year in Illinois, it would be a good arrangement, in which I heartily agree. The great defect of the management is that it is practically in the hands of a clique if not of an individual. – If we could have two men of high position possessing the confidence of the European shareholders passing part of each year on the spot, it would be far better than sending two ordinary English directors to live in New York, where they would of course be always in a minority. – [36]

From time to time after this trip Cobden received letters from Osborn (frequently bearing news of the Civil War); and he saw Osborn again in 1863 when the latter paid him "a sudden visit" in Midhurst.[37] During these years he supported Osborn, giving him the proxies on his stock.[38]

It is clear that Cobden was satisfied with the integrity of the general management. "As respects the character of the management," he wrote to Gilpin on this trip, "I must not omit to say that we have been very foolishly fouling our own

[34] *Ibid.* 43652, Part 5, Cobden to Bright, December 29, 1862. For this statement in its context see n. p. 191, *infra*.
[35] *Ibid.* 43663, Part 2, Cobden to Sale, March 26, 1859.
[36] *Ibid.* 43663, Part 2, Cobden to Ellis, March 12, 1861.
[37] *Ibid.* 43655, Part 6, Cobden to Hargreaves, August 22, 1863.
[38] Gates, *The Illinois Central Railroad*, p. 82.

nest." He found that in the two instances of the board's allowing credit for calls, "it was done for the benefit of the Company & wisely done." He furthermore found that the report of the crop failure was not to some extent an excuse – "But it was a real visitation of Providence. – ... Last year was a most calamitous season – Nothing like it was ever known before in the North West of America or Canada."[39] Regarding the New York directors as a whole, he declared, "they are *as a body*, as respectable as any board in England, & far richer than most of them."[40]

The conduct of the men involved in the Illinois Central was but one side of Cobden's mission. The other part was the railroad itself and the country through which it ran. The opening sentence in Cobden's letter to John Sale indicates something of the extent and nature of his investigation of the physical property: "I have traveled over every mile of the Railway by day light in the Directors car, sleeping in it at night in a siding, & stopping to visit the villages & walk upon the prairie farms."[41] Some of those miles he traversed several times, and miles of other western railroads as well. Steamer and wagon were also employed on his extensive journeys.

His first trip over the Illinois Central Railroad took him from Chicago to Cairo, from which he continued south by steamer and train as far as Holly Springs, Mississippi, to investigate the railroad with which the Illinois Central hoped to connect in a complete Chicago-New Orleans line. Returning to Cairo, he followed the Illinois Central to Dunleith, its terminus on the Mississippi. Crossing to Dubuque, Cobden descended the Mississippi by steamer to St. Louis, ferried to the Illinois side, and took a connecting railroad to Centralia, whence he rode on the Illinois Central to Chicago. On his next trip in the west, he went by wagon from La-

---

[39] Add. MSS. 43663, Part 5, Cobden to Gilpin, April 10, 1859.
[40] *Ibid.* 43663, Part 2, Cobden to Sale, March 26, 1859.
[41] *Ibid.*

fayette, Indiana, to Sullivant's farm in eastern Illinois, and from there by wagon to the nearest station on the Illinois Central, on which line he continued to Cairo. From that point he made his return to Chicago, covering the route of the Illinois Central as far as El Paso. Yet a third separate journey on the line took him to Springfield (via the Illinois Central to Tolono), whence he made a side trip to Jacksonville. In addition to these long journeys, Cobden went on short wagon rides into the country to see the progress of cultivation. On these various trips he observed carefully the land through which the railroad passed, visited villages and emigrant colonies, and talked with individual farmers. He picked up much information on land values, farming conditions, the effects of the crop failures of 1858, the character of the people, and the development of the Illinois settlements.[42]

After such exhaustive inquiries Cobden's conclusions must have been heartening. "In regard to private matters," he wrote to Gilpin, "I have found nothing unsatisfactory since I have been on the spot."[43] To Bright he asserted, "I find no substantial injury done to the Illinois Central railroad by the disasters of the last year. – If our London Comm[ee] [Committee] should be a little more forbearing all may go well. – No good will arise from a violent or arrogant tone."[44] As for the railroad itself, he was delighted with what he saw. Writing to Gilpin he reported:

I have spent some time in Illinois & was over every mile of the railway by daylight. – Unless I had seen it I could not have believed in the existence of such a vast tract of such unvarying fertility. – For at least 670 miles out of 706 the railway passed through land as fertile as the very best soil in England, without an acre of heath, rock, hill, or bog, offering any impediment to the

---

[42] Corliss states that soon after Cobden's visit to Illinois, Osborn directed that the town of South Pass, situated in the fruitful section of southern Illinois, be renamed Cobden. *Main Line of Mid-America*, p. 92.

[43] Add. MSS. 43663, Part 5, Cobden to Gilpin, April 10, 1859.

[44] *Ibid.* 43652, Part 7, Cobden to Bright, April 29, 1859.

progress of the plough. – If 5 miles only on each side of the track were cultivated as it would be by English farmers the railway would not carry off the produce. – The land is like an old rotten English dung heap. – [45]

In the same vein to Sale, he prophesied, "When the history of the railway is written at some future time it will be with a smile of incredulity at the embarrassments which accompanied the donation of this 2½ million acres of the richest tract of land in the world."[46]

Cobden's hopes for the future were high. He was satisfied that the land sold would be paid for. Good grain returns would facilitate this. "As respects the future, all depends on the next harvest," he wrote to Gilpin. "At present the prospect of the harvest is favorable. – The winter wheat is looking well, & the season being early there will be a great breadth of spring corn sown. – With a fair harvest, & the opening of the through line to New Orleans in the Autumn a great change in the traffic will be witnessed before Xmas."[47]

Next to the value of the land-grant, it was on this direct railroad connection with New Orleans that Cobden founded his greatest confidence in the future of the line. This confidence was based on what he learned when he went down to Mississippi "to see with my own eyes" the actual state of the southern railroad which was to give the Illinois Central that connection. All but about sixty miles of the line had been finished; and much had already been done on that section. It was expected that the line would be completed in the autumn. From the facts gathered from the representatives of the road, Cobden "was satisfied . . . that the opening of this line will be a new era in the Illinois Line." A railroad from Chicago to New Orleans would transport one in less than two days from a frigid temperature to a balmy clime – "from the region of thick ice & snow into the midst of orange trees

[45] *Ibid.* 43663, Part 5, Cobden to Gilpin, April 10, 1859.
[46] *Ibid.* 43663, Part 2, Cobden to Sale, March 26, 1859.
[47] *Ibid.* 43663, Part 5, Cobden to Gilpin, April 10, 1859.

& alligators!"[48] It was expected that the shipment of tropical products for the consumption of the lake region would now go up the Mississippi and the Illinois Central Railroad, instead of by New York as formerly. There would also be a great passenger traffic between north and south. Telling Sale of these things, Cobden wrote from the States, "I have always expected much from this great north & south line; for it is a variety of *latitude* & not of longitude which creates traffic & travel. – What I learnt at Cairo (our southern terminus) satisfied me that we are certain to realize the benefits of this southern extension. – . . . If Illinois be blessed with an ordinary harvest, & the New Orleans line be opened by September, I 'guess' there will be a very different opinion of the railway before Xmas."[49]

It was one of fate's ironies that neither of these hopes materialized to change the fortunes of the railroad. The year 1859 brought its crop failures through two unseasonable frosts which destroyed the corn and through a plague of the chinch bug which ruined the wheat. Net land sales for 1859 were the lowest of any of the three-year period from 1858 to 1860; and low collections accompanied them.[50]

Meanwhile, to meet this situation, some of the British representatives and a number of the shareholders were convinced that calls on the stock were sounder finance than more bond issues at high interest and heavy discounts. A favorable arrangement was therefore made to induce the shareholders to make full payment on the shares.[51] It appealed to Cobden who had returned home from America. He wrote to Slagg in July 1860:

I am sorry to see that there is another call for the Illinois Company. – This will make 80 dollars paid out of the 100. – There is a proposal standing still open to enable shareholders to pay up the whole and to be entitled to 4 per ct. preference dividend. I

[48] *Ibid.* 43663, Part 2, Cobden to Sale, March 26, 1859.
[49] *Ibid.*
[50] Gates, *The Illinois Central Railroad*, p. 257.
[51] *Ibid.*, p. 82.

believe I am right in this. If so (*Mr James Walker the share-broker knows all about it*) I should be placed in a much better position if I could possibly raise the money to pay up the rest. I do not know whether any more could be borrowed on the shares for that purpose. I enclose a statement. I have not the least doubt about the due payment of the dividend or the security of the investment. – It is only a question of time, and a very short time to make it a safe and valuable property.[52]

Many shares were paid up by the investors; and these payments helped the Illinois Central to reestablish its credit. In 1860 the economic situation improved; and there was an increase in revenue from traffic and land sales and collections.[53] Cobden wrote to Slagg in August, "A good deal of the rise in the Illinois shares is of course mere speculation. – But it will to a large extent be permanent if the accounts we hear of the prospects of the yield of the harvest of Illinois should turn out correct."[54] Two weeks later things were looking so well that Cobden refused (in response, apparently, to a proposal from Slagg) to dispose of his shares in order to ease his financial difficulties:

I am much obliged by your letter respecting the Illinois. After taking all the trouble I could have done if it had been an ordinary private investment, to understand the value of this property, I would prefer not to part with my shares at present. I do not at all fear their going back in value as they did before, *unless after having reached the same price as they had done by a previous great speculation in the West when shares reached 35 premium.* If that should come again, I might be tempted to sell. – But there is intrinsic value in this property. The State of Illinois is rapidly growing in population & wealth, and the *land* owned by the Company must increase in value proportionately. At all events I should be glad to leave them over for the present.[55]

Undoubtedly it took courage for him to hold on. Returning from America, he had learned that his resources were

---

[52] Add. MSS. 43677, Part 2, Cobden to Slagg, July 9, 1860 [typed copy].
[53] Gates, *The Illinois Central Railroad*, pp. 82, 258.
[54] Add. MSS. 43677, Part 2, Cobden to Slagg, August 27, 1860 [typed copy].
[55] *Ibid.* 43677, Part 2, Cobden to Slagg, September 11, 1860 [typed copy].

practically at an end; and again his friends had come to his aid with a gift of £40,000.[56] During the following year he had neglected his affairs to negotiate the Anglo-French Treaty of Commerce, together with its tariff. Catching rumor of an attempt to vote him money in recognition of his services, however, Cobden asked Bright, who was active in Parliament, to put a stop to such a movement. "It is bad enough to have neglected my affairs till I am obliged to see something of this sort done privately for my family – But the *two* processes would be intolerable."[57] In 1864, the year before he died, Cobden held 441 shares of stock.[58] That he should have retained so much of his stock through the vicissitudes of these last years is proof of his faith in the railroad.

Better times for the railroad continued through the early part of 1861, in spite of the increasingly serious political situation.[59] In a letter to Ellis in March, Cobden wrote, "The news respecting the Illinois affairs seems more hopeful. – If the States can avoid a civil war, I don't think a peaceful separation of North & South will be a great evil to any party, certainly not to Illinois which would in that case attract many settlers from the slave States."[60] Though his statement sounds completely materialistic, his position was based substantially on his love of America and on an idealism of peace.[61] Although he wavered in the beginnings of the conflict, he deplored the war, and was soon to hope ardently for the triumph of the Union.[62] In this same letter he considered that "the worst feature in the concern is that the *land is not*

[56] Morley, *Life of Richard Cobden*, II, 285-286.
[57] Add. MSS. 43651, Cobden to Bright, February 4, 1861.
[58] Gates, *The Illinois Central Railroad*, p. 82n.
[59] *Ibid.*, p. 259.
[60] Add. MSS. 43663, Part 2, Cobden to Ellis, March 12, 1861.
[61] Bright, in referring to the grief which the Civil War had caused Cobden, stated: "He, I think, was more broken down in heart and feeling by the American War, perhaps, than any other man that I happened to know at that time in England." *Speeches of the Right Hon. John Bright, M.P., Delivered in Bradford, on the Occasion of the Inauguration of the Cobden Memorial*, London, 1877, p. 13.
[62] See his many letters for these years in the Additional Manuscripts.

paid for."[63] And things were soon to become temporarily worse. With the outbreak of the Civil War, returns from land sales and collections fell off sharply and the north-south freight traffic was badly hit.[64]

Cobden's high hopes for that other source of improvement, a lucrative Chicago-New Orleans traffic, were temporarily doomed to disappointment. During the 'sixties and 'seventies the north-south trade was altered to east and west. The growing industrial activity of the east and of western Europe, the demand in the east for western food stuffs and raw materials, the development of steam shipping on the Great Lakes and of rail communication, which afforded a cheaper and faster system of transportation between Europe and Chicago, together with the break in north-south communication during the war and the subsequent prostration of the south, all combined to change the course of trade routes along lines of latitude instead of longitude.[65] Inasmuch as in 1859 an enormous traffic passed through Cairo north and south, it is not surprising that Cobden should have anticipated a flourishing trade almost immediately between the two sections. He could not have foreseen the course of history.

In the meantime, the hard days of 1861 were not destined to last long. Transportation of men and supplies for the army, a rise in agricultural prices, and a new demand for land increased traffic and land revenues for the railroad the following year.[66] From this time on, the Illinois Central experienced a period of prosperity. It was ironic that Cobden could not live to witness its future; but his faith in the railroad was justified.

The Trip of 1859

If the extent of Cobden's journey in 1835 was remarkable, the distance covered during the short period of the trip of

[63] Add. MSS. 43663, Part 2, Cobden to Ellis, March 12, 1861.
[64] Gates, *The Illinois Central Railroad*, see pp. 82, 259, 275-276.
[65] Brownson, *History of the Illinois Central Railroad to 1870*, esp. pp. 75-76, 82-86.
[66] Gates, *The Illinois Central Railroad*, pp. 82, 259-262.

1859 was even more so. Within little more than four and a half months Cobden crossed the Atlantic from Liverpool to Boston, made two trips from New York to Chicago, traveled up and down Illinois some five and more times, once as far as Mississippi, journeyed to Washington and Albany from New York, and returned to England by way of Boston, Montreal, and Quebec. Taking into consideration his stops, he traversed these many miles in less than two months of actual travel. Writing to Bright from Washington, with a little over half of his trip completed, he said, "It seems more like two years than two months since I landed in this Country so great have been the changes & so long the distances I have gone through. – In moving through the Country so rapidly I have of course only been able to skim the surface of things."[67]

A brief survey of Cobden's itinerary may help to clarify the complicated nature of his activity.

Sailing from Liverpool on February 12th, Cobden must have been glad that he did not have to depend on the whims of a sailing vessel, for he wanted very much to reach Washington before the adjournment of Congress. Arriving in Boston on the 26th, he stopped but a few hours to see friends; and continued to New York to spend the weekend on Illinois Central matters. On Tuesday he hurried to Washington with only an overnight stay at the home of friends in Philadelphia – in time to observe the final congressional proceedings and to enjoy an additional day or two of Washington life. Upon his return to New York, Cobden resumed his investigation of Illinois Central affairs and, after five days, was ready to leave with Osborn for Chicago – by way of Albany, Niagara, Toronto, and Detroit – there to begin his examination of the railroad at first hand. At Niagara he notes, "This journey of 15 hours travelling would have occupied a week when I was over the same ground in 1835."

Arriving in Chicago for one day, he attended the annual

[67] Add. MSS. 43652, Part 7, Cobden to Bright, April 29, 1859.

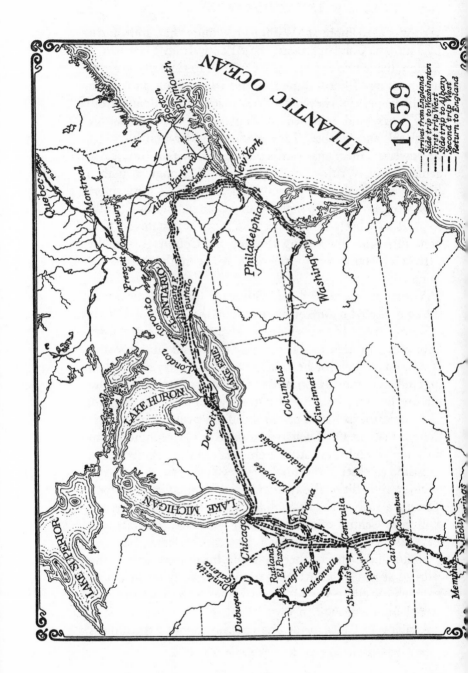

1859

Arrival from England
Side trip to Washington
First trip West
Side trip to Albany
Second trip West
Return to England

ATLANTIC OCEAN

Plymouth
Boston

New York
Hartford
Albany

Philadelphia
Washington

LAKE ONTARIO
Buffalo
Niagara R.
Toronto
London
LAKE ERIE

Columbus
Cincinnati

Detroit

Indianapolis
Lafayette
Urbana

LAKE HURON

LAKE MICHIGAN

Chicago

LAKE SUPERIOR

Dubuque
Dunlette
Galena
Rutland El Paso
Springfield
Jacksonville
St.Louis
Richview
Centralia
Cairo
Columbus
Memphis
Holly Springs

Québec
Montreal
Ogdensburg
Prescott

meeting of the Illinois Central, studied the railroad's business, and then left for an extensive tour of the railroad itself. As indicated above, this trip took him by rail and
steamer to Mississippi, north to Cairo, along the Illinois
Central to Dunleith, and, from Dubuque opposite, down the
Mississippi to St. Louis. A connecting train on the Illinois side
carried him to Centralia whence he returned to Chicago. On
this journey he traversed the entire main line of the Illinois
Central once and parts of it twice. In seventeen days, "Since
Mar 12th the date of my departure from New York I have
travelled upwards of 3,000 miles," he wrote. After five days
in Chicago, he returned to New York, completing his first
extensive trip. "During my absence of 24 days from New
York," he noted, "I have travelled nearly 4,000 miles."

Approximately eleven more days in New York were filled
with business, sight-seeing, and social events, interrupted
only by a four days' visit in Albany at the home of a friend
interested in the Illinois Central. Then began the second trip
west. In Philadelphia Cobden stayed with friends for almost
five days, again combining business and pleasure. Perhaps
the high point of the trip socially was reached in Washington where he visited "our old friend the President & his pretty
niece."[68] Within a week of leaving Washington, he arrived
in Chicago by way of Cincinnati (where he stopped less than
two days), Lafayette (from which point he traveled into
Illinois by wagon), Cairo, Centralia, and El Paso. After a
day of correspondence in Chicago he made the separate journey to Springfield, where he saw various state officers, and
took a short excursion to Jacksonville. Returning to Chicago,
he stayed a final four days winding up railroad affairs.

Upon his return to New York Cobden spent a last nine
days in business and sight-seeing. From there he traveled to
Boston (stopping in New Haven and Hartford) where he
passed over a week with friends, giving some attention to
business, meeting various people, and visiting points of in-

[68] *Ibid.*

terest which included Plymouth, the home of a fellow-passenger of the trip of 1835. Boston was the last American city of importance at which he stopped; he left the States at Ogdensburg, and at Prescott took the steamer to Montreal. There he stayed for five days with a friend who was one of his fellow passengers on the voyage from Liverpool, and, as usual, met stimulating people, saw interesting sights, and discussed Illinois Central affairs. A day in Quebec before leaving impressed him with the beauty of that city. On June 18 he sailed for England, and landed in Liverpool after a voyage of eleven days.

The vast distance covered testifies to the great improvement in the means of transportation since Cobden's earlier visit to the United States. The sailing vessel of a month's voyage of 1835 had given way to the steamship of less than two weeks' crossing in 1859. The stagecoach which pulled him over execrable roads in 1835 was gone; there was rail transportation to practically any place he chose to go.

The even greater differences in the conditions under which the trip was made in 1859 bear tribute to the man. Cobden now did much of his traveling over a line of which he was an important shareholder, riding in a private "Directors" car. He was the guest of other railroads: "Mr Livermore the Treasurer of the Michigan Central gave us the use of the Directors car, & would not allow me to pay my fare. – . . . Started from Cincinnati for Indianapolis & Lafayette in a special train furnished by Mr Church the President of the Line of railroad leading to those places." On one occasion, en route to Cincinnati, "Mr Garrett the Chairman of the Baltimore & Ohio Railroad met us & passed several hours in our company," and on another Cobden was accompanied from Cincinnati to El Paso, Illinois, by Mr. H. C. Lord "President of the Cincinnati & Indianapolis railroad, an intelligent & respectable man." Throughout much of his journey he was escorted by other prominent men, notably Osborn and McClellan.

The twenty-four years had made their difference. The young English business man had become the renowned English statesman. As such he was received. This time he spent nearly half of his trip in America's chief cities of Boston, New York, Philadelphia, Washington, and Chicago, with New York alone accounting for nearly one month of the journey. In these places and others, he was accorded marked honors. Seven years before, as will be recalled, he had told a friend that "[I] should dread the turmoil of public meetings when I arrived there";[69] and his admonition to Bright only three years earlier, when he had suggested an incognito trip to America for Bright's health, reveals his own personal feelings: "But it would be suicide to allow yourself to be feted in the States as they would do if you allowed it."[70] On the whole Cobden was able to avoid official and public entertainment; but his days were filled with private functions.

Instead of comments on American hotel life, of which the journal of 1835 contains many, the diary of 1859 reflects comfort at the homes of various friends such as the Gilpins in Philadelphia, Buchanan in Washington, the Burches in Chicago, Wood in Albany, the Bradfords in West Roxbury (Boston), Young in Montreal, and others. In practically every place Cobden met the principal men of the city and was entertained by many of them. A list of his hosts would include many of the proudest American names of the period. In New York he was wined and dined by such men as George Bancroft, Peter Cooper, Cyrus Field, James Brown, Abram S. Hewitt, William Osborn, Robert Minturn, and John Jay; and at their breakfasts and dinners he met among others Bryant, Cunard, Everett, Astor, Greeley, Tappan, Dana, Mott, Grinnell, John Van Buren, Jerome Bonaparte, General Scott. Some of these and other friends drove him to

[69] Watkin, *Alderman Cobden of Manchester*, p. 165.
[70] Add. MSS. 43652, Part 2, Cobden to Bright, March 8, 1856.

their estates nearby and showed him the schools, courts, and other public buildings and places of interest.

On the second of Cobden's two visits to Washington he was the house guest of the President whom he had known intimately when he was the American minister to Britain. His first evening in the capitol he "was introduced by Senator Mason to many members of both branches of the legislature . . . [and] was allowed the privilege of the 'floor.' " The following day he went "again to the Capitol in both House & Senate, & made the acquaintance of the leading men." The ranking members of the British diplomatic corps, Lord Lyons, minister to Washington, and Lady Napier, wife of the retiring minister, entertained him during his stay; and several American political figures, notably Lewis Cass who was Secretary of State and Senators Mason and Hunter, paid him courteous attention. In Boston he was the house guest of the S. D. Bradfords, though he was entertained and accompanied on some of his days there by John Murray Forbes. Through them and other friends he met among many others: Emerson, Wendell Phillips, General Sumner, George Sumner, Charles Francis Adams, Josiah Quincy, George Boutwell, Senator Henry Wilson, Charles Hale, and President Walker of Harvard, several of whom showed him special favors. Possibly he felt more at home in Philadelphia than anywhere else, for he stayed with the Gilpins, relatives of his friend Bright, and personal friends of his own. The two missing pages of the diary in the Philadelphia section prevent complete knowledge of Cobden's activities there; but he was accorded the usual courtesies and met the prominent citizens.

Tribute was as earnestly paid the famous Englishman in lesser centers. In Albany he was received by Governor Morgan and "attended the Session of the House of Assembly which passed a resolution admitting me to the 'floor'. – . . . Afterwards looked in at the Senate for a few minutes. – Great number of Albums brought me by the 'call boys' for my autograph." On one of his four evenings in Albany "a numerous party of the principal inhabitants paid a visit at Mr Woods," where Cobden was staying; on another evening he went "to General Gansevoorts & met a large party." His one night in New Haven Cobden "put up at the house of Doctor Bacon the leading clergyman of the place a man eminent for his logical eloquence & his courage & honesty. – . . . In the evening a number of the principal people of the Town chiefly professional men came to meet me, – & a serenade was given me by some of the Collegians who sang some excellent choruses, & finished with 'God Save the Queen.' " Continuing to Hartford, he "was invited by the President of the Senate, & the Speaker of the House to take a seat by their side where I observed for a few minutes the course of their [the Connecticut legislature's] proceedings."

The west in its turn honored Cobden. Privately entertained by individual Chicagoans – the J. H. Burches, at whose home he stayed on two of his trips to Chicago, Ambrose Burnside, James Grant Wilson, Isaac N. Arnold, and others – Chicago extended its hospitality semi-officially. On his second arrival there, "a requisition presented to me asking me to address a meeting which I declined, but suggested a private soiree at which I could meet the requisitionists in a conversational tête-à-tête." Two days later he was accompanied by four prominent citizens of Chicago on a visit to the schools of the city, and "in the evening was entertained at a dinner by the principal people in the city." Springfield was aware of the fame of the man in her midst. There he was escorted to meet the Governor and various state officers; and on his second night there "was disturbed by a serenade under my window . . . & was summoned from my bed by the landlord to return thanks from my bedroom window." Cincinnati judges entertained him during his short stop there; in Indianapolis "was introduced to the governor & several private Citizens." Everywhere he received a hearty welcome. Bright, some years after Cobden's death, referred to his popularity with the Americans: "He visited that country twice during the course of his life. He had made, as he made wherever he went, many very earnest and very warm friends."[71]

His stay in Canada was equally pleasant. In Montreal he was the guest of the Honorable John Young, with whom he had crossed the Atlantic on his way to America. There he met among others such Canadian statesmen and politicians as McGee, Rose, and Dorrion; and he seemed to enjoy particularly the courtesies accorded him by the scientists, Ross and Sir William Logan. Friends made pleasant his short stop in Quebec; and the following day he departed from America with "Mr Noad & Mr Forsyth offering me kind attentions at parting."

Sight-seeing appears to have consumed almost as much of Cobden's time as business and social activity. There is much in the diary about the metropolitan scene of 1859. The appearance of some cities is indicated, the remarkable growth and development of others is described. Much of what Cobden saw was seen by the usual tourist; but he was more fortunate than many visitors in having friends who drove him through the suburbs or showed him points of interest not visited by the average traveler.

As the dominating interests of a man are frequently revealed by the ends to which he gives his free time, so it was with Cobden in the places which he visited and the things which he observed. As a practical business man and economist he was interested in commercial establishments of numerous kinds – in such varying details as rentals, income, production, methods, and, particularly, growth. He was constantly impressed by an amazing engineering progress, proved by patent office statistics and evidenced everywhere. The extensive economic survey of Illinois lands and settlements was the main part of his business; and the diary offers vivid glimpses into the life of these days of farm and railroad

---

[71] *Speeches of the Right Hon. John Bright, M.P., Delivered in Bradford, on the Occasion of the Inauguration of the Cobden Memorial*, London, 1877, p. 13.

beginnings. References to land values and to the effects of the depression of 1857, remarks on emigration by small colonies, descriptions of early crude settlements, accounts of individual farms, notes on people encountered, observations of life on the Mississippi reveal the intrinsic worth of a country that was fast coming into its own. He has more to say on the economic conditions prevailing in this section than upon any other single matter.

Being of the political world himself, Cobden was keenly interested in the democratic processes of American national and state government. He made a special point of visiting all of the legislative bodies which he could, – Congress, the New York and Connecticut legislatures, and the Canadian Legislative Assembly. He seems generally to have respected the men who directed the affairs of government. He was doubtless partly reflecting his impression of Congress at this time when, later in 1863, after studying some congressional records which Sumner had sent him, he told Bright: "There is a far higher average of talking & debating talent in Washington than at Westminster. – We have two men in the Commons who have a gift of natural eloquence above any thing in the U.S. Congress, but as a whole we are not to compare with them."[72] Writing to another friend the following year he said, "I have read with interest your allusions to the American Diplomatic papers. My attention has often been given to these, generally, very able documents. I am struck with the number of men in the walks of literature & politics in the United States who are available for the successful conduct of all public affairs in that country."[73] He was, however, critical of the inequality of representation in the Connecticut legislature and of the adjournment of Congress before business was finished, which "would not be viewed so lightly in England."

[72] Add. MSS. 43651, Part 3, Cobden to Bright, September 8, 1863.
[73] *Ibid.* 43678, Part 4, Cobden to Edward Alexander, November 5, 1864 [typed copy].

Cobden's comments on the subject of political integrity are of interest in the light of Ashworth's letters to him from America two years earlier wherein Ashworth had reported widespread political corruption, especially in elections, and stated: "One Gentleman with whom I was conversing on the subject expressed his regret, that you should so freely express yourself in favour of America on this subject, meaning the suffrage. – In his opinion the Americans who read your speeches consider you not recently or well informed on the matter."[74] It is not surprising then that when Cobden got to America he let slip no opportunity of informing himself on conditions. Several specific instances of investigation he recorded in the diary: he raised the question of governmental deterioration before the Press Club of New York; apparently discussed political corruption with Randall in Philadelphia and with Judge McLean of Cincinnati; inquired of Buchanan about it; and questioned Noyes of New York about the reported venality of the Bench. He seems to have drawn varying reactions. In a letter to Bright he reported that opinion at the Press Club dinner was about equally divided; the Whigs favoring the theory of deterioration and the Democrats denying it.[75] The courts he found "pure"; but he was informed that lobbying influences in the legislatures and the House sometimes smacked of suspicion. He learned of irregularities in elections which took various forms, but never that of bribery. He encountered complaints against universal suffrage in large cities of foreign population where the system had been abused; but for the most part he found the smaller communities thoroughly democratic. From his conversations and his own observations, Cobden remained unconvinced of serious political misdemeanor.[76] His faith in America and

[74] *Ibid.* 43647, Ashworth to Cobden, April 7, 1857. Later, upon his return from the States, Ashworth had written Cobden that he had spent his last two months in the north and in Canada, "and I wish I could remember anything which would feel more acceptable relating to the morality of pub[lic] men either in Canada or in the States." *Ibid.* 43647, Ashworth to Cobden, July 10, 1857.

[75] *Ibid.* 43651, Part 7, Cobden to Bright, April 29, 1859.

[76] *Ibid.* For Cobden's emphatic statement, see *infra*, p. 73.

will to believe the best may sometimes have clouded his insight into undoubted evils.[77]

Of all American social institutions, the educational system still interested Cobden most. His admiration of the American schools was intensified by his visits to those of Chicago, New York, Dubuque, and Boston and to a normal school in Albany. The representation of rich and poor alike in practically all schools, the successful employment of female teachers which "was more and more generally adopted in the U. States," and the "salutary effect" of coeducation impressed him. In his visit to the New York school, he concluded his few remarks to the scholars "by hoping that at some future day England would be blessed with a system of public schools similar to those of the United States."[78] Of an indifferent education himself, Cobden had a high regard for things intellectual. He saw the colleges of Yale, Harvard, and Girard, the New York and Chicago libraries, the publishing houses of Appleton and Harper, and the *Times* office. The Geographical Society, Athenæum Club and Century Club of New York, the American Philosophical and Historical Societies and the Academy of Arts in Philadelphia, the Agricultural Museum of Albany, and the historical museum of Plymouth were all visited in turn.

Cobden was as sensitive to beauty as he had been in earlier years; and the sublimity of Niagara, the charm of Vermont Hills, the grandeur of Quebec's Abraham Heights, and the grotesque shapes of Atlantic icebergs moved him as nature at her best always did. Undoubtedly the tragedies of the intervening years had had their effect, and he had matured spiritually.[79] Religion held new meaning for him. Always interested in humanity and in schemes for its betterment, he

[77] Goldwin Smith notes in his journal of his visit to America in 1864: "Abuse of the popular vote in New York. Cobden's view too ideal." Arnold Haultain, *Goldwin Smith His Life and Opinions*, London, [1913], p. 261.

[78] *New-York Daily Tribune*, April 9, 1859.

[79] Several times after the loss of his son, Cobden wrote that the only consolation he could find was in God's plan of another better life to come.

now sought the society of leading American humanitarians. His comment on individuals and groups which he met is evidence of his intense human curiosity and of his fine feeling for human worth.

"This Hellish Republic"

As the nature of Cobden's trip of 1859 was different from that of 1835, so did he find many changes in the country which he visited. The new world did not disappoint him.

Since I landed at Boston on the 26th February [he wrote to Gilpin on April 10th], I have travelled nearly 5000 miles in this Country, & have been amazed at the progress it has made since I was here, in 1835. – Whatever be the case as regards the political character of the people (about which I will offer no opinion on so superficial an acquaintance) there has certainly been no deterioration in any other direction. – The people are better clothed & lodged, better educated, read more of better books, & still more improved newspapers, display better manners, & are more orderly in every way than when I was here before. – Above all I have been struck with the prevalence of temperance principles which probably you will say accounts for much that is otherwise improved.– . . . There has been, according to all authorities, a very great revolution in the drinking habits since I was last here.–[80]

To Bright he wrote in similar vein, stressing several other changes:

Comparing what I now see with what I remember of the America of 1835 the progress in material & moral prosperity realizes all that I had expected to see. . – The people are far better off to my eye as compared with the Europe of today than they were in 1835 as compared with the old world at that time. – What strikes me now even more than it did then is the obviously higher grade at which the social habits of the working class are pitched as compared with the same class in the old country. – . . . I have been very much struck with an alteration in the drinking habits of the people. – . . . From what I see I should say there is far more reading going on now in proportion to the population than when I

[80] Add. MSS. 43663, Part 5, Cobden to Gilpin, April 10, 1859.

was last here.–. . . You have heard of the substantial privileges accorded to the weaker sex in this country.–So far from this high trait of civilization having grown out of fashion it is very much more striking than when I was here before.–. . . Whilst every thing is thus improving & progressing in this Country, it is the fashion to tell us that "it is going back politically."–On this subject I do not pretend as yet to be able to speak with authority.– . . . I[t] would seem to me to be very unlikely that a country which is progressing most rapidly in every aspect of its social life, & where the people are every year growing richer & younger & stronger, should at the same time become decrepit & worn out in its political character–I don't believe it.–[81]

America, on the whole, pleased Cobden mightily. "Comparing class with class the people of the United States are raised to a much higher level than in any other country." The unlimited opportunity which the country offered was largely responsible for this, he believed. In the letter to Bright he remarked, "It is this universal hope of rising in the social scale which is the key to much of the superiority that is visible in this country.–It accounts for the orderly self respect which is the great characteristic of the masses in the United States."[82] Thus, the "absence of servility on the part of servants is one of the characteristics of the West"; and there Cobden found that because of the need for labor "man instead of being a drug in the market is at a premium, & this to my taste constitutes the chief charm of this valley of the Mississippi." As he wrote to Bright, "the political condition of a people is very dependent on its economical fate . . . there must be room to rise in the social scale in order to draw out the better qualities of humanity."[83] He considered America's schools, which afforded equal opportunities to rich and poor alike, tools in this process.

Manners reflected something of this self-respect, as he was informed by a friend in Chicago when observing the courtesy of two drivers involved in a collision, though Cobden be-

[81] *Ibid.* 43652, Part 7, Cobden to Bright, April 29, 1859.
[82] *Ibid.*   [83] *Ibid.*

lieved that they were affected by alcoholic moderation as well. On a Mississippi journey he "was struck with the orderly sober & forbearing demeanor" of a rough Pike's Peak company; on trains he "never heard a dispute about a seat or an angry word pass";[84] and in observing people in questionable places in New York slums he considered their behavior, their dress, and amusements "superior to what we meet in the lowest resorts of similar classes in London." Cobden found the Americans forbearing: "It seems as if the higher level at which every man is placed here than in other countries, by the general assent & claim of the Americans, inspires a greater mutual respect among the people which restrains them from that plainspoken style with which Englishmen call each others conduct in question." If there was little banter in conversation, there were sweeping statements. Though he thought the Americans were to be accounted truthful ("They would not utter deliberate falsehoods."), "their 'fast' habits & their confidence in the future lead them into hasty & exaggerated statements, & make them often very inexact in their conversation when matters of fact are involved."

In keeping with their character, Cobden noticed that the people showed "a great decency" and that they "seem to be careful of their horses & kind to dumb animals." From the many numbers that he saw attending churches in various places and doubtless from the activity of the churches, he concluded in Albany that "a larger proportion of the whole population must attend churches here than in England." One of the most notable features of American society in his eyes was the position of women, abused as it was by the creatures themselves. In his remarks on this subject something of his old antipathy to American women persisted. He considered that the "substantial privileges" granted to women were "highly honorable to the *men* of America & places them, in a most important point of view, in the front rank of civilized

[84] *Ibid.*

nations." But the women took such courtesies too much as a right and if they lost them it would be their own fault. Writing in the mood of the diary to Bright he reported, "The ladies take possession as a matter of course of the best seats every where, & the men never allow a woman to be standing whilst they are seated. – I fancy I can perceive a certain degree of *confidence* in the manner of the ladies which is the result of such prescriptive privileges being accorded to them, & which does not increase their attractiveness in the eye of an Englishman."[85]

Cobden returned to England with his greatest hopes for America realized. In a letter to Parkes in the early part of the Civil War, when feeling was running against the North, he asserted:

... I am convinced that all European Statesmen, from their dislike of the men, the civilization, & the form of government, underrate the *power* of the 20 millions of free men in the North & West, – who, come what may, will be 30 millions in 1870. – I have been twice throughout the North & West, at an interval of 24 years. – And I maintain that nobody who has not twice visited the States can comprehend the vitality, force, & velocity of progress of that people, & their inborn aptitude for self-government. – We talk of mobs. – There is no mob but what we send them, & the way in which they clarify & absorb our Irish & German element is the most marvelous illustration of the value & soundness of their institutions. We talk of the government being a failure. – It is only in places like New York, with its vast foreign sediment & froth, (German & Irish) where some Americans complain of the evil of Universal Suffrage. – In the quiet New England interior towns, the result of democratic institutions is as perfect as human imperfection can hope to be. – Every one of those little Towns contains population enough of men used to self-government, virtuous, religious, intelligent, & industrious men – to furnish the materials for the self-government of an Independent State.–

I wish our rulers knew more of this. – *For the South & Slavery there is no future* – Future America will be in the North & West,

[85] *Ibid.*

where, in the life time of my children, will be 100 millions of prosperous people.—...[86]

The day before, Cobden told Fitzmayer: "I have paid two visits to that Country, at an interval of 24 years between the first & second trip. — I do not believe any body, without two such visits, can form an idea of the power & resources, & the rapid & *sure* growth of that people."[87]

Cobden expressed his faith in America's future, even as America was acting in her own faith in that future. Writing to Ashworth during the Civil War he said:

... nobody can doubt the future of the North & West where free men only are found. — Now you and I, who have travelled through the free States, know how much that young people live in the future. — Their faith in the destiny of coming generations becomes a part of their estimated power when measuring themselves against the old world. — They are the only people who in their statistical works carry on their progress into the future. — Take a table of the past growth of Chicago, for instance, & you will see, in addition to the exports & imports to the present time, an estimate of their increase for a dozen years to come. — Such a people cannot be beaten or humbled by present misfortunes. They take refuge in the future, — which offers them advantages over the whole world.[88]

Some of Cobden's estimates of several prominent Americans of the time, recorded in the diary and in his letters, justify brief digression at this point. As has been stated before, Cobden had known Buchanan well when he was the American minister to London. He did not find the same Buchanan. He was looking "much older ... apparently out of spirits ... not so happy ... [and] disappointed." To Bright Cobden reported from Washington, "The President does not look in such good health & spirits as when we knew him in London.

---

[86] *Ibid.* 43660 [Part 1], Cobden to Parkes, December 4, 1861. Cobden prophesied truly; his last surviving daughter, Mrs. Cobden-Unwin, has died within the past decade.

[87] *Ibid.* 43662, Cobden to Colonel Fitzmayer, December 3, 1861.

[88] *Ibid.* 43648, Part 2, Cobden to Ashworth, June 14, 1862.

– He has been worried to death nearly [?] by the politicians & placehunters."[89]

Cobden records Jefferson Davis' opinion of the man who within little more than two years was to become the foremost general for the North in the Civil War, McClellan. Meeting Davis on one of his trips on the Mississippi, Cobden questioned him about McClellan, then the vice-president of the Illinois Central Railroad. Davis praised McClellan highly and considered him "not merely an able man in his profession, but a gentleman, high-spirited & with an honorable ambition." Cobden's letter to Sale adds to the estimate of the diary: "He [Davis] told me that he had three times selected Captn McClellan for special confidential missions – to Europe, to Mexico, & to the Pacific – & that he had always been satisfied with the result. – He said he was an honorable high spirited gentlemanly man."[90]

Cobden's opinion at this time of Davis himself was that of "a very intelligent man though a strong advocate of Slavery & Southern rights." In a letter to Bright in 1861 he supplements the reference in the diary: "Jefferson Davis the new Southern President is an accomplished gentlemanlike man with whom I found myself for a couple of days on board a Mississippi Steamer. – He fought desperately in the Mexican War, & was afterwards Secretary at War at Washington, & both as an officer in the field & an administrator, friends & foes allow him to be a superior man. – Lincoln whom I saw at Springfield is a backwoodsman of good sturdy common sense, but evidently unequal to the occasion."[91] This is the first indication that Cobden saw Lincoln on this trip. Undoubtedly from his impression of Lincoln the meeting was not worth recording in the diary. In another letter to Bright the following year he stated:

. . . It is useless shutting ones eyes to the fact that the leaders in

[89] *Ibid.* 43652, Part 7, Cobden to Bright, April 29, 1859.
[90] *Ibid.* 43663, Part 2, Cobden to Sale, March 26, 1859.
[91] *Ibid.* 43649, Part 2, Cobden to Bright, March 25, 1861.

the Federal government are not equal to the occasion. – Lincoln has a certain moral dignity, but is intellectually inferior, & as men do not generally measure others correctly who are above their own calibre, he has chosen for his instruments mediocre men. – ... I know the men at the head of affairs on both sides, & I should say that in energy of will, in comprehensiveness of view, in habits & power of command, & in knowledge of economical & fiscal questions, Jefferson Davis is more than equal to Lincoln & all his Cabinet. –[92]

If Cobden was not impressed by his meeting with Lincoln and by Lincoln's policies at the beginning of the war, as the years wore on he was convinced of the President's qualities. The alteration in his feeling was gradual. Even in March of 1863 he did not approve of Lincoln: "Notwithstanding the blundering incapacity of the Republican party, from their President downwards, I will back them to win (as our sporting men say) because they carry the flag of freedom & of human progress."[93] But within the following nine months, Cobden's attitude toward Lincoln changed. A letter to Sumner in January of 1864 explains why:

You will soon begin to busy yourselves with the task of President-making. I hope you will re-elect Mr. Lincoln. He is rising in reputation in Europe apart from the success of the North. He possesses great moral qualities, which in the long-run tell more on the fortunes of the world in these days than mere intellect. I always thought his want of enlarged experience was a disadvantage to him. But he knows our countrymen evidently, and that is the main point. And being a stranger to the rest of the world, he has the less temptation to embark in foreign controversies or quarrels. Nothing shows his solid sense more than the pertinacity with which he avoids all outside complications. His truthful elevation of character, and his somewhat stolid placidity of nature, put it quite beyond the power of other governments to fasten a quarrel on him, and inspire the fullest confidence in those who are committing themselves to the side of the North. I say all this on the assumption that he has irrevocably committed himself to 'abolition' as the result of the war. Any compromise on that question

[92] *Ibid.* 43651, Part 1, Cobden to Bright, October 7, 1862.
[93] *Ibid.* 43660, Part 3, Cobden to Arles Dufour, March 28, 1863 [copy].

would cover your cause with external infamy, and render the sanguinary civil war with which you have desolated the North and South, a useless butchery.[94]

Cobden referred to this and other letters when he informed Bright the following month: "In writing to the States I have for some time expressed a strong opinion that Lincoln ought to be reelected. – I have urged it from a foreigners point of view, because he has evinced an imperturbable good temper & conciliation in his relations with Europe, which has been of the most vital importance in their critical dilemma."[95] By the autumn of 1864 Cobden was asserting:

What may be Lincolns particular defects in the eyes of those who are near enough to judge him as an administrator I am of course unable to perceive, – but as far as we can judge him at a distance, he seems to have honesty, self-control, & common sense, in an eminent degree. – Osborn complains that he does every thing one day too late. But he has had a difficult part to play, for in satisfying the more ardent abolitionists he runs the risk of losing the more moderate Republicans, & drifting from the anchorage of the Constitution which means anarchy in a Country that exists only on a written document – & not as we do, politically through hierarchies derived from hazy antiquity. I should say that as a politician Lincoln is very superior to McClellan who is a professional soldier and nothing more. – By the way L. "stumped" Illinois for the Senate in opposition to Douglas, the ablest debater in America after Clay. – ... It is the fashion to underrate Lincoln intellectually, in part because he illustrates his arguments with amusing anecdotes. – But Franklin was not less given to monologues, & some of them not of the most refined character. – It is quite certain that an inferior man could never have sustained such a contest as he Lincoln went through with Douglas. Presidents are apt to fulfil the second term better than the first. – ...[96]

Cobden's faith in Lincoln was affirmed many times during

[94] Morley, *Life of Richard Cobden*, II, 446.
[95] Add. MSS. 43652, Cobden to Bright, February 24, 1864. Though eager for Lincoln's reelection, he told Bright in the autumn that as a foreigner he would not interfere in the personal choice of a president of the United States. *Ibid.* 43652, Cobden to Bright, October 3, 1864.
[96] *Ibid.* 43650, Part 2, Cobden to Bright, October 4, 1864.

that fall of 1864. On October 10th he wrote to Bright, "I sincerely trust Lincoln will be reelected. – It will be a most interesting test of the intelligence, integrity & courage of the yeomanry class with whom the election rests."[97] On November 9th he said, "Let us hope the vote today for Lincoln will be so overwhelming as to extirpate Copperheadism."[98] His one consuming hope over these weeks in the last autumn of his life was for Lincoln's reelection. "It is the only public incident (the election of President) which for a long time has so engrossed my thoughts that I have had a difficulty sometimes in attending to other matters – I have found myself walking half-way to Midhurst to meet the news boy that brings out my morning papers at 11."[99] In one of the last letters he ever wrote—dated March 15, 1865—he told Bright (apropos of the wrong the Americans would feel England had inflicted upon them during the war): ". . . I will trust none of their leading politicians [Cobden's personal friend, Sumner, included] except Lincoln whose political life closes with his next term."[100]

On this trip Cobden's impression of Chase, then governor of Ohio and later Secretary of the Treasury, was a favorable one, and was the beginning of a continued admiration of the man. He rode with Chase from Columbus to Cincinnati "& found him an intelligent man but not very profound on Usury laws or other questions of political economy." On arrival at Cincinnati, Governor Chase "took his carpet bag like the rest of us, & walked to the nearest omnibus," an incident which touched Cobden so much that he referred to

[97] *Ibid.* 43650, Part 2, Cobden to Bright, October 10, 1864.
[98] *Ibid.* 43652, Cobden to Bright, November 9, 1864.
[99] *Ibid.* 43650, Part 2, Cobden to Bright, November 19, 1864.
[100] *Ibid.* 43650, Part 1, Cobden to Bright, March 15, 1865. (His last letter to Bright was post-marked March 20.) Cobden could not know that not only Lincoln's political life but his own was to close within a month. Cobden died on April 2, Lincoln on April 15. The news of Cobden's death reached America on the day Lincoln was assassinated. Mrs. Cobden was later told by a friend of Lincoln that Lincoln always spoke of Cobden "in the same spirit of kindliness and affection." (Villiers and Chesson, *Anglo-American Relations, 1861-1865*, London, 1919, p. 207.)

it twice again in his diary. Several years later in 1863 he wrote to Bright, "I was pleased with Chase when I saw him in Ohio where he was governor of the State in 1859. – He is in his physical & mental traits not unlike Sumner – a massive, stately, principled man, but more practical & less of the rhetorician than his Massachusetts colleague."[101] And in 1864 Cobden, obviously excepting Lincoln, referred to Chase as "the strongest man of the Republican party, & I sincerely hope Lincoln will bring him back to the Treasury."[102]

Apparently Cobden did not see Seward when he was in the States; but his comment on the man is of interest. Writing to Charles Sumner, May 1, 1860, he said: "Your probable candidate, Mr Seward, did not please me, when I was in America, with a speech in which he declared himself opposed to the policy of *building railroads with foreign iron over your own coal and iron beds.* I suppose this was merely intended for Mr. Bunkum in Pennsylvania, but I don't like it any better for that. I must own that this gentleman did not make so great a mark on society in England as some of your other distinguished visitors have done."[103] Later, during the years of the Civil War, Cobden disapproved many times of Seward's foreign policy.[104]

Cobden includes in the diary a short vivid glimpse of General Scott, "a colossal man," who gave Cobden anecdotes of Whig leaders he had known in England in 1815, and, with a very exact memory, conversed well on the literature of the previous century. Two years later Cobden wrote a friend that Scott "is the Duke of Wellington of the States, is 77, and a very superior man in every way."[105]

---

[101] Add. MSS. 43651, Part 3, Cobden to Bright, October 17, 1863.

[102] *Ibid.* 43650, Part 2, Cobden to Bright, October 4, 1864.

[103] John A. Hobson, *Richard Cobden The International Man*, London, 1918, pp. 341-342.

[104] See various instances in the Additional Manuscripts.

[105] Add. MSS. 43677, Part 2, Cobden to Slagg, December 6, 1861 [typed copy]. Cobden's attitude toward Scott had changed greatly since 1850 when he thought of Scott only as the "invader of Mexico" and a "successful warrior. . . ." (See Hobson, *Richard Cobden The International Man*, pp. 71-72.) Cobden was im-

Finally, Cobden's brief comparisons of Canadian and American life may be noted. Even in 1859, at a supper in Ontario, he observed that the men looked more English than those on the other side of the frontier, that they were more fleshy, had ruddier complexions, with less hair on their faces. Something of the same he noticed on a St. Lawrence boat going to Montreal: his fellow-passengers were more fleshy in appearence "& their movements were slower" than he had been accustomed to on the American side. The great majority of them drank wine or beer at dinner "thus reminding me that I am on British territory." In Montreal he was impressed by the churches: nowhere in America had he seen more "solid structures devoted to religious worship than here." But he was thoroughly disgusted with the evidences of military preoccupation that he saw in Canada: "I have seen more *government* military officers since I have been in Canada than I did in all my travels in the States." The statement which follows in the diary embodied his whole position on the subject of Canadian armament: "I have not met with a sensible man who does not regard the British army posted in Canada as a piece of useless folly. – It is useless in time of peace & would be powerless in case of war with the United States. – The defense & security of Canada must depend wholly on the people." It was the affirmation of this belief, the effort to see that nothing was done which would strain relations between these two peoples, that took Cobden to London six years later to enter the debate on Canadian fortification, a trip that was to cost him his life.[106]

What is to be said, then, of this diary in conclusion? There is reason to believe that although at times it may be too

pressed by his meeting with Scott and, later, by Scott's wise position on the northern blockade and the Mason-Slidell incident.

[106] In the Gladstone papers are two powerful letters which Cobden wrote to Gladstone as Chancellor of the Exchequer in an effort to secure Gladstone's opposition to an increase in Canadian armament during the Civil War. See letters of the following dates: December 11th, 1861, February 14, 1865. Add. MSS. 44136, Gladstone Papers, LI.

favorable in its estimates, it generally constitutes a reliable account of those things with which it deals. These are the notes of a mature man who speaks from a background of vast experience. Thoroughly informed on affairs economic and political, his interpretations of such matters in another society are to be trusted. For years a laborer in behalf of social improvement, his insight into human nature and social relations as he found them expressed in the new world is penetrating.

The record, furthermore, is that of a man who would be objective in his judgments. Cobden is just in his analyses, as contrasted with those of "writers & travellers [who] fall into a great unfairness in comparing the middle & upper classes with whom alone the tourists & the book-writing class associate in Europe with the *whole people* whom they meet at the table d'hotes & in the railway cars in the United States." Petty or snobbish criticisms of things American are totally absent from the diary. A mean spirit could not live in a man who found Niagara "suggestive of ideas of eternity & omnipotence" and was there "almost brought to kneel & pray." Only a fine soul could have penned the eloquent tribute to Joseph Sturge. And what he said of Sturge may be said of him, ". . . a man of great earnestness in the pursuit of some of the highest objects to which humanity can aspire."

The Diary

OF THE TRIP TO AMERICA

1835

The Diary

OF THE TRIP TO AMERICA
1835

Mem[1] Mr. Francias conversation – the Govr of Gibraltar Lord Chatham receives £10,000 p^r ann   resides in England was once in Gib^r [Gibraltar] for a few months – the duties performed by a Deputy Govr.

Consul General appointed at Madrid thro whom all communications from the local consuls to the Ambassadors must be addressed Mentioned that Mr Mead the Consul of Malaga (the only efficient Cons^l of Spain) in answer to his letters addressed to the Consul Genl at Madrid received a mere acknowledgment in an official form stating that "his letter had been rec^d and laid before the Ambassador" Mr F. had seen many of such letters – The Americans have no Consul gen^l & their affairs are better managed

Mentioned the enormous expense of our establishment at Gibraltar – New Police sent over to a fortress that contained 5,000 troops – All done with a view to Patronage – Spoke of an offer that had been made & published from the Town to support & defend themselves without putting this Country to any expense – the fortress additionally fortified with another line of defences lately at a great expense

A trip recommended from Bordeaux to Marseilles touching on the Coast of Spain & Portugal & from Marseilles to Naples touching on the Italian Coast

[1] The original diary has no title. It opens with a memorandum. The consecutive account begins on page 87. This first section shows Cobden's distaste, even at this early date, for large governmental expenditure for military and other purposes which seemed questionable to him. He was to oppose such outlays all of his life.

Passengers on board of the Britannia[2]

Dr Wilsone	Glasgow
” Warren	Boston U.S.
Mr Palsgrave	London
Hunt	Irish
Francia	Gibraltar
Captn Marshall	British
Mr Smyth	Scotch
Walter McKay	”
Captn Gardner	U.S.
Mr Rostron	Man^r [Manchester]
Mr Nash	Essex

Dr Warren a great nephew to the commander of the insurgents at Bunkers Hill

1835.[3] May 25 – Crossed the great Bank of Newfoundland a thick fog & rain with a good breeze – passed within a few yards of a french fishing Smack at Anchor – great danger of running down these small vessels owing to the hazy weather that is generally found to prevail – Severe life for the fishermen besides the risk – from Ap^l or May to Sep^r & Oct^r

The Captain tells me that two or three of these fishing brigs are upon an average found missing at the close of every season – no doubt these are run down in a moment whilst at anchor by larger vessels under a heavy sail (as we were nigh doing to the frenchman) & never heard of again!

Enquired of the Captain as to the wages etc of the seamen – the average pay in the American service is from 12 to 15 dollars per month – the hands on board our ship received fifteen dollars monthly   the beverage of these men is water

---

[2] The *Britannia* was one of the . crack BlackBall packets between New York and Liverpool—the best means of transportation across the Atlantic until steamship service started in 1838. She was built in New York in 1826, and in 1835 was just rounding out nine years of steady service, after which she went into tramp or "transient" service. See Robert Greenhalgh Albion, *Square-Riggers on Schedule*, Princeton, 1938, p. 276, *passim*.

[3] Appears to have been added at a later date.

– their health better at the close of the voyage than on start-ing – engaged for the voyage to Liverpool & home usually about 3 months

Sailors & mates only sleep four hours at a time – first watch – middle watch – morning watch –

June 3ʳᵈ 1835
My birth-day – To fortify a resolution which I have now solemnly made to break myself of an old and ridiculous habit of biting my lips and cheeks in which I have been for twenty years foolishly accustomed [?] to indulge when in cogitat-ing moods I record it in writing here – Surely I can suc-ceed in conquering a propensity which only distorts my features & tends to exhaust the saliva that is designed for the mastication of food & without on the other hand affording in recompense any other gratification than that which arises from the mechanical repetition of the same action of the muscles[4]

Conversation with Mr Francia
Our consul general at Tangiers receives £4,000 per ann – more than all the consuls of the rest of the world together?[5]

On board the Britannia off Sandy Hook 100 miles
June 6 1835
Anxiety to see land increases as we find ourselves a short distance – rise & fall of spirits with every change of wind – enquiries from Captain mates & crew as to the time – hopes & fears –

At 7 o'clock p.m. a delightful breeze springs up that will certainly bring us off the pilot station by day light – reluc-tance of all on board to go to bed

Sunday June 7 4 a.m.
Are up by sun rise – open rejoicing & shaking of hands on

[4] Beginning with "fortify," all of this has been scratched through in ink.
[5] The question mark is in another handwriting. All of the foregoing part of the diary is in pencil; the remainder is in ink.

the Approach of land – small vessels in the distance towards shore – eager look out for the pilot-boat which approaches us – beautiful sailing craft schooner rigged – puts our pilot on board of us at 7 – not like our pilots – all eyes criticize this first American visitor – Rostrons simile in speaking of him   the inexpressible sensations on the first perceiving the fragrance of the shore – sea life not natural   beauty of the bay of New York as it opens out – *Never-Sink* the small hilly spot opposite highest land on the sea-board of the States – the bay would be more interesting if the shores were loftier like Naples or the Bosphorus – pass the narrows & enter the inner bay   beauty of this surpasses the other – number of small pleasure boats with young men taking excursions – Steam boats full of passengers – Staten Island on left with quarantine station a large building (in the distance reminding one of Somerset House or Greenwich) close to the shore – Hoboken to the right on the East river – to the left the Hudson with the heights of the Hudson in the distance – the scene all round animated by the appearance of the small white houses erected on the shores – What beauty will this inner bay of New York present centuries hence when wealth & commerce shall have done their utmost to embellish this scene!

New York as we approach appears flat – only about half a dozen spires visible – get on shore before other people in my brothers boat   first specimen of inquisitiveness on landing   Houses very irregular – red brick – all with outside folding sashes like those of Paris – few negroes met – people brown complexioned.

June 8th – Clintons   Breakfast in public room perhaps sixty people – Not a word spoken except by our own party – the appearance of the Americans more like French or Italians than English – resemble us in nothing but our taciturity & haughty & austere exteriors in which qualities they surpass even us – Struck with the dress of the people superior to that of the English the men stylish & with the advantage of slim

& elegant figures – the women with their mincing gait & French costume reminded me of Paris – struck with the pallid & unhealthy complexion of the American ladies who are too thin for my taste the females generally are *petite* but elegant – deficient in bust & *bustle* – thin lips & attenuated features – Many of these belles so pale & sickly that in Britain they would be regarded as consumptive – Many of the more elegant remind me of the London people of *ton* at the close of the season when worn down & haggard by late hours & incessant visiting

Poets & sculptors will find few inspiring models here, a certain plumpness of feature & figure, which is all but universally wanting in females here, in my taste indispensable to beauty

Henry[6] drives me into the country – vast extent of plan of New York & the high price of land which is sold in building lots even seven miles from the Town – beauty of the country – more thickly wooded than is general in England – great diversity of surface – admirable spots for villas – knolls & valleys – lovely bursts of the Hudson or East river or Haarlem river – verdure surpassing in brightness of tint the English scene – Stopped at Burnhams hotel the country resort of the New York parties of pleasure – pretty garden with a field at the back sloping down to the majestic Hudson – opposite banks of which beautifully wooded – Marble & stone quarries – go on to Manhattan-ville a small village with a primitive looking little church with wooden spire – return by way of Haarlem bridge prodigious number of vehicles of all kinds that were pouring out into the country with company of every degree & color as we returned to New York in England such a scene – in the neighbourhood of even London could only be observed on the occasion of some races in the vicinity – fast-going horses & sulkies people here not particular what kind of carriage they ride in – all ride –

Lafayette place –

[6] Cobden's brother.

In the evening entertain Captn Waite[7] – afterwards walk out – beautiful evening – full moon – look in at Palmos' a new establishment after the manner of the Parisian Cafés – *young* looking men filled this house at 11 o'clock – when in the billiard room at the back of the coffee room was struck with the French-like looking appearance of things   to bed at ½ past 12

June 9th

Take a trip on long Island by invitation of Hardy[8] with a company in four carriages – Cross the Brooklyn ferry – commodiousness of the Steam ferry boats – party comprised amongst others Judge Boardman called in conversation with him "Judge" – Undignified in contrast with the big wigs of our bench in England – jovial over the champagne at lunch – go to Coney Island to eat clams a shell fish – mode of dressing these on the ground by placing them on edge in the sand & then putting a fire on to burn the muscles forming the hinge whilst the sand prevented the shell opening & thus saved the fluid contents – thence to Bath-house another resort for holiday parties – we had a difficulty in making the driver go this extra distance   our Judge threatened to throw him off & drive us if he did not comply – at Bath-House took mint julip – returned by flat bush – the fire-fly or lightning bug – the cricket – frogs & other insects & animals make the woods more noisy at night than day – My American friends anxious to draw comparisons between England or Europe and America in favor of latter – insatiable love of unqualified admiration – conceded that *"cherries do* grow in England as good as in America   as if that were a bit of praise – beauty

[7] Benjamin L. Waite was captain of the *Britannia*. He was around Cobden's age, and, in the words of Fanny Kemble, "a very intelligent, good-natured person; rough and bluff, . . ." Among the crack packet captains Waite ranked high in popularity and ability to make his crossings in fast time. Albion, *Square-Riggers on Schedule*, pp. 160, 343. After his tour Cobden was to see Waite again in New York. See *infra*, p. 126.

[8] Cobden's friend, whom he saw again on his two stops in New York at the end of his tour. See *infra*, pp. 121, 126, 128.

of this part of Long Island which serves as the garden of New York – return again to Brooklyn ferry – Brooklyn is destined to be to N Yk what Southwark is to London – Already are plans laid out for a town large enough for a million of people – Streets placarded on trees by the road side miles from the present Town – the rage for speculation in land in the vicinity of great Towns – *paper money* –

June 10th

Proceed by Steam Boat to South Amboy by the Raritan River which for a great part of the way presents flat banks similar to the shores of the Thames below Gravesend – At Amboy take the rail road to Bordentown on the Delaware Sandy country produces low copse wood with here & there a meagre patch of grain or grass – Joseph Bonapartes house & grounds, anecdote of his passing in a vessel several times along the French Coast during his present residence in Europe to take a glance of that Country which he is prohibited from entering

At Borden town take Steam Boat again for Philadelphia – the Delaware here resembles in width & also in the appearance of the banks the Thames in the neighbourhood of Chiswick or Richmond – Bristol on the right Bank with its wooden houses – & an elegant building painted white amidst willows inscribed in gold "*Bank*"

Burlington on the left – the shores of the river rise a little into gentle slopes as we proceed – very lovely all the way to Philadelphia Philadelphia a tame & uninteresting Town from the water – but with more appearance of maturity & stability than New York United States Hotel – black servants – look into kitchens – blacks in one room dining – white servants in one adjoining – the Exchange handsome – the bank of U.S. – Bank near exchange – beauty of water works – theatre about equal to that of Man[r] [Manchester] in appearance of company & in quality of performance – see a woman of color in pit, on enquiry of Indian blood – blacks in the gallery keep on one side & whites on the other   Museum – the Mammoth Indian ornaments – taste of the savages – N.B. this has been the hottest day I ever knew

June 11
Leave Philadelphia at six morning in Steam Boat   the Delaware rich but flat banks – take railway at Newcastle & go by locomotive power to Elkton – thence by Steam Boat on the Elk river to Baltimore – largest & handsomest Steamer I have yet seen – Cabin 105 feet long – Commodore Chater the Captain a humorist – company of Boston fusiliers going to Washington exercise & play on the top of boat   beauty of the scenery as we advance towards Chesapeake bay – the entrance of the Susquehanna river striking – Chesapeake bay – North Point where battle was fought – spot where General Ross fell   spoke to a man on board who remarked that he could not read or write but that he had thrown in (*voted*) for universal education & that his children were instructed – saw this man who described himself as having been bred a common sailor seated opposite to me & conducting himself with propriety   Conversation with Mr Phelps, a passenger, leader of the Democrats in N. York   intelligent man – his lady & daughter – their horror of black & white amalgamation – Mrs P. tells me that a Physician assures her there is a difference between the structure of the negro & that of the white! – Approach to Baltimore rivals the bay of New York – the city with its cupolas spires & monuments & its amphitheatrical situation with back ground of hills looks well – like an European Town – go to Beltzhoovers Hotel

Call on Mr Brown[9] & find him gentlemanly & intelligent with a fault in over diffuseness & a propensity for amplification long after a little more tact must have convinced him that his hearer was sufficiently informed – corn & flower of the best quality selling as dear here as in England

Call on Miss Lemmon   intelligent woman – Oldfield –

---

[9] Apparently George Brown, railroad promoter and head of one of the country's most important banking firms. See DAB.

At hotel see a little girl quite white with blue eyes &
straight hair the slave of the Innkeeper who tells me the
reported cause of this is in the supposed fact of the grandmother & mother of the child having been successively connected with white men who were father & son! – the blacks
of this state are the first slaves I have seen – am told that out
of 20,000 people of color in Baltimore not a tenth part are
pure unmixed blacks – illicit means will tend to aid amalgamation

Baltimore is the handsomest place I have yet seen – here
are the finest monuments – the prettiest girls and the cleanest City in the Union – A very handsome Doric column 170
ft to Washington & another small one to the heroes of the
North point both of white marble

Am struck with the white & clean appearance of the linen
& white clothes of all classes & colors – No poor people or
beggars – The Theatre (minor) not equal to that of Philadelphia – saw a man in the front seat of the dress circle with
one foot hanging over into the pit

Baltimore is the first of the Southern Cities

Told of a horse that has trotted a mile in two minutes
twenty nine seconds – at N. York

Saw Webster – good forehead – but a heavy tiresome expression of face[10]

June 12

Breakfast at Baltimore before starting – large fans or flap-
pers kept moving over the table during the meal

Leave by the Coach for Washington at 8 – A poor soil all
the way – Companion outside a Virginian – his remark that
the people could not live on that soil we were passing through
except by breeding & selling slaves to the southern planters

Anecdotes of slavery – of the white ladies with mulatto

---

[10] This sentence was inserted by pencil, apparently at another time, and then
traced in ink. Cobden is here referring to the famous senator, Daniel Webster,
who only five years earlier, in his significant debate with Hayne, had delivered
his great exposition of federal supremacy.

offspring – pass by a house & farm belonging to an Englishman – his character for intrigue with his negroes – reputed
father of the mulatto girl he is now living with! – a fortune
left to a mulatto family which cannot be possessed by it
owing to the mother having been a slave – the Maryland
laws do not allow free slaves to remain if manumitted in
that state – great emigration, by purchase, of the negro population into the southern states – continued swearing of the
driver – Approach to Washington not very remarkable – the
magnolia tree – the Capitol – go to Gadsbys Hotel – at dinner twice as many slaves as the free waiters that would have
sufficed for attendance on us – the brushing away the flies by
black boys with bunches of feathers during dinner reminded
me of the west Indies – the chambers of Senators & representatives – each member with a distinct chair & one desk
for two chairs with names of the members   handsome pillars – view from the dome – the rotunda with statue of Jefferson – paintings of celebrated scenes in American History
– in the evening incessant flashes of vivid sheet lightning

June 13

Told by the bar-keeper of Gadsbys hotel that he can make
up beds for 280 persons – Call again on Mr Morfit – receive
his advice for the purchase of some American books as
'Forces National Calendar – Waterson & Vainzants[?]'[11]
Statistics, Niles register – North American & Quarterly Re-
views – leave Washington at 11 o'clock for Frederick – passing through George Town am shown the work-house & told
that the white & colored inmates have separate tables for
meals.

Companions a blacksmith going to the west for work who
can earn 18 dollars a month & be '*found*' – hours of working
from sun rise till sunset or in winter say from sun-up till
eight in the evening – all kinds of journeymen work more
hours pr day in America than in England – A lady & her

[11] Inside the cover of the diary, Cobden refers to the publication as "Watersons
& Van-zants Statistics."

companion who wore gold spectacles who talked about taste & enquired of me about Bulwer Lady Blessington & the Duke of Devonshire but chewed tobacco & spat incessantly, *"clearing" the lady*, out of the window

The Coachman with less of self respect & republican spirit than I had before seen – was not averse to be treated & told use that the person inside (a clerk in the post office) was a mean fellow who rode three times a week eight miles out of the city in the Mail & never gave the driver a 'fippenny'

Heard to day of instances of girls marrying in Maryland at 12 & 13 years of age – Still told that the part through which we are going *'raises'* great quantities of negroes for sale & some families are mainly indebted to this traffic for support – the road to Frederick is principally through a thickly wooded country with poor sandy soil – after quitting the County of Montgomery the land improves & we get a first view of the Alleghany scenery – the road all the way from Washington to Frederick is execrable & the dexterity with which the drivers carry a coach & four horses over roads that for ruggedness & occasional steepness surpass our Derbyshire cross-roads would be enough to make our English *jehus* marvel could they behold it.

Wait three hours at Frederick for another coach in which to proceed on the route for Wheeling – Talbotts Hotel a large establishment for so small a Town – the waiter says they can make up 200 beds

June 14 Sunday – At one o'clock morn^g leave Frederick by Mail – with a lady & her little girl – an intelligent man a coal pit owner from Brownsville a civil companion – a journeyman cooper going to Louisville to work – could earn 22 dollars a month in his last place but expects to get 30 dollars – instances of the homage & attention paid to females when travelling – Am told that the price of Coals of the best Newcastle qual^y at Brownsville is 2^d a bushel delivered at the cellar – sometimes 1½ – the coals are taken from the sides of the hills without sinking shafts – veins are 7 to 8 ft thick. Brownville more favorable than Pittsburgh for manufactur[ing?]

At Union take up a companion with a rifle – his anecdotes of an excursion last year to the furthest lead mine of the Missouri named Debuke – account of the miners – one half fugitives & wanderers from honest courses – out of the States as incorporated then[12] – consequently without laws – they petition to be under laws & are annexed[?] to Michigan – they tried convicted & hanged a man for murder with all the forms of law – they whip a thief – Mode of taking the lead mines from the government

Our road from Frederick through Hagers Town, Cumberland, & Union, by the famous national turnpike has presented one continued scene of almost boundless forests of pine, oak, che[s]tnut, locust etc with only an occasional relief of a little cleared spot – the settlers on the borders of this great thoroughfare are very numerous & they appear industrious & prosperous – modes of destroying or consuming the timber – this is Sunday & the sabbath day is as strictly kept in these woods as in England – saw some negroes going out on horseback well dressed –

My companion the Coal owner[13] tells me he has been to Baltimore with his black groom who is riding outside to sell a string of horses which fetched good prices – his kindness to his man George who is a handsome & smart negro – the night is cold & George at the request of his master is squeezed inside with us – he is quite at his ease – George dines in the same room as ourselves but at a separate table – I quiz his master & ask him how he should have dealt with this repugnance to dining with a man of color had he been in the situation of Robinson Crusoe with only a man Friday! – Mr D. a man of great resources in conversation – en-

[12] The word "now" appeared originally; "then" was substituted in pencil at a later time.

[13] Mr. Dawson of Brownsville.

thusiastic about England – asks about the expense of a visit – talks of Stratford on Avon – Lucy's residence the abode of the descendant of Justice Shallow – he advises me to purchase a farm of 120 acres with buildings & improvements, situated only a mile from Brownsville & containing a bed of coal from 7 to 8 ft thick   price $3500

June 15 Monday[14]

Passing over the last summit of the Alleghanies called laurel hill looked down upon a plain country the beginning of that vast extent of territory known as the great Mississippi valley & which extends almost without variation of surface to the base of the rocky mountains & increasing in fertility & beauty the further it extends westward, – here will one day be the head quarters of agricultural & manufacturing industry here will one day center the civilization, the wealth, the power of the entire world – As we descend laurel hill find the best soil that I have yet seen on this side of the Atlantic – the country hereabout better cleared it has been occupied by Europeans only eighty years – Any number of able bodied laborers may, the moment they tread the grass west of the Alleghanies, have employment at 2⁸/. day & be *'found'* arrive at Brownsville at 4 o'clock the only place I have yet seen that uses coals for fuel We are now in the State of Penns^a Thank God I am no longer in the country of slaves

June 16

Walk through the Town of Brownsville along with Mr Dawson – number of British residing here they are principally the Capitalists – introduced to Mr Geo Hogg from Newcastle who takes us to survey his coal pit – a *'lead'* as the adit is called runs into the side of a small hill & at the distance of twenty yards a vein of coal eight feet in thickness is worked – the labor costs 75 cents or ¾ dollar for working one hundred bushels & the cartage to houses in the Town

---

[14] This date was written in by pencil at a later time, and then traced in ink.

about half a dollar – introduced to the miner employd in
the pit who shakes hands as usual – introduced to Willm
Hogg the richest man in this vicinity reputed to be worth
half a million of dollars – the shabbiest dress I had seen –
he came out 60 years ago & is now in his 80th year – moderate charge at workmans hotel – did not recognize that the
porter here was a man of color – leave at 9 o'clock by the
Steam Boat 'Fancy' for Pittsburgh – beautiful banks of the
Monogahela – appropriate Indian meaning of the word "*the
hanging banks*" – the whole distance from Brownsville to
Pittsburgh we see the mouths of coal pits opening upon the
road on the edge of the water – great probable value of this
district at some future period

first place we stop at for Coals farmed by two Englishmen
who paid two thousand dollars for the use of the pit which
debt they discharged by the produce of coals last year & have
cleared one thousand dollars besides – the praise given to
me of the hard work of these men by one captain – one of
them observed to me that he wished he had left England ten
years earlier

Extreme civility of all the passengers on board to us when
we were known to be English

Graham an Irish emigrant on board who came out 16
years ago without money as a journeyman carpenter & is
now worth he says 16,000$ – speaks unfavorably of his coun-
trymen who come to America – his honest defence of the
country of his birth against every one seeking to disparage
her – the patriotism of the American character exhibited constantly in the praise of the country – indignation of one of
my companions against Hall Trollope Hamilton but especially of Fanny Kemble[15] – his remark that Washington was
the greatest man – I said the '*best*' – that ever lived – nothing
but praise unqualified & unadulterated will satisfy people of

[15] These visitors to the States had published varying critical observations on the
Americans: Basil Hall in 1829; Frances Trollope in 1832; Thomas Hamilton in
1833; and Fanny Kemble in 1835.

such a disposition – Pass by the scene of Bradocks defeat by the French & Indians on turtle creek – our American friends talk of New Orleans – the honest Graham's estimate of the American valor shown on that occasion – A lady, and an American one, exclaims at my elbow – "Ah! the dear English they do fight bravely on open ground."[16] I believe the Americans feel an instinctive attachment & even respect for 'the old Country' which nothing can obliterate – Beauty of the stream of the Monogahela – placid & without an interruption   junction with the Youghiogeny[17] a violent & sudden storm – oblige to run for the bank   bustle of the Town of Pittsburgh as we approach – the Coal smoke reminds me of England   number of splendid Ohio Steam boats lying at anchor – three hundred houses building – are conducted by our friend Graham round the Town   handsome wooden bridge across the Monogahela which is here about as wide as the Thames at London at high water – Another bridge and a wooden aqueduct for the Pennsylvania canal across the Allighany river the same width as the Monogahena – ascend Grants Hill – view of the Town probably one day destined to be the largest in America – the best view would have been from Coal hill on the other side but we had not day-light   our friend Grahams presbyterian bile excited by the Catholic Cathedral   he takes us to view a cotton factory belonging to Allen who he told us had come to this continent from Ireland after failing in business & had returned thither to satisfy his creditors – handsome brick structure which has been erected about 8 years   4500 spindles, & power looms for coarse sheetings – employ about 180 people – hours from five in the morning till half past six in the evening – the children from nine upwards earn from 6ˢ/6ᵈ to 8ˢ/6ᵈ weekly   the mule spinners *net* about 35ˢ/. or 36ˢ/. weekly – (*not at full work*)[18] – Evening, sup with friend Gra-

---

[16] The quotation marks were inserted later by pencil.

[17] Written first in pencil, then traced in ink. Cobden was less successful in his spelling of the word "Monongahela." See instances above and below.

[18] Parentheses were added by pencil at a later time.

ham further anecdotes of Gallatins aristocracy of S. Gerards discrimination give him our address in case he should come to Europe & we separated – Go to the theatre – Mrs Hamblin an excellent actress something after Mad^m Vestris[19] – enthusiasm with which republican sentiments were caught up – "No crowned head in christendom can boast that he ever commanded for one hour the services of this arm" a phrase which was rapturously cheered – A neat little theatre with a bad attendance – pit empty

June 17

Leave Pittsburgh at 4 o'clk in the morning for Salem on Lake Erie – pass along close to the right bank of the Ohio river till we reach Beaver on the Big beaver river & then turn off – pass through the German village of economy[20] beautifully situated on the bottom of the Ohio the establishment was founded by Rapp – on the principle of Owen of Lanark – go into the house – clean appearance of the interior – the inmates appeared to me to exhibit the dull sunken eyes & the *sodden* inflexible features peculiar to all fanatics – the Ohio generally is about 450 yds in width – is not navigable for three or four of the summer months but may be made so – two quiet individuals as companions – the one had no relish for conversation until the other in the course of remarks alluded to the probable gain by a certain speculation in land at which our mute fellow passenger found both ears & tongue – suspect him to be a *Yankee* jobber – a remarkable alertness on the part of all Americans on the subject of investments in land by which owing to the sudden construction of a railway or by means of a canal project

[19] Lucia Elizabeth Mathews, known as Madame Vestris, was a prominent figure on the London stage at this time. (See DNB.) Mrs. Hamblin was probably one of the two actresses (both of whom were called Mrs. Hamblin) with whom Hamblin lived after his divorce from his wife in 1834.

[20] Economy, Pennsylvania. Cobden is here referring to one of the colonies founded on a "combination of celibacy and communism." For reference to such groups, see Robert E. Riegel, *Young America, 1830-1840*, Norman, Oklahoma, 1949, pp. 263-264.

at a particular point vast profits have been realized – two females likewise as companions with no remarkable traits – we approach the Ohio State & find the land all newly cleared but of an excellent quality – the stumps of the trees every where visible above the grass & the corn – the road every where difficult – observe not one black face throughout the days journey – the Ohio law prohibits people of color from entering this state except under particular regulations – the children ever since we passed the Allegheny Mountains have struck us as remarkably healthy & lovely – the population more robust than the inhabitants of the maritime Towns – At the Town of Poland we change Coaches one branch going to Cleveland & the other to Salem – Drunken man & boys twizing him   Poland is a pretty thriving little Town chiefly of wood with two or three good brick houses quite in the English style – Ohio, free from the curse of slavery or of the presence of a black population, is advancing with greater prosperity than any State of the Union – Proceed to Youngs Town six miles off & there again change coaches but have to wait three hours of the night till the branch stage arrives, & lose my temper for the first time in America in consequence! –

June 18 still en route

Our party inside is now increased to nine persons – converse on the Bank, slavery, and as usual on land investments & internal improvements – have remarked that politics are rarely discussed in public conveyances – Here I found, as in every other company, the slavery blot viewed as an indelible stain upon & a curse to the country – an intelligent old gentleman would prefer the debt of Great Britain to the colored population of the United States – all agree in the hopelessness of any remedy as hitherto proposed   hilarity of the party – bad state of the roads – obliged to walk part of the way – the forest scenery on the great Mississippi valley from its sameness & the absence of hilly scenery is tiresome – breakfast at Brookfield – find on enquiry here as at most other places that there are British subjects found amongst the natives – joke with the landlady – pretty daughter – I have always observed that the Americans are glad to partake in fun & good humor – & they bear raillery well though they are not clever in retorting it – pass through Monroe, Kinsman, & to Connéaut[21] on Lake Erie where we arrive at 8 o'clock in the evening having been forty hours in travelling by mail 110 miles – Sleep at the harbor – Yankee tricks upon travellers by the landlord

June 19

Start at six *morning* by the William Penn Steamer for Buffalo – Lake Erie a mediterranean sea boundless to the eye – what could have been the feelings of those first explorers of this continent who after traversing five hundred miles of uninterrupted forests found themselves on the shore of this fresh water ocean! – what a sublime idea would it convey of the magnitude of that continent which contained within its bounds such a lake, and what food for the imagination in the unknown regions beyond it! – the day unfavorable for a view of the scenery on the shore which however appeared monotonous – converse with an old man who appears familiar with the business of settling a new country – Hints for emigrants – a man & wife with family finding themselves in Illinois or Indiana or Michigan certain of comfort & ultimate wealth provided they are industrious & possess a capital of about a hundred pounds – say, buy a government lot of eighty acres at 5^s/. per acre (a credit is given) – two good horses called a team may be had for twenty pounds – or a yoke of oxen for ten pounds – sow a few acres for present subsistence of maize, wheat & potatoes these & cow will yield a maintenance for the first year – Neighbours assist to build the log hut of the new-comer – furniture may be had & carried in an unfinished state from New York

[21] A "y" which originally ended this word was scratched through in pencil.

or Albany shopkeepers in the nearest Town take produce
for goods – if an emigrant is acquainted with a retail business as well as with farming & is active it gives him a better
chance – *best* route by N. York & the lakes

A New England pedlar a youth who had purchased a lot
of land – contrast between the Irish mate of the steamer a
good American citizen by adoption & Peter the sailor another
Irishman who was eager for returing – touching traits in
Peter who is a noble fellow – would give his years wages for
a sight of his old Mother – *his godmother* – he disparages
America because the people do not have spons[ors?] because
they possess no regatta – no Dublin custom house or Bank
Peter is an aristocrat, whilst the mate talks of his son who is
a clever scholar & of the respect he will meet with in America
for his talents though he be not rich whilst in Britain his
abilities without wealth would be neglected Another specimen of New Englandism in the man who volunteered to
carry my portmanteau – A sudden storm compels us to make
for Erie where we land after a great difficulty in making
the harbour & being once aground on the sand shoal for a
few minutes Erie is a prospering little Town – go to the
Mansion house – Major Clarke landlord choleric but obliging & not above his business – the bar presents an appear-
an[ce] similar to that of an English country Inn in the old
days where substantial farmers & tradesmen used to meet in
the parlour – the Steamer sails at 5 in the morning without the Captain's calling us – Henry[22] goes by Coach to
Buffalo – Sale of a horse by auction in the market Square –
Jockies the same animals every where

June 20 (Saturday)
Go by the Detroit Steamer to Buffalo – fine day – the shores
of the lake level for a few miles from the water & then rise
into hilly scenery – the water of the lake blue like that of
Lake Lemon – take up as companions Mr Cunningham a

[22] Cobden's brother.

gent who has travelled in Britain & Mr Church from Pittsburgh – *"No talking to the man at the wheel"* – company
very mixed at dinner but all equally well behaved – have
never seen an instance of rudeness or of even boisterous familiarity between two citizens since I have been in the States
– same respect as ever paid to the ladies – arrive at Buffalo at
11 o'clock at night – go to the Eagle – great number of guests
in the house – no beds – three of us go to another house where
we are offered one bed – return to the Eagle & sleep on a
shake down with three others in the same room – seventy two
arrivals at the Eagle that day – am of opinion that there is as
much travelling in the States as in all Europe

June 21

Breakfast with a party of about eighty at seven – go to walk
afterwards in the Town which is a thriving place that has
sprung up since the last war during which the British destroyed this place – handsome wooden church – the principal
street superior to any thing in Pittsburgh – go at ½ past 8 by
rail road to the ferry two miles & thence cross to Canada in
the first cattle-tread wheel boat I ever saw over the river
at the mouth of the Erie lake which for its blue color might
be taken for the Rhone issuing out of the Lake of Geneva
– take a coach after reaching the Canada shore & proceed
to the falls of Niagara – ragged youth at the Inn although
it is Sunday – Church remarks that even the *"martin houses"*
are in Canada inferior to those in the U. States – Conversation in the Coach upon the enormous advance in the price
of real estate – the bald headed Eagle – Chippewa village –
the *smoke* (as it appears to be) rising from the cataract is
here visible – not such a volume of mist as I had expected
– the noise not great   reach the Pavilion hotel near the falls
at one – go immediately to see this greatest of natural wonders alone – I jealously guard my eyes from wandering until
I find myself on the table rock – thank God that has bestowed on me health time & means for reaching this spot

& the spirit to kindle at the spectacle before me! – the horse shoe is the all absorbing portion of the scene from this point – the feathery graceful effect of the water as it tumbles in broken & irregular channels over the edge of the rock has not been properly described – Nor has the effect of the rapids above the shoot, seen from this point, as they come surging lashing & hissing in apparent agony at the terrific destiny before them – this rapid above the falls might be called a rush of the waters preparatory to their taking their awful leap – the water is thrown over an irregular ledge but in falling it completely hides the face of the perpendicular rock down which it falls – instead of an even sheet of glassy water it falls in light & graceful festoons of foaming nay almost vapory fluid – possessing just enough consistency to descend in various sized & hardly distinguishable streams whilst here & there one of these foamy volums encounters a projecting rock in its descent which forces it back in heavy spray into the still descending torrent above thus giving indescribable beauty & variety to this scene – in the afternoon cross the river below the falls and visit Goats island – at the foot of the stair case have a view of the American fall at a point of rock near the bottom of the cascade – terrific beyond conception and totally opposite to the effect of the horse-shoe fall as seen from table rock – ascend the stairs & pass over the bridge to Goats island – the view from the platform overhanging the horse-shoe fall where you look right down into the abyss & are standing immediately over the descending water is horrible – I do not think people would take any pleasure in being placed in this fearful position unless others were looking on or unless for the vain gratification of talking about it – in the evening again look at the horse-shoe fall from table rock until dark – oh for an English twilight! – the effect of this fall is improved by the water which flows over the ledge being of very different depths – from two to twenty feet, say, which of course causes the water to flow more or less in a mass so that in one part it descends nearly

half way in a blue unbroken sheet whilst not far off it is
scattered into the whitest foam almost as soon as it has
passed the edge of the rock – the water for several hundred
yards below the fall is as white as drifted snow – not a mere
white froth   but as much as it is disturbed it shows nothing
but a white milk-like effect unlike any water I ever saw – in
the evening a laughable incident with the Scotchman who
waited till dusk when he was *fou* for seeing the falls – Conversation with a gent about Canada – Uselessness of the
Rideau Canal

Written in the book kept at the falls which is full of
attempts at rhapsodical praise of the scene

> O, not to yield presumptuous praise,
> In studied prose or artful lays,
> This scene survey!
>
> *Gods* Majesty is imaged here,
> Let vainer homage[23] disappear
> And kneel and pray![24]
>
> [These waters Thundered at His word]
> When first this monument *He* raised
> [heard]
> (Six thousand years ere Europe gazed,
> In Col[ored?] day.)
>
> [When]
> The rocks & forests echoing round
> [Pealed] Hymed His sole praise – [these] they still [re-
> sound?]
> To kneel & pray!

June 22 *monday*
In the morning go in a coach along with Mess.rs Cunningham

[23] The word "feelings" has been scratched out in pencil, and the word "homage"
substituted in its place, in pencil.
[24] The remainder of the poem has been scratched through with ink. Brackets
indicate words that had been added in pencil and also deleted with the exception
of "heard" and possibly "Pealed."

& Church with Henry to see the whirlpool three miles down the stream – was disappointed – I don't know if it be the all absorbing influence of the falls which prevents my taking any interest in other scenes – return to dinner – fifty or sixty at table – afterwards descend to view the horse-shoe fall from behind the curtain of water – Change of clothes – the stunning noise & the heavy beating of the water render this a severe adventure – there is no danger – the effect of the sound is that of thunder – most terrific   very little effect for the eye – go to view the burning well which would certainly light a town with gas – putting a tub over the well produces a complete gasometer – throw a tree into the rapid   – but the effect of coming over is not great – it dropped immediately it passed the ledge more perpendicularly than the cascade & so disappeared – Church tells me that the coal is worked at Pittsburgh chiefly by tenants who pay to the landlord from half a cent to one cent per bushel rent – the coal is del^d [delivered] to houses in Pittsburgh at four cents a bushel – the manufactur[ers?] get it at about 3 cents – in the balcony looking over the falls with a stupid looking man telling a stupid story about a *stupid lord* – assures me that I am amongst my own countrymen again – the negro barber is a run away black from Virginia – am told that on the 10th of last month the river was passable on the ice & now the corn is ripening – currants fit to gather – the tulip tree in flower etc.

June 23 tuesday

Rainbow nearly a complete circle seen from table rock – cross again to the American side with Mr Cunningham – take a bath not one on the Canada side – ferryman told us of a gentleman who swam over three times – feel less disposed than ever to quit this spot[25] so full of ever increasing attraction – were I an American I would here strive to build me a summer residence – in the evening drunken people

[25] Cobden spent more time (approximately three days) at the falls than at any other place, with the exception of Boston and New York.

have seen more intoxicated persons at this first Canada Town than in any place in the States

June 24 Wednesday

View from table rock rather obscured by the mist – at dinner a crowded table which was wholely vacated in 20 minutes

think of sixty persons at an *English* watering place dining & leaving the table in 20 min! – take a last & reluctant leave of this greatest of all natures works! – go in a carriage to Queestown & then cross in a cattle tread wheel ferry boat to Lewiston – Brooks monument at Queenston – the base too small – view of the Niagara river & of the country on the other side as you descend very fine – the falls are supposed by geologists to have once been here & the water to have in the course of time worn the bed of the rock seven miles up to its present site – what [cou?]ntless ages must have elapsed during such an operation!

June 25 thursday

Leave Lewiston by coach at 6 Go through the Indian village of the Tuscororas – first sight of an Indian – strong Tartar likeness – Lockport to breakfast – the Erie Canal is here carried up an ascent by means of 5 double locks – struck me that this work does not equal a similar range of locks on the Man^r [Manchester] & Bolton Canal – go through Albion & Brockport to Rochester – thriving villages – handsome wooden houses – Am struck by the number of Churches with Towers that I observe in these small places – they are usually all built in one quarter of the village – this has been a very dull day owing to our having a stupid vulgar company in the Coach

N.B. *two German* Jews

Brockport & Albion although two small villages each contains three churches

June 26 friday

Left Rochester at 9 morning – after looking at the falls

which however possess no interest after Niagara – go through Victor – pass several times near the Erie Canal – great traffic of boats for goods & passengers fare am told by stage line boats is four cents a mile & *found* – the common boats carry for 1½ cent & passengers find themselves – go to Canadaigua – a beautiful village with handsome houses & gardens kept in excellent order – abode of wealthy people – saw a church with steeple being removed upon rollers – the Lake of Canandaigua as you leave the Village is a pretty view (about 30 miles) – in the coach Judge Wright who has been into Illinois buying 15,000 acres of prairie land – his account of his travels of 10,000 miles during this year – Geneva on the lake of that name another pretty village – in going afterwards from Geneva to Auburn we encounter the most awful storm of thunder lightning & rain I ever beheld – the whole of the surrounding landscape lighted up with the vivid & continued flashes of lightening – at times a long zig-zag streak of forked light more intense than the sheet flame would give the appearance of the heavens opening or splitting by the peal of thunder – terror of our companions – a more sublime sight than I ever before saw

June 27 Saturday

Auburn a flourishing village – go to see the States prison here – the most interesting sight after Niagara that I have been shewn in America – the discipline calculated to subdue even the most obdurate – struck with a similarity of expression in all the countenances of the prisoners does this arise from the identity of their condition, as we see a peculiar resemblance of feature or expression in the faces of almost all *deaf* men? – I thought the men worked faster than any mechanics I had ever seen – told by the keeper that the 25 women imprisoned are not subjected to the same discipline of silence – negroes & whites are here obliged to board together – believe that the salutary system of moral discipline & reformation of which this is the first model will become generally adopted in all countries[26] – leave Auburn at 5 P.M. & travel by night to Utica – agreable & intelligent company   Judge Wright again – Mr Stale to whom I am indebted for a copy of the prison report – a quaker intelligent & philanthropic as usual – Editor of a paper – reach Utica in the morning at 10 situated in the fertile valley of the Mohawk & containing 10,000 souls

Sunday 28th June

Hire a carriage immediately on arrival at Utica & are driven by a little clever flibbertigibbit boy over an execrable road to Trenton-falls – this should be seen *before* Niagara – pretty & picturesque not sublime   on return struck with the beauty of the scene of the Mohawk valley one of the prettiest views I have seen & reminded me a little of the vale of Cloyd   is from an eminence called Trenton Hills – the Town has [spread?] in the bosom of this rich valley & with its canals mail road & progressing rail-ways must be one of the largest in the State

Monday 29th June

Leave Utica at 9 morng – go by way of Herkimer – Little Falls Palatine etc to Schenectady & from thence by Rail way to Albany – on the way for companions Hayes a Captn of the Night watch of Albany his anecdotes of Irish rows – and a Gentn who talked of being a dealer in *lumber* – his aversion to Jacksons party his plan for stopping the breed of the *niggers* – hear on the road from one of the drivers that a row had taken place with the Irishmen on the Railroad who had attacked the drivers of the stages which compelled them to go armed – beautiful scenery of the Mohawk valley down to Schenectady where we arrived at sun-down – take supper whilst the rail-road carriage is preparing – pale faced females – children eating meat at supper – am told that children take

---

[26] The Pennsylvania and Auburn systems were the most progressive of their kind in the country in the 'thirties. For brief descriptions, see Riegel, *Young America, 1830-1840*, pp. 284-285.

meat three times a day – arrive at Albany at 11 o'clock at
night

Tuesday 30 June
At Albany incessant hawking & spitting in the news-room by
the American visitors – At breakfast hear an American snipe-
bill looking little man talking of his recent exploits in Canada by drinking the *'bladder-faced English'* under the table
there over their own port wine

Albany looks more like an English Town than any place I
have seen – go over the City Court house – portraits of De-
witt Clinton a very fine head – of Van Buren a cunning looking fellow – view from the dome a striking one – fondness of
the people here for domes to their public buildings – Go over
the State House – chamber of representatives & senate con-
venient but not handsome – library – governors room – vile
daub of Lafayette   supreme Court room –

Call on Mr Cassidey[27] – a [clever?] sound young man –
who drives us up by the banks of the river to the Cuhooes
falls – & return on the opposite side to Troy to a superb
dinner – beauty of the scenery on returning – particularly a
view about two miles from Albany shewing the Town with
the hills of the Hudson in the distance – in conversation with
Mr Cassidey have found him a well read & intelligent companion, superior in candour & information to nearly all the
Americans I have met with – his excellent memory particularly of the writings of Byron Moore Bulwer & others of the
modern school for which he has quite a passion   in the evening sup at the American Hotel kept by J. Thomas an Englishman, intelligent company met there

Wednesday July 1st
Call on Mr & Mrs Horner – an elegantly furnished house –
talk politics with Mrs H. an agreable & smart little lady who
laments the *ruin* of her country by the Irish & the low de-

---

[27] William Cassidy was a journalist and politician with pronounced literary
tastes. DAB.

mocracy – very small share of republicanism here – most women are aristocrats – I go to see the exhibition of the grand paintings of Adam & Eve at Stanwin[?] Hill – painted by Otis – Adam reminded me of the Saracens head Snow Hill – Eve is made to look in her nakedness that which, considering there was but one man in the world & he her husband, it is impossible she could have been Leave Albany at 11 o'clock by stage for Boston by way of Pittsfield Northampton etc – cross the river in a ferry & ascend the hill on the other side – looking back to the Town from this eminence a striking view of Albany upon the rising ground on the other side of the river which with its golden dome & other public buildings looks striking – in the coach a family scene of young children & a sick mother – stop at Branards Bridge 15 miles to dinner – whilst it is preparing run across to a neighbouring cotton mill & go through it – an Irish manager – the young women here look cleaner more sedate & in all respects more respectable than similar establishments can exhibit in England – the Spinners here of from 26 to 28 nos[?] with mule frames earn from 40^s/. to 42^s/. a week – girls over 16 (no children are employed) get for throstle spinning from 8/6 to 12/6 a week – the same for weaving

coarse printing power looms from 12/6 to 16/8 per wk each woman attends to three looms hours from 5 in the morn^g till 7 p.m. the Country more picturesque & hilly than any we have seen *inland* excepting on the Alleghanies – reminds me of the milder Swiss scenery – pass through the village of Lebanon Springs (a warm spring) most beautifully planted in a deep small valley entirely surrounded with hills prettily wooded – a village of shaking quakers a mile to the right – on leaving the village of Lebanon ascend by a steep road for nearly two miles which affords from many points of view a pretty scene below – companion in the coach from Illinois his rapturous & *superlative* descriptions of the country. reach Pittsfield at 8 o'clock a pretty little village with a square or green in the centre & a large elm tree – the elms of this country are noble ornaments – in the inn – the Coach[?] the streets what incessant spitting – one only consolation every one must have spit himself to death before I again visit America

July 2ⁿᵈ

Leave Pittsfield at ½ past 11 a pretty but hilly country for the first stage – an attempt at the fine gentleman in one of our companions – pass through Goshen – see the effects of a hurricane in passing through a forest which had for sixty miles torn up scattered & broken into fragments huge trees for the space[?][28] of a quarter of a mile in width   some of the trees had torn several tons of earth up with their roots – had still for a companion our friend from Illinois who says his journey to New England will cost him about 60 dollars

number of the splits of the baptists in Illinois described by him – reach Northampton a pretty village described by Stuart – noble elm trees as we approach it – singular hills that surround this village with ranges[?] of bumps like Camels backs – no cold bread to be had at the Inn today

Our Illinois companion gave me some of the prairie Soil

July 3ʳᵈ Friday

Leave Northampton at 2 o'clock in the mornᵍ for Boston – poor country – crops of stones – rich people do not often inhabit the richest soil – industry of the New Englanders in making shoes hats etc for the rest of the Union – arrive at Worcester to dinner – meeting of country people for the purpose of extending the railroad just completed but not yet opened – activity & enterprise of these people – go in coaches ten miles to the rail road & take the cars – after going twenty miles on the way for Boston the engine breaks & we are delayed two hours – reach Boston at 10 p.m. – Tremont House hotel full go to an inferior place & am nearly devoured by the bugs – a fit wind up to a very unpleasant day

[28] The word may be "span."

July 4 Saturday

The anniversary of the declaration of independence in 1776 – am awakend in the morn[g] by the sound of guns & music but no church bells – on going into the street am amused with the display of military – great variety of costume – thin men – day dreadfully hot – go to the old South Church to hear the oration – the Ladies are admitted into the galleries before the procession arrives – meet with D[r] Wilsone[29] at the Church door – we go to the same pew – the ceremony begins with an anthem to the tune of 'God save the King'! – how the egotism of this people speaks in the use of the pronouns *I* & *my* & *me* in this little composition[30] – observe the use of fans by men   the prayer not equal to the occasion – the oration by a young barrister named Hillard[31] an admirable composition – I will order a copy of it when printed – observed that only those portions of this were loudly applauded which conveyed compliments to the ever [?] craving nationality of the audience   on leaving go with Dr Wilsone to call [on] D[r] Warren[32] – house prettily situated on the common   a green surrounded with trees that reminded me of y[e] Green park – go with D[r] Wilsone after dinner to call on Mr Lowell[33] – a cold looking man with a deathy shake of the hand – this is temperament, organization or what you will & does not bespeak *disposition* at all times. Meet with some intelligent men there who have been

[29] Wilsone, a Scotchman from Glasgow, had been a fellow passenger on the *Britannia*.

[30] The song referred to was, of course, "America," which had been written in 1832 and was first used publicly at a Sabbath school celebration of independence in Park Street Church, Boston, on July 4, 1832.

[31] George S. Hillard, twenty-eight at this time, was a lawyer with a promising career in the field of politics, letters and law, which was never quite realized. He was best known for his abilities as an orator. "His occasional addresses . . . were famous in their day." DAB.

[32] Probably Jonathan M. Warren, who after graduating from the department of medicine at Harvard in 1832 had studied in London and Paris. (See *Appletons' Cyclopædia*.) Warren had been a fellow passenger on the *Britannia*. Apparently it was this Warren whom Cobden saw again on his trip to America in 1859. See *infra*, pp. 202, 203.

[33] Probably John Lowell, 1769-1840, lawyer and political writer. DAB. See *infra*, p. 119.

in Europe –, this the only place almost in America where a class of retired people living on their incomes can be found – & the society is accordingly more like that of England than elsewhere in America   Am glad to be told whilst looking out on the crowd in the 'Common' that ten years ago there were ten booths there selling whiskey & the whole field was a scene of dissipation whilst now not one drop of liquor was to be seen on the ground – good effects of temperance societies in this Country – anecdote told me by a gentleman of the order that used to be given 15 years ago to exclude niggers from this enclosure being now altogether forgotten to show the change which even here is going on in the feeling towards the colored people   Balloon ascent same as usual   Boston like an English city – the people like the English, & the surrounding towns & counties I find are named after the English places   At night witnessed no drunkenness except with a sailor or two

July 5 Sunday

After completing my correspondence to Fred[34] & Sherriff accompany my excellent friend Dr Wilsonne to call upon Doctor Warren from whose house we go to St Phillips[35] Church (?) – preponderance in numbers of the females over the gentlemen – the pews of some of the principal people are lined with green baize – walk with Dr & Mr Warren after church on the common – again the scene reminds me very forcibly of the green park London – dine at Dr Warrens along with Dr Wilsonne   after dinner go in a cab with Dr W. to Nahant to tea with his Sister – pass by Bunkers Hill & through Lynn – Nahant a small watering place stands upon a peninsula connected with the main only by a causeway –Mr and Mrs Lyman – Mrs L. Dr Warrens sister is a ladylike person with more embonpoint than is usually to be met with – has been twice to Europe – find that most people here go

---

[34] Frederick, Cobden's brother.
[35] Written originally, the words "St Phillips" were crossed out in pencil at a later time.

to Europe as a finish to their education – Mr Lyman says that one half of the patients in the infirmary & of the inmates of the poor house are Irish – on my return to Boston am bit by the mosquitoes for the first time[36]

July 6 1835[37]

Leave Boston at 9 morn^g for Lowell by the rail road – delayed half an hour midway – on reaching go to the Merrimark House Hotel – a large establishment – present letter for Mr Prince from Harter – go through the print works which employ about three hundred hands   print rather under three hundred thousand [p's?] & pay about £1400 monthly – make all the cloth they print chiefly machine work – only 28 tables & those principally boys – never grass – considers that the sun in the summer would destroy the color & the winter which lasts from Novr to April precludes grass bleaching [?] – says that owing to the *hardness* of the cloth & the dryness of the weather they are obliged to hang their prints before dyeing from three weeks to a month – the block printers get the same wages as in England – considers that heavy 3 [col?] machines cost 1½^d a y^d – *Coals one year £8,000* & yet the power is all by water!   these cost about 31^s/. a ton & the price cannot be materially reduced

Go through a new cotton mill for weaving weft with throstles – beautifully fitted & cleanly kept – am struck by the superior cleanliness & air of the young women who spin & weave – no men employed   the interior of the mill is fresh painted & the *stairs broad & clean* with a lobby at each story for the purpose of hanging bonnets coloshes shawls tc – *this kind of arrangement promotes respectable & decent habits from the young women*

Go over a woollen mill for power loom weaving, a good establishment – all the looms are worked by girls sometimes

---

[36] The small (3″ x 4⅜″), green-backed book (Add. MSS. 43807 A), containing fifty-two folios altogether, is concluded at this point. The diary is continued on loose sheets (Add. MSS. 43807 B).

[37] Added in pencil.

two to a loom – observe the same respectability in their appearance the hours here as in all the other factories are from five in the morning till seven at night with an hour & a half for meals – see the whole of the girls in the village go home to dinner – their orderly & superior manner as compared with our young women of the same class

Go to see the machine shop, – number of machin[e]s & contrivances for abridging labor greater than at Sharp & Roberts, – remark on the cleanliness of the men who are all neatly shaved, – Mr Prince tells me that no man goes home to dinner without washing – *even the Irish* always wash before leaving his work shop

Mr P. tells me of the absurd regulation by which our government interdicted the exporting of copper shells, & that Attwoods formed an establishment at Rouen for working their copper & then exporting the rollers to the United States

Enquire as to the morals of the young women & am told that a *faux pas* is scarcely heard of in the course of a year – & if a female is discovered to be pregnant or if her character should be suspected to be light the others always denounce her & she is removed There are 8,000 to 10,000 young females of the ages of 12 15 & 18 etc working here – they are the daughters of farmers & are lodged & boarded in houses kept by females for the purpose they sometimes return home during the summer & then their places are filled partly with Irish girls custom in marrying for the girls to earn first as much as will furnish the house & afterwards the husband maintains his wife – I do not think the physical condition of the girls is superior to those in England employed upon the like pursuits in *Country places*

Kirk Boott an intelligent gentlemanly man educated in England – his remark that it was a pitiable case for a person to be educated in Britain & then brought out here to live (told me by Prince) – he says they purpose trying the export of twist to Russia – Lowell contains about 15,000 inhabitants

& the water power is only capable of producing about double the present amount of work

In the even[in]g go to Mrs Inglis to see her children perform 'a play of the Corsair'

The part of Seyd well sustained by a young heroine of about eleven & that of Galnore by a girl of 13 years am doubting the wisdom of those parents & teachers who thus bring their young charges before a room-full of flattering spectators to assume the characters & talk the sentiments of cut-throats & concubines

Eaves-dropping a propensity in this country. Dr Wilsone & I are earwigged by a fellow in fashionable disg[uise?]

July 7

Dr Wilsone & I go to inspect the machine for making lasts by power which was not working We go to view a collection of husbandry implements are struck with the remarkable evidences of ingenuity belonging to the New Englanders exhibited in these contrivances for aiding & abridging human as well as brute labor – the scythe much narrower & lighter than in England would not this do in Britain? – the grindstone with axles revolving upon two steel wheels – the press acting by the weight of the article to be pressed (operating on a multiplied lever) – the pump with a circular motion – Civility of the proprietor of this establishment – afterwards go to see the Statehouse – statue of Washington by Chantrey badly placed – not a very good likeness – the face not possessing the serene & dignified expression of the usual likenesses of this greatest of modern heroes the mouth wants energy & severity which a slight compression of the lips would convey – Ascen^d to the top State-house – commands a view of the surrounding city & country – Boston is surrounded by water excepting on one side where is a neck of land – this Town & Lynn must have been named after their namesakes in England being situated on low land similar to that of the Coast of Lincolnshire – Go to look through the Atheneum li-

brary & news room – a quiet & philosophic looking establishment which does not appear to be much used – On leaving
see Governor Armstrong in his carriage   he was originally
a poor boy in a printers employ

Deliver cards of introduction to several people   all impress
me with the belief in the universality of egotism in this nation – Mr Lowell a warm hearted man though with a cold
shake of the hand – the females of Boston decidedly prettier
than those of New York but still deficient in *preface* &
postcript – take leave of my excellent travelling friend Dᴿ
Wilsone with sincere regret at the separation – believe him
to possess more amiability of heart than almost any other
man of equal knowledge & talent that I have had the enjoyment of associating with – May his worth commend him
& his talents protect him through the rest of his long tour!

Leave Boston at 4 p.m. for the rail road – prodigious number of travellers   again are delayed half way an hour for the
train to meet us – the road not finished at another point we
are obliged to walk – the carriage takes fire twice obliged to
tear out all the [?] – Pat souses us with water from the roof
– his glee at our trouble – 'oh! [tis noting?] – "tis [notin ?]"–[38]
The Yankees are too much in a hurry to finish things
properly before they "go a head" – Arrive at Providence find
all the Inns full – sleep at *the City* upon chairs in the assembly
room – this is a large & flourishing place upon a sand-heap yet
it is a rich Town – so much for industry!

July 8 Wednesday
in the morning go by the Lexington Steamer to New York –
fast vessel – the engine with a stroke of eleven feet – go at a
velocity of fifteen miles an hour over & above the three miles
an hour of stream – reach N. Y'k – a distance of more than
200 miles in 13 hours having completed my tour in just four
weeks

[38] This section is almost indecipherable.

July 9 thursday

Call on Mr Lee[39] – Vietor[40] – Robins[41] – Watt[42] – the Americans still maintain their reputation with me for national egotism by their self-glorification on the subject of their country – the stores handsomer than any thing in England – built with granite fronts to the ground floor very open & light & the goods are exposed on the bottom floor – Pearl St & Pine St will at some future time be the two best streets of warehouses in the world unless Man[r] [Manchester] should very much improve the taste of her buildings   Dine at M[r] Burtsalls[43] – the Misses Burtsall intelligent & amiable girls – the dinner of frogs – the misery of bad domestics – go in a carriage to take boat for the purpose of seeing the constitution frigate – are rowed in a man of wars boat – perfect cleanliness of the ship & the order of its arrangement – civility of the officers – the first Lieu[t] Mr Montgomery a fine veteran like looking little fellow – the men employed in reading, sewing, platting – the greater number reading – some books others newspapers – the Constitution has captured four other frigates – her compliment 500 men & 54 guns – bibles placed round on the cans between decks – return to tea at Burtsalls

To day see the bust of Judge Marshall (who died three days ago) in the Exchange covered with black crape – "hands off" stuck on the crape truly American – the bust by Frazee

July 10th Friday

Call on Mr Tho[s] Dixon whom I do not consider to be too

[39] Possibly Henry Lee who was a merchant, publicist, free-trader, and student of economics and statistics. See DAB.

[40] Possibly Frederick Vietor, apparently a merchant who had come from Germany seven years before and settled in New York City. See *National Cyclopædia of American Biography*.

[41] John Robins was an important dry-goods merchant of Pearl Street, whom Cobden probably saw for business reasons. Walter Barrett, *The Old Merchants of New York City*, New York, First Series, 1862, pp. 393 and 375ff.

[42] Presumably the descendant of old John Watt, New York City merchant.

[43] Burtsell was a friend whom Cobden met probably through his brother or through a mutual friend. Cobden was to see the Burtsells again on his return from the Catskills. See *infra*, pp. 125, 127, 128.

warmly polite – afterwards go with Hardy[44] to see the Courts of Justice – Court of Session – the barristers white hats placed upon the table – Judge without robes or wigs – the negroes still confined to one quarter of the gallery and all sit together – go to the supreme Court of the State & found three judges on the bench without badge of any kind and a barrister pleading in a claret colored coat with pepper & salt pants & white stockings – go to the police office – unostentatious manner of the magistrate & his apparent solicitude to give advice to the applicants – then we walk to see an infant school – oh the happy sight, pregnant with hopes of the exaltation of the character of future generations! I hereby dedicate myself to the task of promoting the cause of infant schools in England where they may become an instrument for ameliorating the fate of the children working in the factories whose case I fear is beyond the reach of all other remedies – at 5 in the even⁸ go by the Steam Boat the Ohio up to Westpoint[45] great numbers on board all the steamers – the fact strikes me that there must be a large proportion of the men who do not marry or otherwise they do not give much of their company to their wives – the number of gentlemen found in all the Steamers coaches & hotels is so great & that of the females in proportion so very small that I should argue but little from appearances in favor of domestic life here – By the way am told to day some incredible stories about the prevalence of unchaste wives in this country – this has been told me before but I am always loath to believe such stories – noble sweeps bends & swells of the Hudson – it is dark before I land at Westpoint – lose the first view of the Highlands   On landing at Westpoint am met by three sentinels who demand my name

[44] See *supra*, p. 90, and *infra*, pp. 126, 128.
[45] As recently as five days earlier Cobden had "planned giving two days to the Hudson river, going up to Albany one day, and returning the next. . ." (Cobden to Frederick Cobden, July 5, 1835, Morley, *Life of Richard Cobden*, I, 38). Cobden was probably dissuaded from such a trip by his New York friends, for not only did he not go to Albany but he spent the weekend from Friday evening to Monday morning in the vicinity of the Catskills.

– this is a precaution as the spot is wholly for the military academys use   the discipline could not be preserved without – was reminded of France at the moment by the Apparition of these the first soldiers I have seen in the U.S.

July 11

At breakfast see the only truly handsome girl I have met in America – Enquiring of Mr Cozzens the landlord of the Hotel I find this lovely creature to be the daughter of an *English* gentleman named Oakey – after breakfast converse with Mr Cozzens – he tells me of Capt[n] Hamilton[46] whilst at his house having transgressed the rules of the hotel by smoking in the parlour for which he was called upon to reprove the Author of Cyril Thornton & to talk of ejecting him   go to see the Cadets on parade – am struck with the more than ever lean & tall figures of the young men – in England such a number of thin subjects would excite ridicule – Call on Mr Leslie[47] to present a letter from Mr Burtsall   house in good taste with a very few well selected proof plates hanging on the walls – Mr Leslie a mild & gentlemanly man with a sweet expression of eye and an intellectual smile – find him a gentleman – we go to the point of view called Fort Putnam – a glorious & inspiring sight – below is Westpoint upon a peninsula formed by a bend of the river whose winding stream above & below is seen pursuing its tortuous course till it abruptly disappears behind one of the numerous heights that here constitute the scenery called the highlands – the gradually sloping banks covered with forest trees – with here & there a little glen or valley breaking away from between these mountains & presenting patches of ripe corn or shining green pasture – the innumerable little sailing boats with their white canvas reflecting the morning sunbeams – the lively looking snowy cottages that are sprinkled over the land-

---

[46] Thomas Hamilton, the popular Scottish writer, recorded observations on his American trip in *Men and Manners in America*, published in 1833.

[47] Charles R. Leslie was a painter and author. In 1833 he had served as teacher of drawing at West Point Military Academy. DAB.

scape – all these charms shut in by a near horizon of mountains that formed a rolling graceful outline to the scene make
the view from Fort Putnam one of the loveliest perhaps
though not the grandest in America

Proceed by the Steam Boat at 11 o'clock for Catskill – the
high banks continue to offer an ever varying scene – what
exhiliration there is in the sight of mountains & vallies rocks
& wild forests! enormous cabin – two tables each 110 feet
long at dinner – dexterity of the crew in lowering & hauling
in the boat with passengers at the landing places

Land at Catskill village & go by a coach to the mountain
house twelve miles which takes four hours & a half – coach
the 'Rip Van-Winkle – driver had not read Irvings tale   half
way house – a little hotel & a good church where are the
inhabitants? for we saw no other houses – from this point the
road mounts incessantly – we see the Mountain house in the
cleft of the undulating ridge of the range of hills above – the
road all the way runs through an uncultivated forest no
break in the foliage even to afford a glimpse of the scene
below – met a man with oxen who enquires of our driver for
some rattle snake oil to cure the rheumatism with – on reaching the mountain house a splendid prospect is opened out
upon a vast extent of plain country stretching in all directions
as far as the eye can reach whilst in the midst is seen the
Hudson winding its clear current in a stream of light upon
the bosom of the dark landscape – Large Hotel with 100 beds
– billiard room – handsomely furnished & yet in a position
not tenantable for one half of the year!

July 12

On rising have a fine view of the clouds as they are rolling
in fleecy masses below the mountain its a struggle of the
god of day with the vapours of the morning – now gathering
up the folds of mist as if to leave the whole landscape below
in the light of the morning sun & then again spreading its
shadowy mantle over all – or occasionally breaking asunder

it disclosed a glimpse of the beautiful vale & then once more closing the fissure & piling thicker & thicker its folds of vapour till it seemed like a sea of foam spreading from our feet out into the interminable distance – Go with a party to see the fall of the Catskill – walk through the forest – here is no pasture or garden on this mountain   all provisions are brought from below – the falls are striking – higher than Niagara but with only a bucket of water – first fall 180 feet the one below 80 ft – the projecting rock is a striking feature (70 ft over the base)   here is the scene of Rip Van Winkles dream   the hollow into which the lower Cataract falls must 50 yrs ago have been the most secluded spot in the world & admirably suited for a scene of romantic adventure   to my surprise find my two companions are from Pulborough Sussex (Constable) & one of them the niece of little Knight (Brown)[48] my old schoolmaster – We feel like old friends in a moment – on returning to the Hotel find to our regret that the day is too hazy & wet to allow of a sight of the landscape below   So that we spend the rest of the afternoon in vain regret at the lovely prospect being shut out from sight by the envious clouds   horrible spitting in the drawing room

July 13

Rise at five o'clock – the landscape below the mountain is visible in the light of the rising sun with here & there a fleecy cloud pursuing its course to join its lost fellows from whose side it had been detached by some playful zephyr – breakfast before starting – a sickly-looking little child eating omelet – parents here permit their children to take whatever & whenever they please

Descend the hill with a Coach full of passengers to Catskill

---

[48] "(Constable)" and "(Brown)" were inserted by pencil at a later time. Mc-Gilchrist records an incident which took place nearly thirty years later at Cobden's funeral when an aged eighty-year-old man handed forward a wreath of spring flowers, which together with a French wreath was placed on the coffin. "He had commenced his friendship with Cobden on the Catskill Mountains in America in July 1835." John McGilchrist, *Richard Cobden, The Apostle of Free Trade, His Political Career and Public Services. A Biography*, London, 1865, p. 286.

where I take leave of my travelling companions (Mr Constable – Mr C. Junr & Miss Brown Sussex) – go on board the Erie again for N. Yk – as we descend towards the highlands where the river finds a passage between two hills that approach each other very closely am struck with the same notion that I had formed whilst looking down from the Mountain house viz – that the whole of the upper part of the channel of the Hudson with the surrounding country once was the bottom of a lake which found its exit by some convulsion of nature – could the palisades once have been the bed of a Cataract worn down in the course of numberless ages in the same way that Niagara is said to be now operating?[49] Will geology ever discover the secrets of the earths past changes? – why not?   prodigious length of the dinner table – am told that one of the boats is 240 ft long – the highlands the prettiest river scenery I have seen but as they only extend about 20 miles & the other portion of the Hudson although good is not peculiarly striking I think the Rhine must owing to the greater length of its beauties be a finer river than this – the scene below West-point is the most romantic where the river seems shut in by mountains that make it appear a lake – where as you advance an opening is found between two hills or round the sharp angle of one and you suddenly find yourself again enclosed [?] in a similar manner again to emerge in a similar way into fresh beauties – West point appears a lovely spot to day – An Irishman on board without money his bundle is seized – the Irish are characterised every where by the same traits – the same passions – the same cunning – the same love of fun & drink   the same proneness to riot & fight – On landing at New York go to 2 Beaver St – in the even^g call on the Burtsells[50] in Mercer St – walk with the ladies to a tea garden for ices – how much the place is like Paris – hear to day that there are 250 bright sunny days in the year in N. Yk – this has been a roasting hot day

[49] The question mark is a later pencil insertion.
[50] See *supra*, p. 120, and *infra*.

14 July tuesday

On rising call upon Hunt[51] at the Clinton   take a bath –
then call upon Waite[52] at the ship – thence go to Hoboken –
bars every where – at the ferry resting place – on board the
ferry – in the gardens of Hoboken etc etc   wherever there is
a concourse of Americans you will find a bar & in truth with
such a hot climate the people are excusable in drinking. I
have to day perspired pints & have swallowed quarts of
water – the thermometer 96 in shade – Hoboken a retired
country retreat used much for children to walk in during
the morning & in the afternoon the resort of multitudes of
Cocknies from New York – On a Sunday tens of thousands of
visitors sometimes cross in the Hoboken ferry boats – the
view of the City from this promenade is the best I have yet
seen – the Town is flat – & wants that diversity of effect which
a larger proportion of spires domes or other public edifices
would be sure to give to an European City of the size – walk
down the upper [part?] of the Elysian fields to the point or
turn that looks up the North river – beauty of this scene
– N. Yk the pleasantest situation in the U. States & perhaps
in the world in respect to the surrounding attractions & facilities for making excursions of health or pleasure   Hunts account of the profligacy the indolence & general degradation
of the people of the Slave owning States – on return go to call
on Mr Steele Mr Robbins etc – afterwards go with Mr & Mrs
Hardy[53] to call at Bunkers Hotel on a friend – room full of
ladies & gentlemen in groups   windows open looks like
Paris   Go to the Park Theatre to see a young boy act Richard
3rd – a good building rather gaudily painted

15 July

Call on Hunt   afterwards upon my friends in Pine & Pearl
St and then go to Staten Island along with Hunt & Grover[54]
– a beautiful view of the Bay of N'Yk   the Quarantine Sta-

---

[51] A fellow passenger (from Dublin) aboard the *Britannia* on both voyages.
[52] See *supra*, p. 90 n.   [53] See *supra*, pp. 90, 121, and *infra*.
[54] Cobden's fellow passenger aboard the *Britannia* on the return voyage.

tion where the vessels from all parts are lying – the custom here is for the cabin passengers to proceed up to N. Yk immediately on arrival by steam and the steerage passengers if they exceed 40 in number are detained till their clothes are washed & the medical searcher pronounces them free from disease If the vessel does not contain more than 40 passengers it is not customary to detain her On landing at Staten Island (which we did in 40 minutes, being 8 miles from New York) we go up to the Pavilion a hotel on the high ground & from the gallery erected on the top of this we had a fine view of the whole of the bay of N. Y'k with the city in the distance, Jersey City, Brooklyn, Hoboken etc – the ships & boats passing in by the narrows at our feet or sailing in the outer bay or in still closer array towards the City – On returning in the Steam Boat hear some sailors in talking of the ships from different countries lying at quarantine say that the British ships were dirtier than those of any other nation On landing again at New York go with Henry[55] to dine at an ordinary – the white jackets worn by the young men struck me as being an excellent summer costume Afterwards go to Carvills the Bookseller & purchase some books – his account of Cooper the novelist very fluent in conversation but too egotistical – the publishers in England get from the New York or Phila [Philadelphia] printers £100 for the first copy of the works of such writers as Bulwer etc in order to enable them to bring out the work first – the native authors labor under great difficulty in consequence of the cheapness of the English copy rights Afterwards go with Harry to see the Burtsells – take tea there – pleasant well ordered family – the mother has undoubtedly been an excellent woman Burtsell a generous hearty young man but with some propensity for prose – the young ladies are lively & accomplished & apparently very affectionate towards each other which is the best test of amiability –

[55] Cobden's brother.

In the evening go with Mr Burtsell to a supper cellar kept by a black of good manners where we had fried wood cocks champagne brandy etc Afterwards return home in a hackney Coach in the midst of a furious conflict of wind & rain

16 July

On rising pack my things – after breakfast purchase views of Westpoint – at 11 go on board the steamer with Hardy, Burtsell, Stirling & Harry for the purpose of being put on board the Brittania – Crowd on board – leave taking of friends – some crying – others laughing & here & there a silent thoughtful person – here was a fond parent giving directions to a parting son the scene rendered ludicrous by the tall robust figure of the latter & his mature age – there was an old man commending to the care of the Captain his friend Smith one of our fellow passengers & as he looked upon his charge he smiled at the dumpy figure & weather beaten & rather rosy complexion of the old gentleman who could not be less than 50 – there is a group of steerage passengers whose rubicund noses – reeling eyes & staggering walk show that they had drowned their sorrows the night before in the whiskey bowl – their grey eyes, slightly freckled skin, large upper lip and thick clumsy mouth proclaim these men to be Irish On running alongside the Brittania which had got under weigh our Steam Boat is lashed alongside of her – the passengers go aboard & the baggage is all removed whilst the vessel is at the same time towed along – there is a great celerity of movement observable here Cast off the Steam Bt below the Quarantine Station & we proceed through the narrows – not quite a mile in width – with a light air. The Victoria[56] a transient ship for Liverpool is leaving the port at the same time – we are told that this ship is a very fast sailor & has never been beaten & moreover we learn that some large bets have been made that she will beat the Britannia all of

[56] For information on these sailing-ships, the *Britannia*, the *Victoria*, and the *England* (mentioned on p. 131), see Albion, *Square-Riggers on Schedule*.

Portrait of Cobden, Aged Twenty-six

which has provoked a huge spirit of deadly rivalry in the breast of our Captain who is resolved to conquer the Victoria

Arranging our luggage & settling ourselves into our quarters occupy the afternoon   The seamen are all mustered & the two mates pick each one half of the crew, man by man, as their larboard & starboard watches

After being out a week we found ourselves one morning alongside of the Victoria & the two vessels were in company for three days – preserving exactly the same relative positions   We parted again on the fourth day

All the dismals of a summer passage, – heat & calms the greatest, & the latter the most intolerable of all, – attended us across the Atlantic[57]   At length on the 13th of Augst in the evening we descried indistinctly land (like a streak hardly perceptible along the clouds that hang above the horizon) and all the company were at once on the alert anxious to rest their eyes once more upon terra firma

In the evening the Captain & I were standing upon the deck, – it was dusk, & I pointed his attention to a large vessel that had approached so near to our stern as almost to threaten our spanker boom with destruction – The Captain walked aft with the intention as he said, of 'ordering her off,' smiling at the same time, when to his surprise he found she was the Victoria! – We had each sailed 3500 miles & for three weeks we had not seen each other & yet here we were at the first view of land not twenty yards distant from one another This remarkable coincidence furnishes a striking illustration of the accuracy with which navigation is accomplished in the present day ——14——

Augst 14th a dead calm nearly all the day which provoking circumstance has for the first time given me a desperate fit of the blue devils & as I can always best get rid of ennui by the help of books & my own reflections I retreated into my birth & amongst other occupations I amused my mind by writing

[57] For a good description of ship life on the crossings of the sailing-packets, see *ibid.*

sketches of the characters of my companions which certainly are the most *motley* that were ever brought into so small a compass before[58]

Colonel Galindo	Chargé d'Affaires from Central America }
Rev^d Mr Hall[59]	Boston U.S.
Mr Gordon, wife, & little boy.	Liverpool & New Orleans }
Lieut Wolseley	Reg^t
Mrs Smith (*soi-disant M^rs*)	
Mr Hunt	Dublin
Mr Grover	Maryland U.S.
Mr Goodwin	(Doctor)
Mr Rennie	Louisville Kent V.
Mr Montgomery } Mr Nicod	Partners from Oxaco Mexico[60]
Mr Smith	Irish born American
Mr Haüppoldt	Wurtemburgh – American
Alexr Lopes	a little boy a Jew
Mr Scott	(*soi-disant*) from Isle of Man

during all the day the Victoria is lying a few hundred yards astern of us – about 4 in the afternoon a breeze sprang up aft which brought our rival alongside of us before we caught the air – what a pucker has this put us all into! – We seem

---

[58] See pp. 134-140 for these descriptions.

[59] Cobden saw Hall again when he visited America in 1859, first in Washington and later in Plymouth. See *infra*, pp. 145 and n., 205, 206.

[60] In a letter to Arles Dufour, October 23, 1863, Cobden referred to these two fellow passengers: "I remember in returning from New-York to England, having for my companions, in 1835, two very intelligent men, one a Swiss and the other a Scotchman, who had been living 7 years in the interior of Mexico purchasing cochineal. Their description of the state of ignorance and demoralization and utter extinction of moral sense in that Country was most appalling, and they wound up their narrative of the character of the people by the observation: 'We have been living seven years in a community where there is not one human virtue extant.'" Add. MSS. 43660 [copy].

to be now more intent upon keeping the Victoria in our rear than reaching Liverpool ourselves – by sun-set however we had passed our foe full half a mile – At night we saw the first light called the hook – a floating light

[*August*] 15th In the morning to our delight we saw the Victoria full five miles astern – The coast of Ireland was now, for the first time, distinctly visible – we beheld houses, fields, & trees, & the sun shone full upon the landscape over which our eyes revelled with a delight only to be compared to that with which half-famished sailors who had been subsisting for a month amidst privations & hunger would enjoy the first meal of their natural food   At twelve o'clock we have the Tuscar light house & proceed under a continually improving breeze for Holyhead – hurra for Liverpool to morrow!   at ½ past 10 at night see Holyhead light

[*August*] 16th *Sunday*
At 6 o'clock in the morning we took our pilot on board & proceeded at a spanking rate for Liverpool where we land at one o'clock two hours after the England that sailed 8 days after us with gratefully acknowledging the blessings of Providence in conducting us to terra firma.

Amen

R. Cobdens route[61]

		Miles	
May 1st	Manch^r to Liverpool	32	R^d
June 7	New York	3500	Brittania
	round Manhattan Island	20	⎱ Gig
	to Coney Island & back	20	⎰
	Philadelphia	91	St B^t & [?]
	Baltimore	120	D°
	Washington	37	Stage
	Pittsburgh	260	D°
	to Conneaut	130	D°
	Buffalo	100	Steam Bt
	Falls of Niagara	20	Stage
	Lewiston	12	
	Albany	360	Stage
	Utica to Trenton Falls	30	”
	Boston	166	”
	Lowell & back to Boston	50	R^d
	Providence	40	R^d
	New York	200	St Bt
	Albany & back again to New York	300	D°
	Staten Island & back	16	D°
	New York to Liverpool	3500	Britannia
	Manchester	32	
	Total	9036	

[61] Written on a separate, loose sheet of paper, with Hunt's route recorded on the other side.

Mr Hunt

		Miles	
Apl 29	Dublin to Lpol [Liverpool]	125	St
	Lpool & N Yk	3500	Brita[nnia]
	Philadelphia	91	St & R^d
	Baltimore	120	D^o
	Wheeling	279	Stage & R^d
	Cincinnati	358	Steam B
	Louisville	132	....
	Cumberland River	313	D^o
	Salem	15	horsebk
	Hopkinsville	40	Stage
	Louisville	140	"
	Steubenville	511	St Bt
	Wellsville	30	"
	Ashtabula	145	Stage
	Buffalo	140	Sail Bt
	Niagara Falls	20	St Bt
	Montreal	470	" & Coach
	Albany by Sarratoga	250	St B^t Stage & Canal
	New York	145	St B^t
	Staten Island & back	16	St B^t
	Liverpool from N Yk	3500	Britannia
	Dublin	125	St B^t

$$\overline{}$$
10,465

Dublin 18 Augst

Sketches of some of my fellow passengers under fictitious names[62] on board the "Britannia" – *1835*

Epicurus Ca[boin?] A voluptuous and handsome looking young man of perhaps twenty five, whose lusty but inert person and whose indolent mind render him the beau-idéal representation of luxury & sloth – He rises in the morning just as the breakfast is ready and takes two steps only from his bed to the table, which walk costs him evident labor, he entombs in his already bursting bowels in half an hour more food than would preserve from the grave a famishing widow and her six starving orphans during the whole day!

With pain & difficulty he removes a dozen paces, (reminding one in his movements of a boa-constrictor after an unwonted gorge) . . . He passes the remainder of the morning seated in a listless posture with his swimming and dreamy eyes gazing on vacancy   The bell for lunch startles him like an electric shock – he is the first to seat himself again at the table – he does not utter a word, how could he, his mouth is never empty – mark his posture as he leans over his plate, his shoulders are bent forward his arms extended half way across the table and his face almost touches the plate – his luncheon would have sufficed for a meal for Christ & his 12 apostles – he again returns to his seat where he remains for the afternoon with as little motion or signs of animation as is observable in a huge pumpkin or head of vegetable marrow – He complains that the last half hour immediately previous to the dinner is the longest part of the day – At dinner he avoids the duties of carving & conversation – he is helped twice to soup – he expatiates on the quality of the joints & talks of the mutton being better than he expected from the appearance of the *sheep* – he compounds novel mixtures of sauces & laments the absence of some choice ingredient that he once tasted in another country   in a word his con-

---

[62] The remainder of the heading was added in pencil and traced later in ink, probably by another hand.

versation is a restaurateurs *carte* – after eating of a multitude of dishes (the sight of his omnivorous exploits twice compelled a delicate person sitting opposite to him to leave the table) the dessert is but the signal for fresh attacks he secures a portion off every dish for fear as he says "it should be eaten," & all – raisins, figs, oranges, almonds, – are piled together upon & about his plate resembling a little fricitures shop – Yet this individual talks of temperance in *drinking* with virtuous zeal – he is intolerant in the more subtle questions of faith – in short he is a minister of the gospel – eager for the emancipation of the slaves but a slave to his own belly – learned in the ancients & yet ignorant of himself & sincerely unconscious that he is other than a consistent imitator of the example of his divine master

Mercutio Gulliver – Has a slight but elegant figure which is never for a moment at rest – his face when he talks or laughs is young & effeminate looking & rather prepossessing; – but when in a state of repose which is very seldom it looks old & jaded & you perceive that his nose, a very sharp & prominent one, has got a twist, as the Captain says, towards his starboard ear, & his chin also projects together with his under lip like that of an old man His head is shaped like a Charib Indian's but much larger – his perceptive organs are protruded forward in a projecting ridge that makes his reflectives appear altogether wanting: – the great weight & bulk of his cranium is above & behind the ear He is about 25 yrs old & has been travelling, to believe his own account, ever since he was eleven & in the course of his voyages has visited every corner of the world He talks upon *all subjects* with an extraordinary fluency & has a surprising memory of facts, persons, dates, & places – His tongue never tires – In repartee his quickness is quite formidable. And his store of observation redeems his conversation from insipidity Notwithstanding he has been nearly all his life on board ship according to his own account yet he argues about horse racing, sporting, & Tom-&-Jerryism, as though he had never been out of England – He has never fallen into a wrangle over cards, or other sports, or after dinner, but he has always proved in the right & yet his disputes have been numerous – In conversation he will assert with hardihood that he sailed with the present King! – that he lodged with Brougham for three months! that he once lost £22,000 at play! – that he rode a steeple chase in an incredible short time! – that he sailed from New York to Liverpool in 13 days! & a thousand other equally palpable fictions: – to convict him of these fabrications in nowise disconcerts him I once began to think him crazy, partly from a flickering expression of his eyes, but more in consequence of a disagreeable giggling laugh, sounding like something between the gobble of a turkey & the whinying of a horse, with which he closes almost every sentence he utters, but the stock of information of a genuine kind possessed by him & the happy talent he manifests upon any subject of discussion removed my suspicions   Yet his presence has been viewed as a calamity by all the passengers – he has prevented the conversation of a very intelligent party from flowing in a pleasing or instructive vein – he answers or contradicts the remarks of all he hears, no matter by whom uttered or to whom addressed & his unfailing laugh prevents your treating seriously any thing he says no matter how insulting it may be – He bears quizzing or contradicting with good humor & this induces a similar forbearance from others towards himself – Yet he is at times so insulting that it is a miracle he does escape a serious quarrel, and, indeed, people think that his nose was twisted, *towards his starboard ear*, by the fingers of some person whom he had outraged – One thing is peculiar that I never heard him in conversation utter a *reflection* upon the scenes or persons or events he had encountered   his talk is merely a narrative (one half of which is *apocryphal* & the rest far from wholly *gospel*) of incidents which he has witnessed without advantage or profit perhaps owing to his phrenological development not being suitable for his becoming a traveller or philosopher

Sancho Panza   A little round tubby body with short stuggy legs about a span long from the ankle to the knee: – his face tanned in brandy till the skin looks like red morocco leather: – his sharp grey eyes swimming in a fluid of the consistency of whiskey punch: – his upper lip, the sensualists tell-tale of feature, is thick and long, and (the whole of his upper teeth having disappeared from premature decay) protrudes beyond his mouth, so that, when drinking, it may be seen dipping greedily half way to the bottom of his glass   On coming on board he passed himself off for a water drinker, & referring to his face, the hue of which gave his tongue the lie direct, swore it was only occasioned by poorness of blood – We soon found by the fragrance of his tea that he contrived to mix with it one half brandy; and happening one evening to put my head into his stateroom I found that it smelt like a spirit vault   In fine we were told by the stewardess that he had made her his confederate in his plans – (he is an Irishman & has a smooth tongue for the women) – for being secretly supplied with his usual beverage   The traitress agreed to assist in playing him false, & one evening, at my suggestion, she gave Panza's tea-cup as if by mistake to Mercutio Gulliver who no sooner tasted the contents than he began to splutter & to scream out at the tip top of his shrill voice "what the devil! – Poison ahoy! No, by the Gods 'tis brandy & water!" This was just what we expected & it drew the attention of the whole party to the discovery – Panza now professed to be as much surprised as the rest of us at the circumstance & took the earliest moment that offered for conjuring the Stewardess not to disclose the secret & he chuckled afterwards at the manner in which *he had deceived us*! – He now discontinued taking spirits in his tea, for fear as he said we should smell them, but he took an extra portion in his state-room – One night young Shylock, who was Sanchos room mate refused to go to bed, because as he said 'it stunk so' The scene was a rich one, it was eleven o'clock, we were all in the cabin, & Panza lay in his berth the door of which was open, & the steward was trying to force the little infidel to go to bed, who resisted for a time very stoutly and struggled hard at the door, protesting in a loud voice against sleeping in the same state-room with "old Sancho who stunk so of brandy" We discovered that the way in which he passed for a water drinker was a cunning ruse to escape paying an additional £5 for wine & spirits during the voyage – Yet he could not so far control himself as to abstain from taking the Captains wine during dinner & having been expressly told by the steward not to drink any more he promised compliance but very soon again took every sly means of filling his glass from the decanter before him – At table he loaded his plate with a dozen heterogeneous articles at the same time – meat, molasses, turtle, poultry, butter mush & whoffles all occupied one plate at once – He is fond of ribaldry & his grin of approbation over an obscene joke, when he is half fuddled, reminds one of Bacchus & Silenus united in one person – A compound of gluttony, meanness, cunning, selfishness, lust, & drunkenness!

Young Shylock Evinces at the age of about nine years promise of a large development of Hebrew obstinacy & cupidity; – he delights in thwarting and opposing all who are near him; but nothing seems to give him such pleasure as to be allowed to sit beside one who is playing at cards & to hold his money which he keeps incessantly passing from one hand to the other or rubbing between his palms You scarcely ever see him but he has one or more coins of some kind in his hands; – he plays at shuffle board with young Hamlet, for silver threepences, & wins his money or quarrels if he loses – The avowal of his faith was an interesting & amusing scene to those who were present when it was drawn from him, & he offered, in a characteristic manner, to say it over again, to those who were absent, for six pence, provided it was paid him *first* "I am a Jew" he said "that is true;   I only believe in one God, no more; Jesus Christ is your lord, but not mine: *my grandmother* told me that the old Jews killed him;   they hung him up alive upon a tree, and then made fun of him till he was dead; – but *she* says *she* wasn't one of them, – it was long before *she* was born" Little Shylock has large round eyes, a nose that is more prominent & hooked than usual for boys of his years – his forehead remarkably low & con-tracted and his mouth always closely shut – *the whole ex-pression of his countenance is that of a weazel* – the cra-nium expands towards the upper & back regions & the ears are rather long which altogether adds to the pointed expression of his physiognomy,

Young Hamlet An intelligent & expressive face, full of gentleness & softness, presenting such a contrast to the one above described, as a painter or dramatist would wish to portray – His features are small and all of them full of amiability; – he is very quick & clever & with a scrambling active turn that leads him into all kinds of harmless fun. Somebody gave him a shilling to play with Shylock for, & the next day the amiable child asked the donor whether he wanted any money because he still had the shilling that he gave him the day before & if he wanted it he might have it again – His head is as much in contrast as his dis-position with that of his young playfellow – He is about seven years old & with a good development of the moral & intellectual regions whilst the propensities are moderate

Argus Quixotte Crusoes
    A tall bony figure at least six feet three with a nose out of all proportion long, & which projects forth from a face

otherwise thin & tapering, giving to it the form of a wedge – his mouth is small & generally a little unclosed so as to afford a sight of a couple of very large front teeth; – his eyes have a parboiled appearance they look like half-washed-out blue stains upon two pieces of mother of pearl; – of forehead he has almost none & his head is quite flat at the crown which is the more perceptible from the mode in which he parts the hair at the top bringing it down in stiff long layers on each side reminding one of the old fashioned straw covered beehives: – the extremities of this thatch fall down till they meet a pair of whiskers that are trained to cover nearly the whole of the face which peers out from its hiding place and looks not unlike one of those heads that we see carved out of a cocoa-nut husk Yet this grotesque being is prepossessed with a favorable opinion of his own personal attractions & he believes himself to be the object of regard to all the pretty women he meets He is however an amiable creature – full of honorable feelings & like nearly all British officers a gentleman in principle. . . .

Aspasia – An intriguante – impatient of the least neglect & eager for the admiration of all on board – with pretty features & yet ugly from the effects of ungovernable passion – alas lust like ambition can convert an angel into a demon!

Angelica – Mild, unsuspecting, simple-minded

The Diary

OF THE TRIP TO AMERICA

1859

The Diary

OF THE TRIP TO AMERICA

1859

Visit to America
1859

Feby 12 1859

Left Liverpool by the Cunard Companys Steamer "Canada" Capt Lang for Boston, United States via Halifax. For the first day the weather in the Channel was very fine. – In 30 hours we passed Cape Clear & found ourselves on the broad Atlantic where we encountered head winds, causing a rolling & pitching of the ship which gave me a sea-sickness for several days. – My companions were chiefly Canadians returning from the transaction of business in England. – – Hon J. Young[1] – Hon Mr Dawson   The voyage had its usual monotony – We saw only three vessels, & two of them were near the shore – The Captain says he sometimes makes the passage without seeing a sail. – This gives one a striking idea of the immensity of the ocean & of the insignificant amount of Commerce still borne on its bosom. –

Reached Halifax at 7 o'clock in the evening of the 24th – This principal place in Nova Scotia seems full of barrels of fish, which is its great staple. – Left again for Boston in a couple of hours crossing the Bay of Fundy, & arrived at Boston at daylight on the 26th –

Remained at Boston till the afternoon – saw Mr Franklin Haven[2] – & Mr S.D. Bradford[3] of West Roxbury, nr Boston

[1] Cobden visited Young in Montreal. See *infra*, p. 211 and n.

[2] Haven, a director of the Eastern Railroad and a New England bank president, was one of the promoters of the Illinois Central Railroad and owned Illinois Central securities. Gates, *The Illinois Central Railroad*, pp. 37, 50. See *infra*, pp. 201, 203.

[3] See *infra*, p. 201 and *passim*.

whom I promised to visit on my return. Left Boston at 3 p.m. for New York, where I arrived about 11 o clock, & stopped at the Brevoort House. –

27th *Sunday* – Dined at Mr Osborns[4] after accompanying him & his wife to church

28th Attended a meeting of the Board of the Illinois Railway Company – found that the Annual Report which had been sent forth contained passages obnoxious to the London Committee of shareholders which I advised the Directors to alter –

Mar 1st. From New York to Philadelphia where I passed the night at the house of Mr H.D. Gilpin.[5] – Met there in the evening some of his intelligent neighbors. Mr McAllister[6] who has investments in Illinois. – Left the following morning Mar 2nd by express train for Washington where I arrived at 5 o'clk. – Call on Lord Napier[7] – the President [Buchanan]. – In the evening went to the Capitol to witness the closing scenes of the session of Congress. – Was introduced by Senator Mason[8] to many members of both

---

[4] William Henry Osborn was president and director of the Illinois Central Railroad. More than any one man, he was responsible for the successful administration of the railroad over approximately thirty years. See *ibid.*, p. 77, *passim*; and Corliss, *Main Line of Mid-America*, pp. 38, 39, *passim*.

[5] Gilpin was a Philadelphia lawyer, author, and patron of the arts, who had served as Attorney-General. (DAB) Half English and a relative of the Brights, he had become a friend of Cobden. See *supra*, p. 41 n., and *infra*, p. 172.

[6] McAlister was a member of the McAlister and Markoe Land Company, a Philadelphia firm which owned extensive holdings in Illinois. (Gates, *The Illinois Central Railroad*, p. 318). He was the McAlister whose opinion on the state of the Illinois Central Railroad Ashworth quoted to Cobden in his letter of May 19, 1857. *Supra*, pp. 44-45.

[7] At this time Napier was upon the point of relinquishing to Lord Lyons his duties as British envoy to the United States. From Washington he went to the Hague, and became successively British Ambassador to St. Petersburg and Berlin and governor of Madras, serving temporarily as governor-general of India. DNB.

[8] James M. Mason represented Virginia in the Senate from 1847 to 1861, serving for ten years as chairman of the Senate's foreign relations committee. (DAB) He was later of fame in the Mason-Slidell incident, to which Cobden referred in a letter to Henry Catt, December 16, 1861: "I happen to know Messrs Slidell & Mason personally, and to the latter I am indebted for many courtesies at Washington; and although, as they must know, I can have no sympathy for their cause,

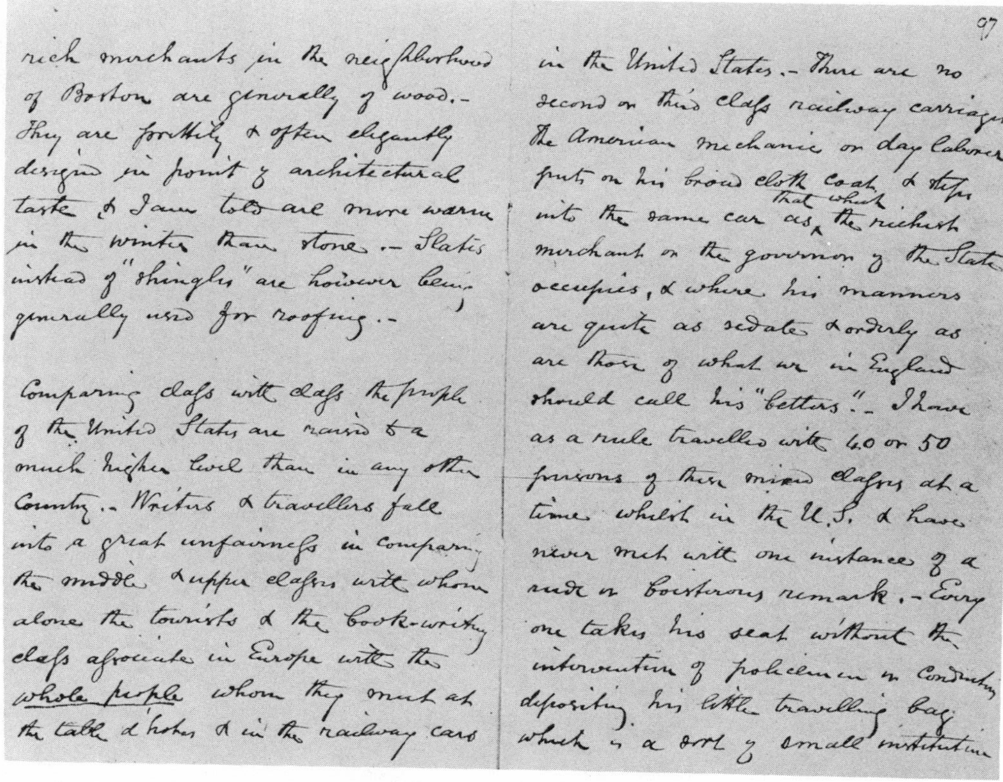

A Page from the Diary of 1859

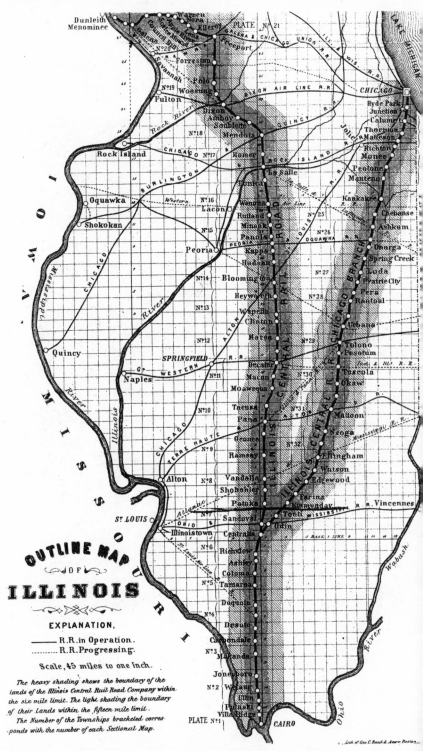

The Illinois Central Railroad in Illinois

branches of the legislature (after he had taken me to his private committee room to take a glass of brandy & water with him), & I was allowed the privilege of the "floor." –

3rd Again to the Capitol in both House & Senate, and made the acquaintance of the leading men. – Great confusion in the proceedings. – The session terminates by the Constitution at 12 o'clock of the 4th March A great portion of the business of Congress was thrust into the last week. – It was doubtful whether some of the most important measures would not be lost. – Both House & Senate sat up the whole night, & the President was in attendance at the Capitol to sign the bills as they should pass

Mar 4 – Met Mr R.B. Hall[9] now a member of Congress with whom I made the voyage across the Atlantic in 1835. Promised to visit him at his house near Boston – Dined with Lady Napier & afterwards accompanied her to the theatre. – Owing to a jealousy on a point of etiquette between the House & Senate, the Session was brought to a close before the appropriation for the post office service was made. – People with whom I conversed on this subject treated it lightly remarking that the government would find a way out of this difficulty – It would not be viewed so lightly in England. –

Mar 5 – Breakfasted with Senators Hunter[10] & Mason –

---

few persons would more rejoice than myself to see them released from an irksome confinement." Add. MSS. 43678 Part 2 [typed copy].

[9] Two years earlier Ashworth had written from America to Cobden: "The inclosed Card of Mr R.B. Hall of Plymouth, Massachusetts may remind you of a fellow passenger in 1835. – This Gent^n I happened to meet at a dinner party in Washington and it was quite refreshing to hear him relate the agreeable impression he still entertains of the friendly intercourse you enjoyed together in crossing the Atlantic and the kindness and hospitality you showed to him whilst in Manch^r as well as in casting out for him very elaborately a travelling route over the Continent." Add. MSS. 43647, Ashworth to Cobden, February 28, 1857. See *supra*, p. 130, and *infra*, pp. 205, 206.

[10] Robert M. T. Hunter was senator from Virginia from 1847 to 1861, serving for a time as chairman of the Senate committee on finance. He was later one of the leading statesmen of the Confederacy. DAB.

afterwards called on Doctor Bailey[11] then met' Mr R.J. Walker,[12] late governor of Kansas, & formerly Secretary of the Treasury with whom I took a walk & called at Bradys the photographer where we both had our portraits taken – Dined with General Cass,[13] & met a large party, sat beside Senator Mason who amused me with some disparaging & original remarks on the characters of Washington, Franklin, Jefferson & the other heroes of the Revolution Promised to send him one of the stamps intended for taxing the Americans. – Met "general" Henningsen.[14] – Remember to see Mr. J.M. Forbes[15] when at Boston –

Mar 6. Sunday – Breakfasted with the President [Buchanan][16] at 8 o'clock found him looking much older, & apparently out of spirits, & not so happy as when I knew him in London. Having attained the highest object of his worldly ambition he is disappointed with the result. He invited me on my return to Washington to take up my abode at the "White House." – Left Washington at 3 o clk by the train for New York. – Travelled at night which I found to be

[11] A physician, Gamaliel Bailey carried considerable influence as an anti-slavery agitator and publisher of the national anti-slavery weekly (the *National Era*) in Washington. *Ibid.*

[12] Although able, Walker had worked unsuccessfully as representative of the Illinois Central to negotiate an early loan with English banking houses. See Gates, *The Illinois Central Railroad*, pp. 69-73; and Corliss, *Main Line of Mid-America*, pp. 32-34.

[13] Lewis Cass was Secretary of State at this time. He had been eminent as a soldier, governor of the Territory of Michigan, minister to France, and Secretary of War. (DAB) Some years earlier, Cobden's opinion of Cass was not high. In a letter to Sturge, April 15, 1851, he referred to Cass as "the bellicose enemy of England." Add. MSS. 43722, Bdl. 1, Part 6. For this statement in its context, see *supra*, p. 35.

[14] Of British citizenship in his early years, Charles F. Henningsen was famous as a soldier, writer, and "man of the world." DAB.

[15] See *infra*, p. 202 and n. and ff.

[16] Buchanan had served from 1853 to 1856 as American minister to Britain, where Cobden had known him well. In connection with Cobden's disappointment at the *Manchester Examiner* siding with the "slavery party," which was supporting Buchanan in his campaign for the presidency in 1856, Cobden wrote: "I speak impartially – for with Buchanan I was on very intimate & friendly – indeed most familiar & confidential terms." Add. MSS. 43658, Part 2, Cobden to Richard, September [?] 7, 1856.

very uncomfortable as we had some ferries to pass over –
reached New York at 3 o'clk a.m.

Mar 7. – Attended a meeting of the Illinois Comm[ee] & found
them willing to expunge the part of the Annual Report
which was likely to be offensive to the London Comm[ee].
Dined with Mr Osborn – met Mr Cyrus Field[17] who laid
the electric telegraph across the Atlantic – Mr Bryant[18] the
poet tc – Mr Dana[19] of Tribune –

Mar 8 Called at Appletons the great publishers – Stuarts
the great silk mercers. –In the evening dined at Mr Barlows[20]
met Mr O'Connor[21] the leading barrister, Mr Sherman,[22]
Mr Cunard[23] etc. –

Mar 9 – Mr Noyes[24] a barrister called & took me to the
Criminal Court where a person was being tried for mur-

[17] Field, a New York capitalist, promoted the laying of the first Atlantic cable
in 1858. It soon failed to function, and not until 1866 was a permanent cable laid.
(DAB) Field profited by this and another meeting with Cobden. Three years later,
February 20, 1862, Cobden wrote to Gladstone for an appointment for "my
friend Mr Cyrus Field from New York upon the subject of the Atlantic telegraph
Cable." Add. MSS. 44136, Gladstone Papers, LI.

[18] The well-known poet, William Cullen Bryant, was editor of the Republican
Evening Post and a leader in New York civic, social, and charitable activities. DAB.

[19] Charles A. Dana, in his fortieth year at this time, was managing editor of the
New York Tribune, Greeley's paper. Later he served as special commissioner at
Grant's headquarters; and after the Civil War he became owner and editor of the
New York Sun. DAB. See *infra*, p. 166.

[20] Samuel L. M. Barlow, head of an important firm of lawyers in New York
City, was particularly skillful in corporation law involving large financial interests.
He was well-known as a private collector of books, art connoisseur, and epicure.
DAB.

[21] Charles O'Conor, in his conduct of the Forrest divorce case in the early
'fifties, established himself as one of the leading members of the New York bar.
Later he was famous in the Tweed litigation. DAB.

[22] Possibly John Sherman, youthful leader in the House of Representatives at
this time, later senator, Secretary of the Treasury, and Secretary of State; but more
probably Watts Sherman, the managing partner in the firm of Duncan Sherman
& Co., Bankers. See M. V. Beach, *The Wealth and Biography of the Wealthy
Citizens of the City of New York*, New York, 1855, p. 66. See *infra*, pp. 166, 171.

[23] Edward Cunard, son of the founder of the Cunard Steamship Line, was for
thirty years agent for the Line in New York. *Appletons' Cyclopædia*.

[24] William C. Noyes was eminent as a philanthropist and lawyer who helped to
codify the laws of the state of New York. DAB. See also *infra*, pp. 193-194.

der. – The witnesses *sit* while giving evidence, & the prisoner was also accomodated with a chair. – – Went over Harpers great publishing establishment – then to a famous tailors establishment where I saw a number of men cutting out their garments under the vast dome of a house larger than an ordinary church. – Dined at Mr Sturges,[25] met Mr Bancroft[26] & a party. –

Mar 10 – Dined with Mr Wiley[27] at the St Nicholas Hotel – an old fashioned party, & an old fashioned dinner. –

11 Breakfasted with Mr Bancroft – met Mr Everett[28] & Mr Astor[29] the millionnaire. Dined with Mr Cyrus Field who is said to have first devised the plan of an Atlantic telegraph – met also Mr Church[30] who is called the Turner of America from his style of painting – one of his greatest productions is a painting of Niagara. –

12 March – – Started for Albany by the river shore railway, the river being still obstructed by ice – the view from the rail by no means equal to that by the water. – From Albany by N.Y. Central railway to Niagara Falls, passing along the

[25] Jonathon Sturges was an incorporator, director, and important shareholder of the Illinois Central. He was the father-in-law of William H. Osborn, president of the company. See Gates, *The Illinois Central Railroad*, pp. 37, 49, 122, *passim*; and Corliss, *Main Line of Mid-America, passim*.

[26] George Bancroft was the distinguished American historian, political writer, cabinet member, and United States minister to Berlin and London (1846-1849) where Cobden had known him well. (DAB) For some specific references to Cobden's previous association with Bancroft, see Add. MSS. 43659, Part 2, Cobden to Sturge, January 22, 1849; *ibid.* 43660 [Part 1], Cobden to Parkes, May 30, 1856.

[27] Leroy Wiley was an incorporator of the Illinois Central. Gates, *The Illinois Central Railroad*, p. 50n.

[28] Cobden had known Edward Everett when he was the American minister to St. James (1841-1845). Everett had a brilliant career as teacher and statesman, but, more particularly, as one of America's most effective orators. DAB. See *infra*, p. 201.

[29] Cobden is referring to William Backhouse Astor, son of the first John Jacob Astor and heir to his fortune. He was the wealthiest man in the United States, his fortune at his death estimated to have been from $45,000,000 to $50,000,000. *Ibid.*

[30] Although only thirty-three when Cobden met him, Frederick E. Church had achieved marked distinction as a landscape painter. The canvas of Niagara Falls, painted in 1857, has been rated as his masterpiece and constitutes "the first satisfactory delineation of the Falls in art." *Ibid.*

Mohawk Valley, & the Gennessee valley, & arrived at Niagara at 3 o clk on the following morning. – This journey of 15 hours travelling would have occupied a week when I was over the same ground in 1835. –

13 Mar – Went from the Station Hotel two miles to the Falls. All around is changed since I was here before. – The quiet natural landscape is covered with Inns, houses, railways & bridges. – But the great & glorious cataract seems alike unchanged in its grandest & minutest features. – It is a spectacle suggestive of ideas of eternity & omnipotence. – One is almost brought to kneel & pray. – I wish Byron had seen this the most sublime of moving scenes that he might have given us a companion verse to his description of Mont Blanc which is sublimity in repose. – – Mr Hadf[o?]ld & his daughter from Buffalo came down to see me. –

Monday Morning Mar 14 – Left Niagara Falls in the morning for Toronto – crossed the wire chain bridge a few hundred yards below the Cataract. – The Country very wooded, but passed many cleared farms which I was told were chiefly 200 acres. – All the way to Hamilton I passed through a good wheat district – Mr Merritt a member of the Canadian Parliament introduced himself to me. – Stopped an hour at Hamilton a flourishing Town on an estuary of Lake Ontario. – At its back a good wheat tract – Thence to Toronto the Capital of Upper Canada where the Governor General resides & where the Parliament was in session. – Popped into both houses for an hour whilst they were presenting petitions. – Was pleased with the appearance of both Assemblies. – Afterwards saw Sir Edmᵈ Head[31] for a few minutes who appeared a sensible man. – Proceeded the same afternoon by train to London. – I have today passed through more good wheat land than in all my travels on the Atlantic coast of the States. – Slept at a huge hotel large enough for the British metropolis. At supper thought that the men

---

[31] Head was Governor-General of Canada from 1854 to 1861. DNB. See also *infra*, p. 215.

looked more English than those on the other side of the
'American frontier – they are more fleshy, have ruddier complexions, with less hair on their faces. –

Mar 15 – Left London at 10 o clk by the Great Western Railway for Detroit – passed through a forest for a great part of
the distance with but a strip of cleared ground along which
the rail was laid. – Passed by Chatham. – The latter part of
the journey was through a poor country generally flat, &
often covered with water – On arriving at the narrow strait
which connects Lake Erie with Lake Huron we were ferried across in a boat in which there was a plentiful dinner
preferred for us – There were many emigrants some of them
women & children – the countenances of emigrants always
seem to me to wear a sad & thoughtful expression. – Detroit
is a fine young city, rising to an elevation & containing many
good streets with handsome houses & substantial stores. – In
a quarter of a Century this will probably be a splendid City
of a quarter of a million of inhabitants. – Mr Livermore the
Treasurer of the Michigan Central gave us the use of the
Directors car, & would not allow me to pay my fare. – Left
Detroit for Chicago at 3 passing across the State of Michigan. – Flourishing towns & villages with school houses forming prominent & handsome objects. – Reached Chicago at
3 [?] in the morning. –

Mar 16 – Chicago   attended annual meeting of the Illinois
Central Railway, & passed the day chiefly with the officers
of the Company. – Chicago a more substantial & older looking City than Detroit but does not stand so well, – the situation being flat –

Mar 17 & 18 – Left Chicago in the morning with Mr Osborn[32] & Cap^n McCllellan[33] for Cairo by the branch of the
Illinois Central Railroad, having the Directors car & sleep-

---

[32] See *supra*, p. 144 n. and *passim.*

[33] George B. McClellan, later general in the Civil War, was vice-president of the
Illinois Central at this time. See *supra*, p. 50, and *infra*, p. 153. See Corliss, *Main
Line of Mid-America, passim.*

ing at night in the car in a "siding," & being brought forward the following day to Cairo. – After passing over 20 or
30 miles we came upon the Great Prairie over which the
road was carried four years since when there was scarcely
an inhabitant upon it. – Now it is dotted with small farm
houses built of wood. – Not a tree is visible excepting here
& there a few fruit trees around the houses. – The soil is a
very rich black mud almost impassable in wet weather there
being no stones or other materials for roads. – The men
wear boots outside of their loose trowsers, & with their long
hair & beards they remind me more of Poles or Wallachians
than members of the Anglo-Saxon family. From Mattoon
to Centralia a distance of nearly 100 miles we passed through
a country of mixed wood & Prairie We saw open tracts of
land varying from a few hundred to many thousand acres,
bordered with belts of forest timber or interspersed with
groups of trees just sufficient for variety & shelter against
winter storms or summer heats. – The open tracts were free
from shrubs or detached trees or stones or stumps, just in
that level state in which an English farmer likes to have his
land. The soil is of the best quality for wheat, & would let
in England for £2 an acre. – Here it is on *Sale* at from 40⁸/.
to 50⁸/. with long credit, & with a railroad running through
it. We reached Cairo in the evening of the 18th – This em-
bryo City which stands on the tongue of land at the junction
of the Ohio & Mississipi & which from its situation may be
expected to be some day a populous seat of commerce, was
almost a sheet of water owing to the overflow of the rivers. –
There was at one house a ladder standing which offered to
the inhabitants the opportunity of escaping from the first
floor in case of a sudden flood, & a boat was moving from
one wooden hut to another, the only mode of communication. – Half of a brick hotel had been swept away during
the late storm, & we were glad to sleep in our railway carriage. – Still, notwithstanding the disasters from flood & fire
which Cairo has gone through, to say nothing of its threat-

ened dangers from earthquake, & despite of the ridicule which tourists & novelists have heaped on it, I predict that its favorable site will lead eventually to the creation of a great commercial mart at Cairo. In walking through the accessible parts of the town & taking some supper at the wooden building called a hotel I observed that the people had a wild amphibious aspect, wearing high boots outside of their trowsers & which seemed never to have been cleaned, whilst their long hair & beards gave them a Sclavonic aspect. –

Mar 19, Left Cairo in the morning by a large Mississipi Steamer for Memphis. – This huge floating hotel besides accomodation for more than 100 passengers takes 1200 tons of freight. – The banks of the river present the same uniform monotonous aspect of forest trees growing almost close to the waters edge – the water, which was high, over-flowing the banks & spreading over the Country for 20 30 or even 80 miles & sometimes forming large lagoons This overflow of the lower Mississippi accounts for the escape of the vast volume of water which from so many great rivers pours into the upper Mississippi through so apparently small a channel as the bed of the river presents towards its termination at the sea where it hardly seems broader than do some of its tributaries 2000 miles above. – Stopped at Columbus 20 miles below Cairo the present terminus of the Mobile & Ohio railroad. – The site of this City is more favorable than that of Cairo having a high bank or bluff at the back of the Town where healthy sites for residences may be found. – Stopped at Hickman a town in Kentucky from whence tobacco is largely shipped. – Went on shore to see the process of packing the tobacco in hogsheads, & found myself for the first time among a gang of slaves. A number of small negro boys were employed in carrying the tobacco from one room to another, & as we entered the premises we found the white overseer engaged in the characteristic employment of whipping one of these urchins. – This little river port from which I was told a large amount of produce the growth of a very rich tract of country is shipped for New Orleans presented a most neglected appearance. – It reminded me in many respects of a Spanish Town. – Four mules were required to draw a cask of tobacco through the deep mud of the streets which might be made perfectly hard for a few hundred pounds. – The people had a sort of slouching Spanish air – & even their hats & their high-pommelled saddles had a similar resemblance. – Senator Jefferson Davis[34] from Mississippi was on board. – A very intelligent man though a strong advocate of Slavery & Southern rights. – He had been Secretary at war in Taylors administration, & bore the reputation of being a very able & honest administrator. In reply to my inquiries he spoke in the highest terms of Capt Mc Clellan saying that he left West Point with a first-class character, that he had been selected by him (Col Davis) when Secretary at war for three successive employments of[?] requiring the highest qualities & that he had been quite satisfied with the result, & that if the Service had presented any opening for his talents he should have tried to keep him in the army that he is not merely an able man in his profession but a gentleman, high-spirited & with an honorable ambition. Since I arrived in the States I have dined at large table d'hotes in all parts, & have never seen a drop of any thing but water drunk with the dinner. – Here on board the Steamer we have no other beverage than the muddy water

[34] For further reference to Cobden's opinions of Davis, see *supra*, pp. 75, 76. Davis later became the president of the Confederacy. An amusing reference to Cobden's meeting with Davis is to be found in a letter from Cobden to Hargreaves nearly four years later, January 19, 1863. In connection with an article in the London *Times*, he wrote: "You know that for the sake of my mental health I do not read that paper. – But the Times has for some time been insidiously sapping the anti-slavery feeling in this Country – It has long been popular in the Southern States of America. – When I travelled in the Steamer from St. Louis to Memphis in the spring of 1859 with Jefferson Davis, he offered me the Times, the very latest file, which he carried with him, but I told him I preferred to watch the banks of the Mississippi to the perusal of that paper – though it contained later news than I had seen from England." Add. MSS. 43655, Part 4.

of the river. – The captain of the Steamer was a mild intelligent man, & not like the *fire eaters* that formerly filled his post. – Observed that the ladies on board occupied one extremity of the large saloon which extended from almost end to end of the vessel, & none of the male portion of the Community – excepting those who accompanied the ladies on board seemed any more to presume to join them than if they had been in their own drawing room. – The real deferential respect paid to women & the solid privileges accorded to them is apparently as much the characteristic of this country now as it was when I was here in 1835. –

Sunday 20. – Landed at Memphis, & after walking for a short time in the town which seems to be a very flourishing place standing on one of the very few bluffs or rising grounds which we had seen since we left Cairo, we left by train for a place called "Junction" where two railroads cross one another & where we slept at a very dirty looking house kept by a dirty ragged looking man & in the morning Mar 21st proceeded forward to *Holly Spring*, upon the line of the Cairo & New Orleans railway, – where we stopped for the day to see the parties connected with this undertaking. – Mr Goodman the President was from home but we saw his son who drove us in his carriage into the Country to see a small estate where he grows cotton – saw for the first time Whitneys Cotton gin. – Holly Spring is a neat little town with 2500 inhabitants, & containing many pretty white wooden houses. – After dinner as I sat along with a group of Citizens at the door of the inn an old man of the party informed me that he "let" his negro men for 240 dollars a year, the hirers finding them in clothes & victuals. – I was also told by a railway engineer that he paid for the hire of slaves (of course to their masters) 20 dollars a month finding them in food but not in clothing. – To skilled negro mechanics he paid from 4 to 500 dollars a year – The food he gave to these hired negroes is as follows –

5 lbs of bacon a week
a peck of Indian meal Do
a quart of treacle – a lb of tobacco D°
1 lb soap, salt. –

Left Holly Spring at 9 o clk for Cairo –

Mar 22 at daylight found ourselves passing through a wood on the borders of Tennessee & Kentucky which extended to the bank of the Mississippi at Columbus where we got on board a steamer for Cairo at which place we arrived at noon. – The junction of the Ohio & Mississippi is not a striking scene – The two rivers approach each other between low banks & with [?] winding courses so that the point of junction is like the reach of a river. – Cairo will become a busy place of transhipment, but not the residence of rich merchants. – Villa Ridge about 10 miles from Cairo on the railway may become the suburban abode of wealthy traders. – Took the train up the Central Railway to Centralia where I slept in the Directors car in a "siding." –

Mar 23 – Left Centralia in the morning & proceeded up the Illinois Central Railway through a rich & thinly settled country to Rutland where we found a colony of settlers from Vermont. – Was introduced to Mr Burns[35] the leading person in the Community who with another person had been deputed by his neighbors to travel through the Western part of the States to choose a residence for about 200 Vermont families. – After visiting Iowa, Minnesota, & other portions of the West he made choice of this spot in Illinois, bought 20,000 acres from the Railway Compy [Company], & named the new Colony Rutland after the place from whence he & his neighbors emigrated in New England. – He tells me that less than 100 families have at present reached – that they are satisfied with the change. – He told me that he had himself

[35] William B. Burns was leader of the Vermont Emigrant Association which brought approximately two hundred families to Rutland. See Gates, *The Illinois Central Railroad*, pp. 131 and 228-229.

entered on his farm in May, & that the next autumn twelve-month he had sent to Market 5000 bushels of wheat the produce of his land. At one of the small stations an Englishman accosted me who said he was from Petworth[36] a tall person named Slater – He introduced me to a Polish "Count" an old gent[n] who gave me a couple of Prairie hens for my supper.

Mar 24 – Passed through a country of the same unvarying fertility until I came to the neighborhood of Galena where the Country assumed a broken hilly appearance. – An Englishman, a servant of the Company, named Woolley got into the carriage at Dixon   he had been formerly in the employ of Sir E. Armitage. – He said that several Englishmen were residing in that neighborhood   Reached Dunleith on the Mississippi in the evening. –

Mar 25 – Dunleith the terminus of the Illinois Central railway on the Upper Mississippi stands on a high bank of the river opposite to Dubuque. – Crossed over to the latter place of about 15000 to take a boat down the river to St Louis. – In walking up to the heights at the back of the town met a person carrying a bag of shavings whom we accosted by accident & he turned out to be a well educated intelligent person who took us to his genteelly furnished house, & afterwards accompanied us to see the schools of the town. – In the "ward" school for primary instruction there were eleven rooms in which boys & girls were taught together. – With one exception the teachers were all females who seemed to perform their duties in a very efficient manner – Was told their salaries were from 35 dollars to 50 dollars a month – The children were of all classes   blacksmiths sons & physicians daughters performing the same tasks together. – On inquiry was told that the practice of teaching the children of both sexes together was more & more in favor. – In regard to the mix-

---

[36] Petworth is a village near Midhurst, Sussex, where Cobden lived. See *infra*, p. 187.

ture of classes Mr Spalding observed that public opinion in America would frown down any attempt at exclusiveness, that there had been an attempt to create a "codfish aristocracy" but it had quite failed. – "Every boy in this school" said he "is eligible to become the President of the United States. – Then went to the High School where youths were completing the higher branches of study – Found on the ground floor a very lady like superior person who had young people of both sexes under her – Youths with moustaches & full grown young women were in the room. – Her moral influence & very superior attainments seemed to surmount the apparent disadvantages of her sex. – She told me she preferred teaching boys to girls as they were more ready & comprehensive in imbibing instruction. – In an upper room we found also boys & girls being taught together. – A female teacher was giving lessons in geometry to youths of 18 years. – Was told that there are scarcely any private schools in Dubuque – that all classes attend these schools. – Heard the boys declaim from Grattan, Patrick Henry, etc. – Judge Clark made a few remarks & introduced me when I also offered some observations Went on board the Steamer the "War Eagle" & left for St Louis at 3 o'clk. – A number of emigrants for the new gold diggings at Pikes Peak came on board with their waggons & oxen commencing a journey of upwards of 1200 miles. – The River has picturesque high banks with occasional islands giving it a varied character contrasting greatly with the scenery of the lower Mississippi which is low & monotonous. –

26th & 27th – on board the War Eagle descending the Mississippi passing on the east bank along the State of Illinois which from Dunleith our starting point to Cairo a distance of nearly 600 miles forms the left bank of the river, – on the west side lie the States of Iowa & Missouri. – The small towns on the banks at which we touched, & where we alighted, had been in an excited state of prosperity up to the summer of 1857 when they had been prostrated by the commercial crisis of that year since which they have been subjected to the additional calamity of an almost total failure of the wheat crop. –Property in the towns had in many cases fallen to one half. – The Iowa side of the river seemed to have more dismal tales of distress to tell than its opposite neighbor – The company on board the Boat comprised a great many rough bearded men with coarse dresses of uncouth fashion, some with loose trowsers tucked into their dirty boots others with their pantaloons rolled up above their shoes like our "navigators," – these men most of them young & full of animal spirits were on their way to the new gold mines at Pikes Peak – all of them carrying the baggage & provisions & small fire arms required for a journey across the plains to the foot of the Rocky Mountains. I was struck with the orderly sober & forbearing demeanor of these men – Not a rude or boisterous word fell from any one of them. – This I attribute to the sobriety of all on board. – With only one exception I observed that nothing but water was drunk at the table – Every body smoked & chewed tobacco but these habits, however nauseous to others, are sedative in their influence on the temper of those who indulge in them. – It is the drinking of intoxicating liquors which leads to excitement & collisions. – Such a company as I find on board this boat if assembled together in England under similar circumstances, with the incessant drinking of beer & spirits which would be resorted to for companionship & pastime, would be attended with boisterous rudeness, & inevitable collisions. – The superior education in America will be thought by some, & the concealed bowie knife & revolver will be said by others, to account for the courtesy & forbearance of my fellow passengers, but I think the absence of stimulants to be the one great preserver of the peace. –

Mar 28th Arrived at Saint Louis at 6 in the morning. – The voyage has been a pleasant one, the weather fine, & I have

had a constant resource in the conversation of my fellow passengers who have preserved to the last their good temper &
decorum. – Among them I have found men from almost all
parts of the Union from Maine to California, & many from
foreign Countries. – The Captain (Gavett) a sensible & amiable man, his clerk a very civil fellow, & the old pilot an
amiable creature. The character of the men whom I have
found in authority on board the Mississippi Steamers con-
trasts most favorably with the ideas hitherto entertained of
them, as a rude & violent class of men.[37] – I have found them
intelligent men of business & very obliging & amiable to all
committed to their charge. – The ladies on board occupy an
extremity of the Cabin fitted up as a drawing room, into
which nobody appears to intrude, though access to it is not
prohibited in the day time. – At night a wooden screen is
drawn across which cuts off all communication with this
privileged quarter, & the married couples & the females are
alone allowed to pass the night within this barrier. – As we
went on shore at St Louis we found a row of stately steamers
at the quay extending almost a mile in length, & the wharves
were encumbered with all kinds of produce & merchandise
ready to be put on board. – Many of these vessels had notices
hung out that they were destined for the Missouri & "Pikes
Peak" the newly discovered El Dorado to which so many adventurous spirits were now pressing forward probably in
most cases to be grievously disappointed. – We were told that
the emigration for these gold regions was probably as great
as 2000 persons a day, but this is probably an exaggeration
The city of St Louis is, in the solidity of its buildings, the
extent of its commerce, & the reputed wealth of its capitalists the third in importance in the States. – I have seen no
place in the interior which gives the same impression of solid
wealth & extensive commerce. – It is the centre from which
nearly all the trade & emigration for the Great West radi-
ates. – There are here also very extensive manufactures which

[37] They were so described by many earlier travelers, notably Dickens.

are constantly increasing. – Called on Mr Chouteau[38] the old established fur trader. – Here as in nearly all the towns on the Mississippi I observed that the most prominent & conspicuous looking buildings are the colleges & schools. – Left St Louis in the afternoon & crossed by the ferry to the opposite side of the river where we took the railway which crosses the State of Illinois – the Ohio & Mississippi – & proceeded to Centralia where we took the Illinois Central railway for Chicago. – The prairie fires which lighted up the horison presented a very striking spectacle at night. – Arrived at Chicago at noon of Mar 29th – Since Mar 12th the date of my departure from New York I have travelled upwards of 3,000 miles. – On arriving at Chicago a requisition presented to me asking me to address a meeting which I declined, but suggested a private soiree at which I could meet the requisitionists in a conversational tête-à-tête.

Mar 30. – Was driven by Mr Wilson[39] through the city & along Michigan Avenue the principal street leading into the country with good residences, some of them of stone, stretching for more than two miles to the south of the city, along the shore of the Lake – returning by Wabash Avenue running parallel. – This city is said to contain more than 100,000 inhabitants, & is literally the growth of 30 years – surpassing in the rapidity of its increase any place in America with the exception of St Francisco. – The principal streets contain some shops & warehouses rivalling in style, & far surpassing in rental, any thing to be found in London or Liverpool. – A large book store, more extensive than any in Manchester or

[38] A merchant of wide-spread business operations, Pierre Chouteau was at one time one of America's foremost financiers. (DAB) He was one of the two persons who had been allowed credit on the assessments of his Illinois Central stock, an arrangement which Cobden found justified. Add. MSS. 43663, Part 5, Cobden to Gilpin, April 10, 1859.

[39] A young man at this time, James Grant Wilson was editor of a monthly Chicago magazine. He later became prominent as author and editor of numerous biographies and biographical sketches, his most comprehensive work being *Appletons' Cyclopædia of American Biography*, of which he was joint editor. DAB. See *infra*, p. 163.

Liverpool. – Called on Mr Steele,[40] Mr Anderson,[41] Mr Burch,[42] Judge Dickey.[43] –

Mar 31ˢᵗ. – Went, accompanied by Judge Drummond,[44] Mr Haven[45] Mr Burch, Mr Arnold,[46] to see the schools of Chicago – two primary & one high schools. – In the former, which comprise several rooms under one roof, female teachers are generally employed, with the exception of one room which is always under the charge of a master. – Again observed that many of the boys & girls are of an age beyond that at which they would be found in the same classes in England, or at which boys would be still found under the charge of females. – Asked an intelligent teacher, & she told me that so far from finding these big boys unmanageable, she would prefer teaching them to girls – observing as did a lady at Dubuque that she found them more easily to comprehend *the whole* of what she taught them. The gentlemen who accompanied me stated that the system of employing female teachers was found to succeed so well that it was more & more generally adopted in the U. States, & every where I find the opinion to prevail that mixing the boys & girls, even up to the age when in this precocious clime they are young men & women, in the same schools & classes has a salutary effect on both sexes in softening & humanizing the manners & feelings of the boys, & imparting the stimulus of self-respect & love of approbation to the studies of the females. – In the

[40] See *infra*, p. 191. [41] See *infra*, pp. 191, 192.

[42] J. H. Burch was a partner with Walter Newberry in the banking house of Newberry and Burch. Cobden stayed at the Burch home when later in Chicago. See *infra*, pp. 188, 190, 192.

[43] Theophilus L. Dickey had served as circuit court judge; afterwards he had practised law in Chicago and Ottawa, Illinois (his home); and later he was to become a Civil War cavalry commander and assistant United States Attorney-General. DAB. See *infra*, p. 191.

[44] At this time Thomas Drummond was United States judge of one of the two judicial districts of Illinois. *Appletons' Cyclopædia.*

[45] Possibly Joseph Haven who was professor of systematic theology in the Chicago Theological Seminary (DAB), or Franklin Haven, on one of his periodic visits to Chicago.

[46] Isaac N. Arnold was a lawyer and political figure of city and state prominence, later of national fame. *Appletons' Cyclopædia.* See *infra*, p. 192.

High School I found delicate lady-like teachers who hardly seemed older than some of their scholars, in a class room with 40 to 50 young persons of both sexes, & among the males were youths whose moustaches were beginning to develop themselves. – In England this would be impossible in the present state of feeling – the youths would be ashamed & afraid of the ridicule which would attach to their being, "like babies", under the care of women. – The schools have an ante-room for receiving the cloaks & bonnets of the children, & in the high schools the boys take off their shoes, & wear slippers during their studies – Am struck with the great respect shown to the teachers by my companions who are the principal men of the city (Judge banker, & barrister) & which may account greatly for the high moral sway which they exercise over their pupils. – Am told that all classes mingle in these schools that a gentlemans son may be found sitting beside the son of his coachman. – "All are equally eligible to the Presidency." – No boy can be admitted into the High School excepting by the process of examination in which rich & poor are placed on the same footing. – On returning in a carriage from the schools to the house of Mr Arnold, & observing a collision in the muddy streets between two waggons, & remarking on the very great forbearance & courtesy of the drivers towards each other, the question arose as to what was the cause of this respectful demeanor under the most trying circumstances of the American working population. – My companion the banker[47] started the theory that the fact of every man hoping & expecting to rise gave to them the manners of those of a superior grade in society. – An ingenious & perhaps to some extent a correct theory. – In the evening was entertained at a dinner by the principal people in the city. Dr Brainard[48] in the chair. – A great many little

[47] Burch.

[48] Internationally famous in surgical circles, Daniel Brainard helped to establish Rush Medical College in 1843, where he held the chair of anatomy and surgery. For two decades he greatly influenced the affairs of the school and surgical thought in Chicago. DAB.

speeches made upon the past history & progress of the city. – Every body in America seems endowed with the faculty of speaking in public with self-possession. –

Apl 2. Went with Mr Wilson[49] to see the public library & news room. – About 2000 members chiefly young men paying a subscription of about 8ˢ/. – Saw the process of raising a large brick hotel of about 100 feet frontage. – 800 screws are put under the building, & a man gives a turn to one after another. – This is going on with a larger number of workmen at the bottom of the building whilst the inmates above are following undisturbed their usual avocations. –

April 3 – Sunday – In the morning accompanied Mr J.H. Burch[50] to the Presbyterian Church where I found a large & respectable looking congregation The singing was performed by four persons – two males & two females – in the gallery. – Went in the afternoon with Mr James Grant Wilson to the Episcopal Church where two clergymen officiated with a good deal of ceremonial & who in conformity with the custom of the country wore beards. – The singing performed by four persons in the gallery the same as in the morning One of the females had a very remarkable voice. – Mr Burch invited me to his house if I should return to Chicago. – Left at 8 o'clock in the evening by the Michigan Central railway for Detroit, whence I proceeded by the Great Western of Canada line to Niagara where the train crossed over the chasm about half a mile below the Cataract on the wire chain bridge, thence by the New York Central line to New York – where we arrived at 10 o'clk on tuesday morning. The sleeping cars enabled me to pass these two nights on the rail with little fatigue. – During my absence of 24 days from New York I have travelled nearly 4,000 miles. – Called on the British Consul Mr E.M. Archibald

[49] See *supra*, p. 160 and n.
[50] See *supra*, p. 161 n., and *infra*, pp. 188, 190, 192.

April 6. – Called on Mr Lewis Tappan.[51] – Went to hear an anti-slavery address by Mr Cheever[52] – to the theatre to see the amusing play of our American Cousin[53] –

April 7 – Went to see the Subtreasury where the duties on imports & other payments to government are made in cash & where the bullion belonging to the government is kept. – The head of the establishment a very intelligent person informed me that during the 5½ years he had held the post there had not been an error of a cent in the accounts that from its foundation nearly 20 years since there had been no defalcation in the establishment that there was 2 or 3 millions sterling in the vaults nearly all in gold, that the appointm[ent?] to all the subordinate posts was in the hands of the Chief who was responsible for their integrity – was of opinion that by each ship from California $300,000 was brought by passengers beyond the amount entered in the ships manifests. – Dined at Mr Hiram Barneys[54] & met Horace Greeley,[55] Lewis Tappan, Mr Mott,[56] of Ohio. – In the evening to the Athenæum Club & the Geographical Society. –

Apl 8 = Went with Dᵣ Thompson[57] to see some of the Common Schools. Was told that all classes send their children to

[51] Tappan was a successful merchant (founder of "The Mercantile Agency," America's first commercial-credit rating agency) and an abolitionist of international influence. *Ibid.* See *infra*, pp. 170-171.

[52] George B. Cheever was a Congregational clergyman, a fearless reformer, and a prolific writer. *Ibid.*

[53] This was the play which Lincoln was attending six years later when he was assassinated.

[54] Barney, the son-in-law of Lewis Tappan, was later appointed by Lincoln collector of the port of New York. See Barrett, *The Old Merchants of New York City*, First Series, p. 235; Third Series, p. 246.

[55] Greeley, the well-known abolitionist, reformer, and political leader, was owner and editor of the *New York Tribune*, which at this time was possibly of greater national influence than any other paper in the United States. (DAB) Cobden had met Greeley in England and discussed with him the advisability of establishing there a penny press in the interests of peace, free trade, and reform. See *supra*, p. 30.

[56] Cobden probably meant James Mott of Pennsylvania, the reformer and abolitionist.

[57] Cobden had had some correspondence with Thompson several years earlier. In a letter to Bright, August 20, 1853, he refers to Thompson as "the American parson, who wrote that excellent letter to me from the Nile on education. . . ."

these schools – with the sole exception of the millionnaire class of the 5th avenue – that even in the girls schools which seemed to be as well attended as the boys the daughters of professional men & judges sit side by side of the daughters of washerwomen   The schools were crowded – the buildings were well ventilated, admirably kept for cleanliness, & there is an air of gentility & finish about them quite different from the make-shift buildings which we have in England. – A handsome piano stood in the school room, & there was frequent resort to music to give time to marches & movements of the children.   Was told an anecdote of the sons of a judge of the Supreme Court & of an excavator or sewer-digger competing for honors in one of the High Schools. – Went with Dr Thompson to see his new church a handsome stone structure – adjoining to it was a reception room furnished like a drawing room with a piano etc where the clergyman could hold his weekly soirées – Dined with Mr Hewitt[58] met an intelligent party – sat beside Mr Bellows[59] an Unitarian preacher. –

April 9. – Went with Mr Peter Cooper[60] to see a building erected & endowed by him for public purposes intended for lecture rooms, school of design, exhibitions, etc – The lower

---

(Add. MSS. 43650) Joseph P. Thompson served for twenty-five years as pastor of the Broadway Tabernacle, one of the most important of the Congregational churches. He was an editor and author of many works, mainly theological, biographical, and historical in nature. DAB.

[58] Abram S. Hewitt, at this time thirty-seven years old, was an iron manufacturer. Later, he was prominent in philanthropy and political life. *Ibid.* See *infra*, pp. 169-170, 197-198.

[59] An outstanding Unitarian minister of his day, Henry W. Bellows published church periodicals, and worked for the reorganization of his denomination and for civil service reform. He was the founder of the United States Sanitary Commission and was a leading figure in the establishment of various civic and academic institutions. *Ibid.*

[60] Cooper was one of America's foremost business men, having built up his fortune in manufacturing (he constructed the first steam locomotive built in America). A philanthropist, active in the cause of civic welfare, he founded Cooper Institute in New York. *Ibid.*

portions of the building to be let off for about £5000 & which sum is to serve for endowment. In the evening dined with the members of the Press Union or club of the newspaper press. – Mr Dana[61] of the Tribune in the Chair – Mr Young[62] of the Albion in the Vice Chair. – Governor Raymond[63] of the Times, etc – I submitted the question whether in politics the character of the country had deteriorated, & which gave occasion for a long & interesting discussion. – Afterwards to the Century Club for a few minutes. –

Sunday 10 Apl – Went to a church where a large Episcopal congregation assembled under a D[r] Tyng[64] who is one of the best preachers in New York Was told that this clergyman receives about £1000 a year for his salary, besides a house & other advantages. – He has a rich congregation from whom he draws enormous contributions for sundry schools missions etc –

Apl 11 – Dined with Mr Sherman[65] met Mr Jno Van Buren[66] – Mr Bancroft[67] etc

Apl 12 – Dined at Mr Jno Jays[68] & met Mr Davis (Major Jack Downing).[69]

[61] See *supra*, p. 147 and n.

[62] British-born, William Young published for nearly twenty years *The Albion*, a paper which dealt largely with British news and interests. *Appletons' Cyclopædia.*

[63] Henry J. Raymond was joint founder, owner, and editor of the *New York Times.* He had been lieutenant-governor; and from 1856 on, for over a decade, he was one of the most influential forces in the Republican party. DAB. See *infra*, p. 195.

[64] An Episcopal clergyman, Stephen H. Tyng was considered one of the two best preachers of his denomination in the country. He was among the first to discern the value of Sunday Schools; and his New York church was the earliest to institute mission chapels for the underprivileged of the East Side. *Ibid.*

[65] See *supra*, p. 147n., and *infra*, p. 171.

[66] John Van Buren, son of Martin Van Buren, was a barrister and politician. *Ibid.*

[67] See *supra*, p. 148 and n., and *infra*, p. 171.

[68] Jay, lawyer and grandson of Chief Justice Jay, was possessed of wide humanitarian interests. He was a distinguished figure in the anti-slavery movement, and, considerably later, in the cause of civil service reform. He was founder or able supporter of many learned and civic organizations. *Ibid.*

[69] A New York merchant, Charles A. Davis wrote effectively on economic mat-

Apl 13 – Mr Dudley Field[70] drove me to call on Miss Ashburner at Brooklyn. – Crossed the Ferry & went down the shore of the Narrows to Hamilton Battery a point looking out in the Atlantic – The view of New York harbor with the city in the distance & the adjoining heights crowned with houses very fine. – Dined with Mr Leupp[71]

Apl 14 – Went by Hudson River Railway to Albany to visit Mr Bradford R. Wood[72] – Rain & mist during the whole journey prevented me from seeing the scenery. –

Apl 15 – At Mr B.R. Woods   Called on governor Morgan.[73] Looked in at the Senate & Assembly where the legislative labors of the session were being brought to a close   The constitution provides that the Legislature shall sit for 100 days every year at the end of which time the pay of 3 dollars a day ceases. The Assembly appeared a sedate dignified body. – The Senate chamber has no strangers gallery & the floor is crowded with spectators close up to the seats of the members. – The House has 128 members & the Senate 32. – Looked in at the Court of Appeal, the highest tribunal – The judges receive £700 a yr – Visited a normal school belonging

---

ters. In the "Peter Scriber Letters" and "Major Jack Downing's Letters" he discussed his conversations with Jackson and the plans for destroying the United States bank. *Appletons' Cyclopædia.* See *infra,* p. 171.

[70] Field, an eminent New York lawyer and brother of Cyrus Field, was at this time engaged with Noyes and Bradford in codifying the laws of the State of New York. Though not accepted in entirety by the legislature, the codes were later to be adopted by many states. Field worked for international law codification as well. DAB.

[71] Charles Leupp was a hide and leather merchant. Barrett, *The Old Merchants of New York City,* First Series, p. 251.

[72] Bradford Ripley Wood, a lawyer of strong religious leanings, had been a leader in temperance societies and the Y.M.C.A. and was a founder and trustee of the First Congregational Church of Albany. Earlier he had served as congressman, and later was to become minister to Denmark and one of the founders of the Republican party in New York State. *Nat. Cyclo. Am. Biog.,* XII. See also p. 198.

[73] Edwin D. Morgan became governor of New York in 1858, and gave the state a wise and beneficent administration. Later he was elected United States senator, twice declining cabinet position. A man of wealth, Morgan gave generous financial support to many deserving institutions. DAB.

to the State to which each County has the right of sending 3 pupils. – Young men & women were being taught in the same room. – Am told that two-thirds of the teachers in the State are females & that they are constantly in increased demand being found more efficient than the men. – In the Evening a numerous party of the principal inhabitants paid a visit at Mr Woods.

Apl 16 – Attended the Session of the House of Assembly which passed a resolution admitting me to the "floor." – No cheering allowed in the debates here or in Congress. – Each member being seated at a separate desk gives the appearance of great order & dignity to the assembly. – The members are more neatly dressed than in the House of Commons. – Hats never worn. – Afterwards looked in at the Senate for a few minutes. – Great number of Albums brought me by the "call boys" for my autograph. – Went to the agricultural museum, & saw monster specimens of vegetables & grain from California – Mr Johnson the Director. After dinner drove to Troy which seems to promise soon to be united to Albany. – Went over, on my return, a leviathan steamer which plies between Albany & New York in the night – makes up 600 beds, & is adorned like a palace   Called on Mr Corning.[74] – In the evening to General Gansevoorts[75] & met a large party. – A hotel, the *Delwan* [?], in Albany lets for $25,000 a year. – It is much less extensive than the New York Hotels. –

April 17 – Sunday – On returning from church at 12 o'clk observed the streets crowded with people returning from the various places of public worship. – A larger proportion of the

[74] A wealthy merchant and banker, Erastus Corning was an outstanding figure in the development of the New York railroad system, becoming president of the early Albany-Schenectady line, effecting its extension, achieving consolidation of the several companies into the New York Central, and (when Cobden met him) serving as president and director of the New York Central Corporation. *Appletons' Cyclopædia.*

[75] This was probably Peter Gansevoort, who, though a judge and not a general, has been described as "an enthusiast in military matters through life." One of Albany's first citizens at the time, he was extremely active in public affairs. *Nat. Cyclo. Am. Biog.,* I.

whole population must attend churches here than in England. – Called at Mr Palmers[76] the Sculptor who showed me his studio which contains many beautiful productions. – Small pieces *night* & *morning* were particularly good. – He gave me a photographic copy of his bust of Commodore Perry

April 18 = Left Albany at 7 in the morning for New York. – Very few passengers travel by water by day as they prefer the railroad. – The night boats are however filled sometimes carrying 600 persons. – The view of the Hudson not so good in descending as ascending. – The banks of the river every where dotted with new houses & villages built since I was last here. – An Irishman on board who had come up the river for the view of the scenery, carrying a black bottle in his side pocket which evidently contained something stronger than water & who disappeared from time to time & always returned on deck with his nose & face a little redder entered into conversation with me respecting the character of the American people among whom he had been about 3 weeks & bore solemn but not sober testimony to their "shocking immorality." – The passengers on board perceived his weakness & tittered as he passed by them with his bottle protruding from his pocket. – Arrived at New York at about ½ p 4.

April 19 – Went with Mr Hewitt in his fast trotting wagon to the Croton aqueduct which crossed the Harlem river 10 miles from New York. – Passed through the Central park which was being laid out & the roads formed. – About 700 or 800 acres have been purchased at a forced valuation in the centre of the island & which will cost 5 to 7 million dollars, whilst the laying out & planting are expected to come to as much more   There is to be a lake of 120 acres to serve as a reservoir for the Croton water to supply the city. – The money for this outlay is to be provided by taxation on the

[76] Erastus D. Palmer, sculptor, was particularly skillful in the creation of portrait busts, though his finest work, "White Captive," was a full-length figure. DAB.

Town. – The ground intended for the park is uneven & rocky & admits of being laid out with much beauty & will form when planted & completed one of the largest & most beautiful parks in the world. – [Mr H. explained to me that he had agreed to take some shares in the Illinois Central R.R. at the pressing instance of the Directors who had agreed to take a bill drawn by another Company in payment. – This was the only transaction of the kind he had had. – On another occasion he had given the Company his bill *in advance* of his call.[77] – He told me that Mr Wiley[78] & he had paved the way for O's [Osborn's] withdrawal from the Presidency[79] when Moffatts unlucky suggestion & the attack made on him at the meeting of shareholders made it a point of honor with the Board to support their president. – Is of opinion that O. is not fitted for the situation of President that he is deficient in judgment etc, and he thinks he may be induced to resign when he finds the finances of the Company put in a proper state.] Dined at Mr Minturns,[80] & met Mr Grinnell[81] who sent a vessel at his own expense under the direction of Doctor Kane to search for Sir John Franklin, Mr Aspinwall, Mr Belmont, Mr Sherman & other capitalists –

April 20 – Saw an establishment for inquiring into the character of mercantile houses originally founded by Mr Tap-

[77] See *supra*, p. 165n. Hewitt, like Chouteau, had been allowed credit on Illinois Central investments, which, as in the case of Chouteau, Cobden found justified. Add. MSS. 43663, Part 5, Cobden to Gilpin, April 10, 1859.

[78] See *supra*, p. 148n.　　　　[79] Of the Illinois Central.

[80] Robert B. Minturn, together with the Grinnell brothers, was head of one of the strongest commercial businesses in New York. He was one of America's greatest ship-owners of the time, his firm operating regular packet lines to England and engaging in an extensive trade to many parts of the world. Minturn generously assisted many needy causes and was active in the founding of humanitarian institutions. DAB.

[81] A brother-in-law of Minturn, Henry Grinnell controlled with him their widespread shipping business. Retired during the fifties he later engaged in the insurance business. A wealthy philanthropist, Grinnell twice furnished ships to search for the lost Franklin Polar Expedition and helped to support further polar explorations. (*Ibid.*) Grinnell was an incorporator of the Illinois Central. Gates, *The Illinois Central Railroad*, p. 50n.

pan[82] – a great number of clerks employed in posting up the latest accounts of the character & financial position of the houses of business throughout the U. States   An annual subscription entitles parties to all the information contained in this inquisitorial institution. – Heard what appeared to be fabulous accounts of the rents paid for business premises in Broadway & other leading streets. For a store 50 feet frontage by 200 feet deep, a corner situation, the rent was $25,000 – the landlord paying all rates & taxes including the water. Called & had a long conversation with Mr Sherman[83] & saw copies of his letters to Mr Moffatt[84] respecting Ill Central affairs. I strongly advised Mr S. & his capitalist friends to come in & take a large interest in the railroad. – Dined at Mr Jas Brown[85]   Met Mr Astor[86] said to be the richest man in the world – reputed to be worth from 30 to 50 millions of dollars, all at his own disposal

Apl 21 – Breakfasted with Mr Bancroft.[87] – Afterwards went with Mr Jas Brown to his country house in New Jersey.   At Mr Wrights[88] his near neighbor who has a large picture gallery saw the celebrated "horse fair" by Rosa Bonheur – a very large & striking painting, wonderful & strange for a lady both in the conception & execution. Today was pointed out a store in *Broadway* measuring 62 feet by 175 ft which is let for $50,000 – & another which is being built & is bespoke for a dry goods store & which measures 75 ft by 150 ft which is to let for $50,000 – The landlord pays rates & taxes including water rate & which amount to abt 10 per Ct of the rental. – Dined with Mr C.A. Davis[89] "Major Jack Down-

---

[82] See *supra*, p. 164 and n.
[83] See *supra*, pp. 147n. and 166.
[84] Either George Moffatt, the English broker, or William Moffatt, M.P., the English investor.
[85] James Brown was head of the influential New York banking house of Brown Brothers & Company, a railroad promoter, a trustee of other business firms, hospitals, and colleges, and founder of various philanthropic institutions. DAB.
[86] See *supra*, p. 148n.   [87] See *supra*, pp. 148n., 166.
[88] Possibly William Wright, manufacturer and senator. *Ibid*.
[89] See *supra*, pp. 166-167n. In the diary the phrase, "Major Jack Downing," is set below.

ing" & met General Scott[90] a colossal man who commanded the American army in the Mexican war & who also distinguished himself against the English in 1814. – He was in England in 1815, & mixed with the Whig leaders of that time & gave me anecdotes of Romilly, Macintosh, Brougham, & Horner. He conversed well on the literature of the last century & has a very exact memory. – Broached the theory that Horne Tooke was himself the Author of Junius! – Met also *Jerome Bonaparte*[91] son of old Jerome by Mrs Paterson whose resemblance to the Bonaparte family is striking. It was droll to hear "Mr Bonaparte" talking in a strong nasal tone & with a Yankee idiom of his fast trotting horses & other Americanisms. – His horses travel "2 – 40" – that is a mile in two minutes & 40 seconds which seems to be the standard of first rate merit. Some horses are however now doing a mile in 2 min 30 sec

April 22. To the Astor library, containing about 100 000 volumes, founded by the late Mr Astor with an additional endowment from his son. – The librarian Mr Cogswell showed me a list of British patents from which it appeared that from the year 1617 to 1852 there had been granted 14,354 patents, whilst since the latter date more than 15,000 had been obtained. – Probably the great increase had arisen from the reduced cost to some extent. – But the immense number during the last few years shows a vast activity in the inventive faculty of the country.

April 23 – Left New York for Philadelphia where I arrived at 4 & put up at Mr H.D. Gilpins[92] 300 South Eleventh St –

[90] At this time Winfield Scott was seventy-three. In 1852 he had been given the office of lieutenant-general, the first person since Washington to be so honored. *Ibid.* See also *supra*, p. 79.

[91] Nephew of the former Emperor Napoleon I. Jerome's father, the elder Jerome, when nineteen, on a visit to Baltimore, had married the eighteen-year-old Elizabeth Patterson, lived with her for less than two years, permitted the marriage to be annulled on insistence of his brother, Napoleon I, married a Württemberg princess, and was made king of Westphalia. *Ibid.*

[92] For Cobden's reference, before he left England, to a possible visit at the Gilpins', see *supra*; p. 41n. See also p. 144 and n.

In the evening Mr Ingersoll[93] – Mr Kortright the British Consul called. – Went afterwards to a philosophical club[94] where I was introduced to Dr Bache[95] the great grandson of Dr Franklin – Mr Carey[96] the protectionist etc –

Apl 24 Sunday. To the Episcopal Church – large congregation – the clergyman here as elsewhere in America makes announcement of a variety of meetings of the congregation for prayer, for charitable & missionary purposes, all showing a great activity in the congregation – Collections of money are very frequent. – The Bishops see extends over the whole State. – It is the custom here to hang a black crape scarf to the door handle or bell (with addition of white in case of the young) to announce a death in the house. – The streets filled at noon when the congregations leave church. – Went 6 miles into the country to dine with Mr Fisher.[97] –

Apl 25 – Walked in the city & made calls. – Chestnut Street the principal street contains some splendid shops equal to any thing in New York or London. The houses generally set off with white marble window frames & door steps & posts which make even the brick houses look stately. – The City contains memorials of Franklin in a library founded by him & 24 mechanics & other traces of the great philosopher. Here is the hall where the declaration of independence was

[There are here two pages of the diary missing.]

[93] See *infra*, p. 176. Charles J. Ingersoll had been a lawyer, author, and congressman for a time in the forties, holding the position of chairman of the committee on foreign affairs. DAB.

[94] The American Philosophical Society.

[95] Franklin Bache, a chemist, professor of chemistry, and physician, was for thirty years an officer of the American Philosophical Society, serving as president from 1853 to 1855. *Ibid.*

[96] Leader of the American school of political economy which urged protection, and an intense, anti-British nationalist, Henry C. Carey was the antithesis to Cobden. See *Ibid.*

[97] Possibly Joseph Fisher, the investigator sent over by the British shareholders, or the Philadelphian, Joshua Francis Fisher, who is described in Wheeler Preston's *American Biographies* as an "author and humanitarian," a "student of history and of political systems."

to him. Yet they are now perfectly good friends. – Speaking of the mode of conducting elections in America Mr Randall[98] said with much emphasis that he had been an active party politician for nearly 40 years, & that he had never known a bribe to be given or received. – Falsification of votes, personations, stuffing of the ballot boxes, & violence in a variety of forms may have been witnessed in many places, but bribery never. – – Saw a procession of Odd Fellows today with their scarfs & banners looking very much like a similar exhibition in England. –

April 27 – Went to see the Girard College which was founded by Stephen Girard,[99] a rich merchant of Philadelphia who left a vast property by will to build & endow an institution for the support & education of poor orphan children. – The main building which is of white marble is perhaps the noblest structure in the world, & it is certainly devoted to the noblest purpose. – The cost of the college & out buildings was upwards of £400,000. – The annual expenditure is about £20,000. At present about 330 boys are supported, but it is expected there will be eventually when the coal lands owned by the Trust are realized an income to support 1000 orphans. – By the terms of the Founders Will no clergyman is admitted on the premises. The following is an extract –[100]

EXTRACT FROM THE WILL
OF STEPHEN GIRARD.

There are, however, some restrictions, which I consider it my duty to prescribe, and to be, amongst others, conditions on which my bequest for said College is made, and to be enjoyed, namely . . . . *Secondly,* I enjoin and require that *no ecclesiastic, missionary, or minister of any sect*

[98] Probably Josiah Randall, lawyer, friend, and political adviser of Buchanan. See DAB under "Randall, Samuel Jackson."

[99] For a sketch of 1867 of Stephen Girard and his college, see James Parton, *Famous Americans of Recent Times,* Boston, 1867.

[100] The following extract is a printed statement which has been pasted into the diary at this point.

whatsoever, shall ever hold or exercise any station or duty whatever in the said College; nor shall any such person ever be admitted for any purpose, or as a visiter, within the premises appropriated to the purposes of the said college: — In making this restriction, I do not mean to cast any reflection upon any sect or person whatsoever; but, as there is such a multitude of sects, and such a diversity of opinion amongst them, I desire to keep the tender minds of the orphans, who are to derive advantage from this bequest, free from the excitement which clashing doctrines and sectarian controversy are so apt to produce; my desire is, that all the instructors and teachers in the College, shall take pains to instill into the minds of the scholars, *the purest principles of morality,* so that, on their entrance into active life, they may *from inclination and habit,* evince *benevolence towards their fellow creatures,* and *a love of truth, sobriety and industry,* adopting at the same time, such religious tenets as their *matured reason* may enable them to prefer.

STRANGER'S TICKET.

Went to the Academy of Arts to see an exhibition of painting & sculpture by American artists. – I predict that in less than a quarter of a century the Americans will beat all modern competitors in painting & statuary. –

> Miss Dilworth, Hill Side,
> Under Castle Wall, Lancaster.
> Sister of old Mrs Gilpin
> Aunt of Mr H. D. Gilpin
> Mr Trist, friend of Mr Tolmé

Philadelphia is famous for its schools, prison, & other public institutions. – Every young person here rich & poor can be well educated gratis in the public schools where children of the highest as well as lowest class meet on a perfect footing of equality, – always excepting the poor colored race. – These latter are excluded from participating in the benefits of the Girard College the founder of which expressly limits its advantages in his will to "*white* orphan children." – Mr Gilpin tells me with expressions of regret that the feeling of hostility towards the free negroes is growing stronger, in the Free States, that the gulf which separates socially the African from the white race is constantly widening & deepening. – This is probably in part owing to the natural repugnance which seems to check the amalgamation of races even much less dissimilar such as the English & French – & which draws a line of demarcation more impassable than the Rhine between the French & Germans. – But it is still more owing in the case of the negro to the sense of superiority on the one side & the consciousness of inferiority on the other which forbids that sentiment of equality which is essential to confidence or friendship between races as well as individuals. – It is this which in a great degree probably accounts for the constantly increasing alienation which exists between the native & anglo saxon races in India. – Dined at Mr C. J. Ingersolls[101] formerly in the diplomatic service in Europe is now 77 – When a boy he saw Washington & his cabinet smoke the calumet of peace with some Indians with whom he had negotiated a Treaty of peace. – Met his brother Mr J. R. Ingersoll. – Mr Rush formerly the minister at the English Court sent an apology. – Speaking of S. Girard, the rich old merchant, he mentioned the anecdote of a less prosperous neighbor having once remarked to him in conversation "I wish Mr Girard you would give me the secret how to get on in the world as well as you have done" – "That I will" replied the old millionaire in four words – "mind your own business." – Saw Mr Ashbell Welsh[102] & had a long con-

[101] See *supra*, p. 173 and n. Under Webster's influence the Senate refused to confirm Polk's appointment of Ingersoll as minister to France. DAB.

[102] A civil engineer, Welsh during these years largely directed the engineering work of the Delaware-Raritan Canal, began the design and construction of the

versation with him respecting Illinois Railroad matters in which he is interested. – He is quite confident of the ultimate success of the undertaking, thinks the President [Osborn] an honest man but too impulsive & wanting in judgment, & would like to see a better man in his place, but deprecates any hasty or violent proceeding to get rid of him. – Mr Fisher speaks of Mr A. Smith as the most reliable man for integrity & talent, & the most valuable in every way in connexion with great public works such as railroads or canals that he knows in the U States, & he suggested that he would be a proper person to represent the English shareholders at the Board. – Saw at the Historical Society the *wampum belt* which was given by the Indians to Wm Penn when he made his celebrated treaty with them under the elm tree – "the only treaty not ratified by an oath & the only one never broken." –

April 28 – Left the house of my much esteemed friends Mr & Mrs Gilpin, & started at 12 o clk by the train via Baltimore for Washington where I arrived at 6 o'clk, & proceeded to the "White House" on a visit to the President of the United States Mr Buchanan.[103] – In the course of conversation in the evening he expressed the hope that Lord Palmerston would not again become Prime Minister as it would be unfavorable to the maintenance of friendly relations between England & America – that although personally partial to Lord P. he (the President) regarded him as hostile to the United States & as of a belligerent character – that he (Ld P) was unpopular with the people of America who considered

---

Chesapeake and Delaware Canal, and built several of the New Jersey railroads. He later achieved consolidation of the competing New Jersey lines; and served as president and administrative officer in charge of the properties until they were leased to the Pennsylvania Railroad in 1871. *Ibid.*

[103] Hearing the news of Buchanan's election to the presidency in 1856, Cobden wrote to Parkes, November 23, "So old Buchanan is returned. – I have a smaking liking for the old democrat, & should nt be surprised if he were to throw overboard his party as Peel did." Add. MSS. 43660, Part 1. For further reference to Buchanan, see *supra*, p. 146 and n.

him dictatorial, & that he (the President) could in any negotiations make concessions to Ld Aberdeen which he would
not dare to make to Ld P. – The President, in reply to my
enquiry, declared with much emphasis his belief in the purity
of the judicial bench throughout the whole Union – that
probably the State legislatures may have been subjected to
"lobby" influences, & even the representatives at Washington
may not have been always wholly pure, but he did not believe the man lived who could assert that he knew an instance of a judge having received a fee; – and as regards the
Supreme Court, he would be a bold person who ventured
even to talk to one of its judges upon the subject of any suit
which might be pending before them: – the President adding
that he should as soon think of proposing to Saint Paul, if he
could appear on earth, the commission of murder as of at-
tempting to influence the mind of Chief Justice Taney upon
any cause pending before the Supreme Court. – [104]

April 29 = Called on Lord Lyons[105] our minister at Washington. – Went to the Patent Office. – The number of patents
taken out now is double that of the year 1845 & previously. –
The cost of a patent is about £6. – There are 250 sewing machines patented & the models arranged in the museum. –
Here are several relics & curiosities of the revolutionary period; – the original declaration of American Independence the
signatures to which are nearly obliterated owing to the bad

---

[104] This position found an echo five years later in a letter from Cobden to Slagg.
Apropos of a suggestion that a specific case before the Supreme Court could be
influenced by the Washington government, he declared such an idea entirely a
delusion. "That Court is as pure & inaccessible to corrupt influences as our House
of Lords." Add. MSS. 43677, Part 2, Cobden to Slagg, February 12, 1864 [typed
copy].

[105] Lyons had been appointed to the post in the previous December; he served
throughout most of the Civil War. (DNB) Cobden's comment on Lord Lyons
in a letter to Bright, November 1, 1861, is of interest: "I have no faith in Lord
Lyons in his present delicate position.—He ought to have been a man of mature judgment & large experience instead of a Lord without any antecedents.—
If we may believe a paragraph in the papers a dry nurse has been sent out to
him from the Foreign Office." Add. MSS. 43650, Part 1. For further reference
to Lyons, see *infra*, p. 180.

quality of the ink. – Washingtons clothes – in which he took leave of his army, Franklins walking stick bequeathed to Washington, etc. – At dinner met the Secretary of the Interior & the Postmaster General. – After they had left I accompanied the President to his room for a gossip. – He spoke of the unpleasant task which every President has to undergo of dispensing the patronage – he having upwards of 20,000 places directly & indirectly to fill up – the time which is required for the task, to say nothing of its irksomeness, will necessitate a change – he mentioned the case of the appointment to the post of district marshal for Pennsylvania in which there were 22 applicants for the place of whom 15 were so equally elligible that he might have put their names in a hat & drawn out one at random, & they had all equal claims on him owing to their political views & their services to the party. – In selecting one of these he alienated the greater part of the remainder. – He gave me some curious examples of the way in which the newspapers anticipate his public acts. – Yester day the New York Times contained a very tolerable summary of what he was going to say to Senor Mata the Mexican minister which was printed 10 hours before he had decided in his own mind what he should say! – To day the New York Herald announces the Presidents intention to remove the judge of the territory of Utah, several hours before it was decided even to introduce the subject to the consideration of the Cabinet. – All this may be accounted for. – The newspapers are as cognizant as the President of the public grounds for taking certain courses, & it is not to be wondered at therefore that they often come to the same conclusion as himself as to what should be said or done. – The public visit the President with little ceremony & certainly without servility. – Formerly & down to the present week [?] there was a constant thoroughfare for strangers all through the day in the White House. – But he had put a restriction on the time of such visits by declining to receive visitors before 1 o'clock

Apl 30 – Accompanied Miss Lane[106] in a drive into the country – near the "soldiers home" – the view of the surrounding country & the broad Potomac very fine. – Dined at Lord Lyons,[107] the minister, met Hon Mr Ashley & Ld Edwd Cavendish who have been travelling a year in the States. Afterwards to Mrs Senator Uhlers. soirée. –

May 1 – To the Episcopal Church The President dined to-day, being sunday, at 2 o'clock. – The "White House" or *Executive Mansion* in which the President resides was built about 50 years since, & is a commodious & very comfortable house larger than any private residence in the country, but with none of the retinue of servants in gay livery which would characterise the house of a nobleman of the first class in Europe. – The few men servants are either Irish or German, the old housemaid is from Derbyshire in England – Native American Citizens will not (at least the better part of them) undertake the duties of a menial servant even for their president. – They will attend upon horses, or even pigs, but will not wait on the person of their fellow man.

May 2 & 3rd – Left Washington in the morning at 7 for Cincinnati by the Baltimore & Ohio railroad. – This road passes over the mountains of Virginia & ascends an incline plane to the height of 2700 feet (in 15 miles the ascent was 1600 feet) crossing the blue ridge where the river Potomac forces its way through the rocky mountain pass at Harpers Ferry, & which Jefferson in his "Notes" says is worth coming from Europe to see. – The scenery for more than a hundred miles is beautiful & in many places quite sublime. Slept near the summit, & on the following day descended on the other side

---

[106] Buchanan's niece and hostess, famous for her social grace and charm. In connection with the news of Buchanan's election to the presidency in 1856, Cobden had written to Parkes, November 23, 1856: "How happy his pretty & elegant niece Miss Lane must be in the prospect of being lady president at the White House without any alloy of responsibility in the appointment of a Cabinet." Add. MSS. 43660, Part 1.

[107] See *supra*, p. 178 and n.

of the mountain to the Ohio river; the streams changing their direction from the time when we began to descend, & running towards the Gulf of Mexico. On reaching the level of the Ohio river which we crossed on our way to Cincinnati the country became cultivated. – Mr Garrett[108] the Chairman of the Baltimore & Ohio Railroad met us & passed several hours in our company. – On reaching Columbus the Capital of Ohio which is a pretty place with good public buildings we were joined in our car by Governor Chase[109] the leading man of the Republican Party, & governor of the State. Travelled with him in the same carriage, & found him an intelligent man but not very profound on Usury laws or other questions of political economy. He is the popular candidate for President in this State. – Every body seemed to recognise him & talk familiarly, but there was no appearance either of rudeness or servility. On our arrival at Cincinnati he took his carpet bag like the rest of us, & walked to the nearest omnibus. – In the railway car a fellow passenger in good humored jocular style complained to me that though he had worked hard for the governors election he had been entirely overlooked in the distribution of the patronage at which the governor & the rest of us joined in a hearty laugh.–The disappointed partisan added that he should go to work for the governor in hopes of making him President, & he hoped by speaking in good time to have better luck when the high offices were disposed of. All this passed in good humor & from the appearance & manner & age of the person it was quite clear that he had no place-hunting views & that he was merely indulging in a little good humored banter with the governor who seemed to be of that thoroughly genial nature which enjoys a joke

---

[108] Although but thirty-nine at this time, John W. Garrett had been elected president of the Baltimore & Ohio Railroad the year before. He vastly extended the system over approximately the next twenty years, at the end of which time he had established autocratic control of the railroad. DAB.

[109] Later, Salmon P. Chase was appointed by Lincoln successively Secretary of the Treasury and Chief Justice. See *ibid.* See also *supra*, pp. 78-79.

May 4th – Judge Piatt[110] drove me through the town & for three or four miles into the country ascending a ridge at the back, & passing along good roads among a succession of villas reminding me of the neighborhood of Highgate – The City has a substantial & prosperous appearance – Like Philadelphia it depends very much on its manufactures, besides being the centre of a very rich agricultural region   its pork market being the most famous in America. – Lying along the right bank of the Ohio river, with its wooded banks on both sides & its graceful reaches as it winds its course below the City, it is one of the most beautiful sites for a town I have ever seen. – The population is about 200,000 of which nearly one half are Germans & Irish. – Am told there are 60,000 Germans who have newspapers in their own language, & who are well spoken of for thrift & industry. – At dinner at the hotel heard a discussion as to the number of people in Cincinnati who are worth $500,000, when it seemed to be the opinion that there were from 20 to 25 persons owning that amount of property. – It was thought there were hundreds possessing $100,000. – Went to see Mr Longworths[111] wine cellars in which there was a large stock of *Catawba* wine the name of the produce of a grape grown in this country of which he is the chief cultivator. – He began to grow grapes in the neighborhood of Cincinnati on the steep banks of the Ohio river 35 years ago. The cultivation of the grape is now rapidly extending, & is in the hands of many persons who are producing a very peculiar & agreable wine – Mr Longworth paid last year in taxes to the City government $35,000. – Rents are very high in the principal streets of Cincinnati. – Was shown premises 25 ft by 70 containing 3 stories which

---

[110] Donn Piatt had been judge of the Hamilton County court of common pleas in 1852-1853, and, later in 1854-1855, had served as secretary and chargé d'affaires of the American legation in Paris, in which connection Cobden may have known him. See *Lamb's Biographical Dictionary of the United States.*

[111] Nicholas Longworth, wealthy lawyer and outstanding figure in the beginnings of Cincinnati's commercial and cultural life, is best known as one of America's most skillful horticulturists. He was the first to make the growing of grapes on a large scale commercially profitable; and he was remarkably successful in strawberry cultivation. DAB.

were let for $6000 for a ready made tailors shop. And another 30 by 125 which was let on lease for $7,000 (7,000) & $10,000 had been offered for the 10 years lease. In the evening went to a wedding at Judge Estes'[112] where I met a very large party The ceremony was performed by Bishop Macilvain[113] without the prayer book, & in a much briefer form than in England. After the conclusion & the usual greetings of friends & relatives the newly married pair continued to mingle in the crowd of visitors to a late hour. – All marriages even of the poorer classes are performed by ministers of religion at the homes of the parties. – Had some conversation with Judge McLean[114] of the Supreme Court who was in a desponding mood upon the subject of the political prospects of the Country. – An elderly person at the supper table called my attention to the fact that the young men of the present day are much shorter in stature than their fathers. –

May 5 – Started from Cincinnati for Indianapolis & Lafayette in a special train furnished by Mr Church the President of the Line of railroad leading to those places – Passed through a rich country partially cleared & well suited for the growth of wheat & indian corn. – Indianapolis the principal city in Indiana & the capital of the State contains the usual public buildings & about 25,000 inhabitants. – Was introduced to the governor & several private Citizens. – From thence proceeded to Lafayette 60 miles further north a place containing about 12,000 people For the last 20 miles the country became open prairie which is the commencement of those vast untimbered tracts going by the name of prairies which extend with occasional interruptions to the base of the Rocky Mountains nearly 1000 miles. – The country was rich & all under culti-

[112] Of the prominent Cincinnati family of that name.

[113] After becoming bishop of Ohio in 1832, Charles P. McIlvaine had served as president of Kenyon College and of the divinity school at Gambier. On a trip to England during the Civil War he won many friends for the North. *Ibid.*

[114] John McLean, earlier a congressman and Postmaster-General, served from 1830 until his death in 1861 as Associate Justice of the United States Supreme Court. *Ibid.*

vation. On arriving at Lafayette was called on by several Englishmen who were residing there & who were careful to warn me against universal suffrage. – I found that at an election for the municipal offices which had taken place the day before the democrats had returned a "ticket" comprising with only one exception a list of "full blood Irishmen." – At this the Englishmen who called on me were very indignant & one of them thought he should emigrate. – The exception I was told was a low drinking fellow a plasterer by trade who had been elected to the post of assessor. – It seems that the Irishmen are here so numerous as to be able to control the elections. – An Englishman told me that at the election of the previous day a drunken fellow a plasterer was elected assessor along with the Irish ticket his name having been added to the list in pencil as a sort of joke. The Irish generally belong to the Democratic party & as they are generally very prompt in their attendance at the primary meetings they exercise great influence in the choice of candidates. –

May 6 – Left Lafayette at 7 a.m. & after travelling about 60 miles in the railroad took a waggon & pair of horses & travelled 30 miles principally over the open trackless prairie to visit a large Illinois farmer named "Mike Sullivan."[115] The prairie was covered with rich herbage, & studded with beautiful wild flowers. – We disturbed many Prairie hens & other wild birds. – Arrived late in the evening at Mr Sullivans who seemed to be living very much like a Wallachian landowner or an Australian squatter. –

May 7. Mr Mike Sullivan, as he is generally called, owns 16,000 acres of land, & his son has about 4,000 adjoining, making 20,000 which surround his temporary wooden residence in an unbroken mass – A portion is still in wild prairie – When the whole is brought under cultivation he expects to sell year-

---

[115] Michael Sullivant was one of the famous large-scale farmers of this period. Cobden undoubtedly is referring here to "Broadlands," one of the most extensive farms in the state. For an account of it and of large-scale farming in general, see Gates, *The Illinois Central Railroad*, p. 294ff.

ly about 6000 head of cattle, – & a proportionate number of pigs & other produce. – He pays his laborers $15 a month, & board & lodging (£3) – He pays this amount for 26 days of labor, deducting wet days for which he gives food but no wages. – A ploughman & pair of horses plough 2 acres a day. – A number of harrows fastened together & drawn by 8 bullocks abreast do 40 acres in a day. – The farm will be 6 miles by 5. – After inspecting the farm young Mr Sullivan drove us in his "waggon" across the wild open prairie 26 miles to the nearest station of the Illinois Central Railway. – Saw several herds of deer, & flights of wild geese, ducks, & other birds – gave chace to a badger, & saw a wolf in the distance. – At the station met young Lord[?] Grosvenor who was on his way to California by way of California [sic]. – Proceeded by railroad to Cairo where we arrived on sunday morning. – The flood of the Mississippi was higher than usual, & the intended site of the town was filled with water. – Saw a boy who was fishing with a rod & line on a "town lot." –

Sunday May 8 – Cairo though so much reviled has a church & two sunday schools the larger being attended by 75 children. – Left after church time by train up the Illinois Central R. passing through Jonesboro (the neighborhood of which is the garden of Illinois[?] Duquom [Du Quoin] etc to Richview where we slept. –

May 9. Richview The station master at this small place which has only been in existence four years says there have been more than 150 reaping machines sold here, the price varying from 140 to 200 dollars. – Took a drive into the country to see a small colony of New Englanders settled upon the prairie, accompanied by a preacher who had been chiefly instrumental in organizing the settlement. – The colony has been quite successful. – Mr Miner[116] our clerical companion

---

[116] Ovid Miner was one of the ablest traveling agents of the Illinois Central. Through religious organizations in particular he encouraged emigrants to settle in groups, and helped them establish their colonies. See *ibid.*, pp. 186-187.

says he would advise the promotors of emigrant colonies not to make them too large, that about a dozen persons are more likely to agree together than 40 or 50, when the number is large there being a greater risk of the colony breaking up into feuds & factions. – The settlement comprises farmers, shopkeeper, blacksmith, joiner etc   Each of them had some capital varying from £100 to £200. – They generally took an eighth or a quarter of a section (80 or 160 acres). – Persons having a larger capital can have a very neat house built by contract containing four bed rooms at from £160 to £200. Mr Miner thinks very highly of the plan of associated emigration similar to that which he has promoted. – Never knew it to fail. – People moving into a new country with a body of companions with whom they are familiar & whose sympathies they share, experience none of the loneliness of exiles, & are generally contented in their adopted home. – Proceeded in a wagon with a couple of mules to Centralia where we took the train of the Illinois Central Railroad & proceeded to El passo at the junction of the Peoria line passing through Bloomington & several other thriving station towns, all the growth of the last 5 years. – Observed every where a great show of agricultural implements of various descriptions. The country throughout our ride of upwards of 100 miles presented the usual appearance for Illinois of an unvarying richness & fertility. Every where the population was busy at the plough & in planting Indian corn. – Saw the ploughs going till 7 o'clk as long as the day light lasted. – "Corn" can be planted till the 1ˢᵗ June & even later. – From one & a half to two gallons of seed will produce a crop of from 50 to 70 bushels to the acre – This is a far larger increase than is got from any other cereal crop. – Parted with Mr H.C. Lord, President of the Cincinnati & Indianapolis railroad, an intelligent & respectable man who had accompanied us from Cincinnati. –

May 10   Elpasso. – Slept in the car, in a siding, & in the morning breakfasted at a little hotel at the station kept by an old

Polish refugee called the "Count," the same that gave me some prairie birds on my former visit. – Met a 'seedy' looking Englishman named Slater from the neighborhood of Petworth. – [117] Drove out for seven miles in a "wagon" on the Prairie to observe the progress of cultivation. – Conversed with a man occupying 80 acres who sowed 25 acres of wheat last year from which he thrashed only 35 bushels. – His "Corn" had also failed; sickness fell on him, & he was unable to collect hay enough for winter fodder for his yoke of bullocks which he exchanged for a pair of poor small horses; his neighbors who were strangers like himself recently settled in Illinois refused to give him credit for some seed corn, & he had not money to pay for it. – He crawled to a farm house & worked at shelling corn till he earned enough to buy some seed. – His family suffered much from insufficient food during the winter. – Yet we found him turning the furrow with a resolute hand & in answer to my remark that he did not seem to despair he replied in a cheerful tone "I mustn't lose hope for that is the only thing I have to live upon" – This mans case is I believe that of many thousands of settlers in Illinois consequent on the bad harvest of last year. A good crop this year will set him on his legs. – Talked with another man at harrow who was cultivating a quarter section 160 acres (the square mile or section which is 640 acres, is divided into half sections, 320 acres, quarter sections, 160 acres, & eighths, 80 acres,) for the proprietor, paying him one third of the produce for rent. – On returning to Elpasso found a telegram from Chicago announcing the commencement of the war between Austria & Sardinia, & which may probably lead to a general conflagration in Europe. So little has Europe advanced in intelligence or real self-government that after an interval of 60 years we have another Buonaparte playing over again the game of his uncle, disposing of men like pawns on a chess board, & millions of human beings giving themselves up to his will as tacitly as though they were a flock of sheep.

[117] See *supra*, p. 156, for Cobden's earlier experience at El Paso.

– Three crowned heads can plunge 130 million of Russians, French & Austrians, into deadly strife with each other with the same absolute will as that with which Xerxes or Alexander swayed their hosts. – And yet we are told that we live in an age of progress. – If I were a young man I would sever myself from the old world & plant myself in the western region of the United States, where the "Balance of Power" is not an article of political faith, & where the voice of the people can alone determine peace & war, – & where fillibustering crowned heads are unknown. – At the junction of the Peoria line with the Illinois Central Branch I inspected a pretty looking wooden house containing four bed rooms, & four rooms on ground floor including kitchen with a separate stair leading to a servants bed room, all completed for $950, & with a stable at back which cost $130 making together £216. – This is really a pretty looking house with verandah & venetian blinds complete. – Reached Chicago at 11 p.m. & proceeded to the house of Mr J.H. Burch.[118] –

Chicago, *May 11th.* – Spent the day at the Illinois Central Railway Office in writing letters to England. At 11 at night left by train for Urbana where I arrived at 5 in the morning. – Met there a Scotchman named Mc Guffie who is come with his family to settle in the Prairie who told me the land in this neighborhood would let for £5 an acre in Scotland. – He had been in Canada with the view of buying a farm there but was deterred by the labor of clearing the timber. – Went to see a large farmer named Curtis, & a Mr Dunlap,[119] a nurseryman. – Caught in a thunder storm on the prairie & returned to the inn very wet & dirty. – Proceeded by a special train to Tolono the junction of the Great Western Line which I traversed to Springfield the seat of government of the State of Illinois. –

[118] See *supra*, p. 161 and n., and *infra*, pp. 190, 192.

[119] Probably M. L. Dunlap, editor of the *Illinois Farmer* and contributing editor to the *Chicago Press and Tribune*, who gave much favorable publicity to the agricultural promotion work of the Illinois Central, and strongly supported Osborn's management. Gates, *The Illinois Central Railroad*, pp. 289, 290.

May 12, Springfield. – Called on the Secretary of State, Mr Hatch, at the "Capitol" where the business of the various departments of the government of Illinois is carried on. The office of the Secretary of State is opened at 7 in the morning where he professes to be in attendance till 6 or 7 in the evening. – Mr Hatch accompanied us to wait on the governor Mr Bissell[120] whom we found in bed owing to bodily infirmity. – His salary is $1500 a year. – Having to keep up a large house in Springfield he incurs considerable pecuniary sacrifices by accepting the office – which few persons are prepared to do –

May 13 Went at 7 in the morning by train to Jacksonville passing for 60 miles through a rich tract of country pretty well cultivated & every where abounding in cattle & pigs. – Mr Wiley & Colonel Dunlap accompanied me. Jacksonville a pretty town of about 10,000 inhabitants its streets planted with trees, & its suburbs containing many neat villas. – In this neighborhood there are a considerable number of English settlers occupying farms which they cultivate successfully living in a kind of Colony in the vicinity of a village called Lynnville, & looking up as I am told to the largest landowner of their body as a leader. – This is another instance of the success of the plan of emigrating in colonies of at least a dozen families together. – A large cattle farmer in this neighborhood named Strawn has 6,000 acres in cultivation. – The country for many miles round Jacksonville is so rolling as almost to be called hilly, & it has a lovely intermixture of open farming land & forest scenery. – The land which is about the very best in Illinois sells for about $50 an acre including buildings & improvements. – Returned to Springfield at 6 o'clk. – Was the guest of Colonel Dunlap at Jacksonville. At night was disturbed by a serenade under

[120] William H. Bissell had been elected Republican governor of Illinois in 1856; but his administration was generally ineffective because of Democratic opposition. (DAB) Previously, he had acted as lobbyist and solicitor for the Illinois Central. (Gates, *The Illinois Central Railroad*, p. 242.) Bissell was crippled for many years before his death.

my window (at Springfield) & was summoned from my bed by the landlord to return thanks from my bedroom window. – The leader of the band sent an apology for not playing "God save the Queen," regretting that his performers did not know the tune. –

May 14 Left card at the governors. – Called at the Capitol to see the Auditor & other State officers, & met a party of Senators & other politicians who sat round in a circle & expectorated towards a common centre in a very undignified way. – An English youth took me to be introduced to his employer a respectable old established storekeeper in the drapery business. – The young fellow joked with his master in a very familiar fashion, & in terms of perfect equality, but without any rudeness or sense of indecorum on either side. – This absence of servility on the part of servants is one of the characteristics of the West. – Life is easy, & the opening for the employment of labor more than commensurate with the supply of workers, & the result is that man instead of being a drug in the market is at a premium, & this to my taste constitutes the chief charm of this valley of the Mississippi. – Another young Englishman took me to have my photograph taken. Left at 12 for Chicago,[121] & passed through a country of the same monotonous richness as before. – Passed the farming land of Mr Funk who is said to have 26,000 acres fenced. – Had for companion in the car a person from Ohio who had purchased for $6,000 the patent right of a new description of clothes horse, & he was travelling to dispose of the right. – He had not yet visited half the States & had realised $50,000. – This is an illustration of the way in which a patentee succeeds in introducing an invention among this novelty-loving people. –

May 15 – To Church with Mr Burch[122] & family. –

[121] Cobden had intended to visit the public schools while in Springfield but was prevented from doing so because they were not in session. *Illinois State Journal*, May 17, p. 3.

[122] See *supra*, pp. 161 and n., 188.

May 16 – At the office of the Railway – Met Mr Newbury[123]
to converse with him on the affairs of the Illinois Central. –
Dined at Major Burnsides.[124] – Mr Newbury, who is one of
the oldest native-born inhabitants of the State, mentioned
that he witnessed, in 1833 an encampment of 5000 Indians
around Chicago which at that time contained only 500 white
inhabitants, & that twelve years later he saw an omnibus full
of Indians drawn through this City who were distributing
handbills advertising an exhibition of themselves, in the evening at a circus at 25 cents admission fee. – So sudden &
complete had been their disappearance from the home of
their forefathers. They were the tribes of Chippewas & Potta-
wotamies. – He related an anedote of a massacre of the
whites by the Indians on this spot when a young woman was
saved by a young Indian who walked into the Lake with her
& under pretence of drowning her kept her with her
face above water until the dusk of the Evening & the departure of the tribe enabled him to convey her in safety to a
White Settlement. The population of Chicago is now variously estimated at from 100,000 to 120,000. –

May 17. – Mr Steele,[125] Mr Anderson,[126] Judge Dickey,[127]

[123] Walter L. Newberry (born in New England!) settled in Chicago in 1833 and,
over the following thirty-five years, became one of her most distinguished citizens.
He made his fortune primarily in Chicago real estate; but, as merchant and banker,
he engaged in various important business projects, among which was the Galena
and Chicago Union Railroad, of which he became president in 1859. He was a
leader in the civic affairs of Chicago, and provided in his will for the Newberry
Library. DAB.

[124] Between 1857 and 1861 Ambrose Burnside held successive positions in the
land office of the Illinois Central Railroad and as treasurer of the Company. He
was later a general in the Civil War. *Ibid.*

A reference to Burnside in a letter which Cobden wrote to Bright, December
29, 1862, is of interest: "I knew Burnside at Chicago.—He was the Treasurer &
McClellan the manager of the Illinois railway when I was there—And, singular
enough, Banks succeeded McClellan for a short time as Manager.—I should not
have considered Burnside equal to McClellan intellectually, or in a professional
point of view.—Both were thoroughly educated soldiers, from West Point.—But
Burnside was singular for his high *moral* qualities which attracted Cairds notice
as well as mine.—I should say he is as truthful & honorable a man as could be
found." Add. MSS. 43652, Part 5.

[125] See *supra*, p. 161.   [126] See *supra*, p. 161.   [127] See *supra*, p. 161 and n.

etc called – Mr Arnold[128] & Mr Joy[129] dined with us. – Mr Joy is a leading lawyer of the West, a clever man. – Talks of removing from Detroit his present residence to Chicago, & Mr Burch suggests that he may become interested as a shareholder in the Ill Central & be made a local Director.[130] Mr Anderson is also suggested. – Mr Joy, Mr Burch & Mr Anderson would make an excellent local Comm[ee]. Passed the chief part of the day in the Land Office of the Ill C. Company with Major Burnside & Col Foster.[131] – Made an estimate of a "budget" for 1860. –

May 18 – Saw Mc Cormicks establishment for manufacturing Reaping Machines where he makes 5000 a year which he sells at $140 for pair horse & 155 for 4 horse instruments. – Mr Burch estimates his ann[l] profits c £20,000. Drove round the Town with Mr Burch to see the suburbs. – Miles of lumber on the river banks. – There are 5 miles of wharfage on the two sides of the river which branches into two arms in the City limits. – Saw a mechanical bread baking establishment where bread & biscuits are baked kneaded & yeasted by steam power. At the railway station saw about 600 Morman emigrants on their way to Utah. – They comprised 2 to 300 English & Scotch, & a similar number of Scandinavians, a few Welsh, & some Germans & French – a large proportion of women & children. – All seemed very healthy, & the young ones were in boisterous spirits. – The young unmarried women appeared shy & shrunk from observation as if conscious that their principles were open to remark. – Was told by their leader that they expected to reach their destination in September. – They were going by railroad as far

---

[128] See *supra,* p. 161 and n.

[129] The railroad builder, James F. Joy, began his career by effecting the sale of the Michigan Central to a private company. He then negotiated the extensions of the lines west of Chicago (which he had largely achieved by the time Cobden met him), and finally constructed and purchased additional roads to form a junction with the Union Pacific and to extend into the far reaches of Kansas. DAB.

[130] Cf. Gates, *The Illinois Central Railroad,* p. 75.

[131] An eminent geologist, John Wells Foster was Land Commissioner of the Illinois Central. *Appletons' Cyclopædia.*

as Saint Joseph on the Missouri, after which they would have nearly 1000 miles to traverse over the plains & across a desert tract, the men chiefly on foot & trailing after them their worldly goods in handcarts. – Left Chicago in the evening by the Michigan Central railroad which passes through the wooded portion of that State to Detroit where we arrived in the morning, & breakfasted in the Ferry which crossed the narrow neck connecting the two Lakes. Took the Great Western Railway of Canada to Buffalo where I slept. – Walked through the town which derives its importance principally from being at the junction of the Erie Canal with lake Erie. – Observed whole streets which judging by the names on the signs seemed to belong to Germans

May 20th. Started at 5 by the Erie Railroad for New York & passed through a picturesque mountainous scenery all clothed in wood. – For a considerable distance we skirted the banks of the Delaware & Susquehanna rivers which were covered with trees down to the waters edge, winding among precipices, & across ravines & torrents of water, often presenting views of great grandeur. – Arrived at New York at ½ p 9. –

May 21 – New York – Met at dinner Mr Noyes[132] a leading barrister of this State. – In answer to my inquiry whether there was any foundation for the belief entertained by many persons in England that the Bench in the United States is venal he stated that there was no recorded instance of a judge having been proved to have been guilty of receiving bribes, & he knew of only two cases in which there had been grounds of suspicion, that he did not believe there existed in the world a purer body of judges than in the United States – one proof of which might be found in the fact that they uniformly closed their career in unprosperous pecuniary circumstances. – He stated also his belief that in no country was the decision of the courts more respected than in America – nowhere could great mortgages be more readily foreclosed. In

[132] See *supra*, p. 147 and n.

illustration he mentioned the great Van Rensaller case which involved a claim of rents from the farmers & landowners of several counties of New York & which had been disputed for more than ten years & had been made the ground of a political movement. – The claim which was derived from the English law, & was particularly obnoxious to the population as being founded on an old feudal custom, involved a pecuniary issue amounting to probably half a million of dollars per annum besides arrears of 5 or 6 millions, was decided a few weeks since at Albany by the Court of Appeal: – "Eight plain looking men" said Mr Noyes "sitting in a quiet room none of whose salaries exceeded £800 a year decided in favor of the claim, & the next day every man interested submitted without a moments hesitation to his fate, & the question which had been agitating the State for so many years was settled for ever. – It never entered any bodys head in New York State that the judges had been bribed by the Van Rensaeller family." – Having been by accident myself in Albany when this decision was come to, I could corroborate the above statement. –

May 22 (Sunday) Went to hear Mr Henry Ward Beecher[133] a celebrated preacher, brother of Mrs Beecher Stowe the authoress. – He is affectedly unaffected, wears a surtout coat & black cravat whilst preaching. – Instead of a pulpit of the ordinary kind he has a platform on which he paces to & fro, throwing great action into his delivery, & raising his voice out of all proportion to the weight of the ideas it has to utter. – He is loud, denunciatory & arrogant in his style. His figures & illustrations were sometimes good but often otherwise, & there was a comic expression in his eye which coupled with the grotesque action in which he occasionally indulged made

[133] Powerful preacher and ardent advocate of many social reforms, Beecher was wielding vast influence at this time. Highly emotional and somewhat spectacular, it is not surprising that he failed to appeal to Cobden. For a colored contemporaneous account of Beecher, see Parton, *Famous Americans of Recent Times.* Cobden had entertained Harriet Beecher Stowe at breakfast when she was in England in 1853. See her *Sunny Memories of Foreign Lands,* London, 1854, pp. 176-177.

me afterwards think he ought to have been an actor on the boards of a theatre. – On the whole I was greatly disappointed by this celebrity for whom a new church is now in the course of erection to hold 3 or 4,000 persons.

May 23 – Mr Hugh Williams[134] arrived from England. – Saw Mr E.C. Hamilton[135] respecting the Sackets harbor scheme of railroad. – (Mr Church thoroughly well acquainted with the State of New York who purchased on speculation a large part of the Van Rensaellers rents tells me he was offered by government a large tract in the interior of the State for 8 cents an acre – that he made a fortnights inspection of the proffered territory on foot & had hoped to make a fortune but eventually declined the land thinking it dear at the price)

May 24 – Saw the process at the "clearing house" where all the banks of New York adjust their balances with each other every morning at 10 o'clk. – The whole of the balances are struck in 7 minutes. – Obtained from the President of the New York Bank a collection of the engravings used for bank notes, many of which are beautiful specimens as works of art. – These engravings have been in great demand owing to the number of small notes circulated in this country, & a school of vignette engravers has been created to furnish the supply. – The demand extends even beyond this country. – An order to the amount of $25,000 for Bank Note forms for *Athens* has been lately received of which the Engravers here are proud. – [Went with Mr Hamilton to see Mr Mc Caw, Mr Bidder, Mr How, Governor Raymond, etc upon the subject of the New York railroad[136]]

---

[134] Cobden's brother-in-law, the brother of his wife.

[135] Cobden had been requested, by interested British parties, to investigate the advisability of investment in the construction of a railroad in New York State, projected by Hamilton. Cobden's unfavorable report to Henry Rawson from New York, written May 27th, outlines the results of his conversation with Hamilton and others and reveals his own reasoning on the matter. For Cobden's letter, see Watkin, *Alderman Cobden*, pp. 197-198.

[136] Cobden's brackets. These are doubtless the people to whom Cobden refers in his letter of May 27th to Rawson. See *supra*.

May 25 – At a large tailoring establishment in Broadway saw young women employed sowing with a machine by which they earn six dollars a week. – Women working with a needle in the ordinary way earn from 3 to 5 dollars a week. – A shop was shown me in Broadway where sewing machines only were sold, & the rent was said to be $20,000. – The name *Singer* one of the most successful patentees. – Accompanied Mr Robins, Mr Steels [?] friend, to his country house "Throgs Nest" on the East River, where I dined & passed the night. – This country residence about 12 miles from New York resembles an English house of the same description.

May 26th In the evening went to see a spiritual "rapper," a young woman who with her mother seems to get her living at this profession. – A company sat round a table & in answer to their questions certain raps were heard on the floor. – It was evidently an imposture almost too childish to be seriously resented. –

May 27. – Went to see the Subtreasury where the govern^t keeps its gold deposits. – Mr Cisco the Subtreasurer, a fit man for his post, showed me over the establishment & explained the process of chemical analysis & refinement. – With ordinary work the establishment refines about 10 millions sterling annually Attended the "Brokers Board" where the stocks & shares are sold by auction, a place which corresponds with our Stock Exchange. – The clamorous bids for the various stocks put up reminded me of Tattersalls. Then to the Electric Telegraph where messages are printed off on strips of páper by a person sitting perhaps 500 miles away & fingering an instrument which resembles a small pianoforte This is perhaps the most wonderful of all modern inventions & looking to the speed with which messages are transmitted may be considered to be the nearest to perfection of any human contrivance – for it is difficult to see how intelligence can be communicated quicker than lightening. – If Doctor Franklin could come to life again he would I dare say declare this invention to be

the greatest which the world had made during his slumber.
Dined with Mr Hewitt,[137] & afterwards accompanied him
with the Mayor Tiemann & Captain Leonard of the police to
inspect the low haunts of the City. – The "Wapping" of New
York contains numerous dancing rooms some of them very
commodious with a raised orchestra where music generally
by Germans was performed, & where sailors boatmen &
others resort to dance with the loose women who are kept as
a part of the attraction of the house. – The conduct of all
present at these saloons seemed more decent & orderly than
I expected   The absence of liquor in the room (the drinking
being confined to the bar at the entrance) accounts partly
for the absence of all violence & noise in the dances. – On the
whole the demeanor of the people in these low haunts & their
dress, & amusements are superior to what we meet in the lowest resorts of similar classes in London. – Afterwards went to
some places of a similar character but which are frequented
by a superior class of persons. – The Irish & Germans furnish
the greater proportion of prostitutes. – Looked in at the
"Folks garten" where the Germans enjoy their Lager bier –
Then to the Bowery theatre where a rather broad comedy &
farce were provided for the amusement of a very crowded
house. – Observed that the people in the pit who seemed to
be of the mechanic class were all without coats seemingly as
though it was a fashion. – Lastly to the "Times" printing
office where a machine was printing 10 to 15,000 copies an
hour. – A busy day!

May 28   Dined at Mr Abram S. Hewitts.[138] – At his father
in laws Mr Peter Cooper[139] the philanthropist. –

May 29. – Called on Mr Graham.[140] Accompanied Mr Hewitt

[137] See *supra*, pp. 165 and n., 169-170, and *infra*.
[138] Referred to just above.   [139] See *supra*, p. 165 and n.
[140] Possibly the lawyer, John Lorimer Graham; though Cobden conceivably may
be referring to the youthful James Lorimer Graham who early enjoyed a reputation as a connoisseur in literature and art (see *Appletons' Cyclopædia*) or N. B.
Graham, President of the Metropolitan Insurance Company (see Barrett, *The Old
Merchants of New York City*, Fourth Series, p. 228).

& Mr P. Cooper to hear Doctor Bellows,[141] an eloquent Unitarian, preach. Then went with Mr H. to Brooklyn & drove down to "Owls Nest" near the "Narrows" to call on Mr Theodore Sedgwick[142] who married Miss Ashburner – now deceased – Saw the Misses Ashburner. – Passed over land which 25 years since was worth $100 an acre & is now worth $35,000. – Mr Hewitt has lately come into possession of land worth $4,000 which is 5 miles distant from New York Exchange – Mr Bradford R. Wood[143] came to see me from Albany. –

May 30 – Left New York at 8 in company with Mr B.R. Wood from Albany for Newhaven. The country when we passed the frontier into Connecticut was thickly populated, small farms & small factories abound. – A general appearance of thrift & comfort, & equality of condition characterises the New England States. – No very large mansions & no squalid hovels meet the eye. The houses are generally built of wood the same as in Illinois which considering the great superabundance of stone every where is somewhat surprising. Reach Newhaven one of the first of the New England settlements at 10 o'clk & put up at the house of Doctor Bacon[144] the leading clergyman of the place a man eminent

[141] See *supra*, p. 165 and n.

[142] Sedgwick had been a lawyer and writer, president of the Association for the Exhibition of the Industry of all Nations, and district attorney of the southern district of New York. DAB.

[143] See *supra*, pp. 167-168.

[144] A leader in the anti-slavery movement and one of the foremost Congregational ministers of his day, Leonard Bacon served as pastor of First Church, New Haven, for forty-one years and later as a faculty member of Yale Divinity School. *Ibid.*

Cobden had known Bacon in England where he made several addresses in 1850 on education. Writing to Sturge, November 2, 1850, he referred to Bacon: "Read Dr Bacons speeches. He is from Connecticut & is a Calvinist minister whose congregation have subscribed a large sum of money to enable him to visit Egypt & Palestine with his son, & to pay for a substitute for his pulpit. So highly is he esteemed that not only his own congregation but his neighbors generally contributed to the fund & amongst the rest a Roman Catholic priest gave 10 dollars. I hope what he said will be calculated to remove the scruples of our evangelical dissenters." Add. MSS. 43722, Bdl. 1, Part 5.

for his logical eloquence & his courage & honesty. – Drove round the neighborhood to see the village life of the farming population, & a specimen of the manufactures of "notions" which consist of all kinds of small iron wares & innumerable patents. – A stream of water is intercepted, a dam made, & the fall converted into the motive power of a miniature manufactory As the business increases by the addition of one "notion" after another to the articles of production a steam engine is added & larger buildings follow, until it grows into a considerable establishment Was told that skilled workmen earned from five to six shillings English a day, & the unskilled four shillings. – Coals 24^s/ a ton. – Passed by a cave in which it is said the regicides Goff, Whalley, & Dixwell found a hiding place & were fed by the people of Newhaven. – In the Town there is a handsome monument to the memory of Dixwell bearing an inscription commemorative of his patriotism honesty & christian virtues – There are the vestiges of two old tombstones which are supposed to have marked the resting places of Goff & Whalley. The memory of these "patriots" seems to be preserved with great reverence by the people of Newhaven who are proud of the asylum which was here afforded them. – Three avenues leading out of the town in the direction of the Cave are named after them. – This place is the seat of Yale College where 5 to 600 youths from different parts of the Union receive their education. There is a picture gallery containing a collection of the original paintings by Trumbull commemorative of the scenes & incidents of the Revolution. – In the evening a number of the principal people of the Town chiefly professional men came to meet me, – & a serenade was given me by some of the Collegians who sang some excellent choruses, & finished with "God Save the Queen"

May 31st – Left Newhaven at 8 a.m. for Hartford on the way to Boston. – The Connecticut legislature sits alternately at Newhaven & Hartford, at which latter place it is in session this year. – Was invited by the President of the Senate, & the Speaker of the House to take a seat by their side where I observed for a few minutes the course of their proceedings. – The House consists of 235 members one of the largest assemblies in the Union for one of the smallest States. – I find to my surprise that here there is the same inequality of representation which prevails in England. – Newhaven with about 35,000 inhabitants sends two members whilst a small town of 600 has the same number of representatives. – The municipality & not the population is considered to be the constituency, which is the identical fiction on which our old rotten borough system was founded. The small towns have successfully resisted the efforts to reform this system   Find that the members are changed almost every year – it being considered fair to give each man of a certain standing the chance of being for a year a representative of the people. – Am told that not more than 25 of the present House sat in the last legislature. – Elections are annual – The proceedings of the body were very orderly – no expression of feeling allowed towards the speakers. – The members seemed to be nearly all in attendance, & the aspect of the assembly resembled that of a country vestry or county meeting in England, excepting that the fashion of beards seemed to be more general than in the old Country   Was told the majority are farmers occupying generally from 50 to 150 acres of their own land. – Their pay is six shillings a day. – – Left Hartford for Boston at 12 o'clock. – The aspect of the country nearly all the way from New York to Boston is uninviting to the agriculturist presenting a broken uneven surface & strewed with boulders & stones which impede the progress of the plough. – Yet the country appears to be thickly peopled. – The population are generally employed in manufactures. – Saw a manufactory by the side of the railway upon which was inscribed in large letters "manufactory of sewing birds" which are small screws in the form of birds to be fastened on a table at which ladies sew or stretch their work. – Was told that the manufacturer had made his fortune. – Arrived in Boston at 5, & was met at the station by Mr Bradford[145] who took me to his house at West Roxbury. –

June 2. At dinner today at Mr Bradfords met Mr Everett[146] formerly American minister to England who is now delivering lectures on Washington for the benefit of the "Mount Vernon Fund" for purchasing the House where the great patriot died. – After dinner the Company adjourned to a neighboring garden where I planted two sugar maple trees for my host

June 3 – Went into Boston to make calls – Saw Mr Franklin Haven,[147] Mr S.G. Ward,[148] (agent of Baring) – At dinner met Mr Boutwell,[149] formerly governor of Massachusetts, who is now at the head of the Educational department of the State with a salary of £500 a yr. –

June 4 – Met at Breakfast Mr Paul Morffley[150] the famous chess player who has just returned from Europe where he has vanquished all opponents, & has entitled himself to the rank of the champion of the game. – He plays 8 games at the same time blindfolded. – Phillidore [Philidor] the famous player performed the same feat I believe with three opponents. – He is a small young man of apparently 22 years with a pale countenance & rather an abstract air, but with a pecu-

[145] See *supra*, p. 143, and *infra*.

[146] See *supra*, p. 148 and n.   [147] See *supra*, p. 143 and n., and *infra*.

[148] Ward was the American correspondent of the London banking firm of Baring Brothers. Gates, *The Illinois Central Railroad*, p. 72, n., *passim*. See *infra*.

[149] George S. Boutwell had been active in the organization of the Republican party in Massachusetts; and upon the election of Lincoln was appointed by him to organize the new department of internal revenue, of which he became the first commissioner. In later administrations he was destined to prominence as advocator of Johnson's impeachment, Secretary of the Treasury under Grant, senator from Massachusetts, and commissioner to revise the statutes at large, under Hayes. DAB.

[150] Morphy was one of the most brilliant chess masters of modern times. (See *Encyclopædia Britannica*, 13th Edition.) Upon his return to America from his European triumph, he was fêted on all hands, receiving considerable attention from the press. For an account of his New York ovation, see the *New-York Daily Tribune*, May 26, 1859.

liarly modest bearing. – In answer to my inquiries he said that the efforts he made in playing with the first masters in Europe occasioned him no mental suffering or inconvenience; that he was not conscious that the possession of his peculiar faculty for chess gave him any advantage in any other mental avocation; that he had no special aptitude for mental calculation, engineering, or logic; that great mathematicians were often not good chess players, though the latter generally had some aptitude for mathematics; he spoke modestly of his rare gift, describing chess as a mere amusement & nothing more, – but differing from a mathematical problem inasmuch as it called the imagination as well as the reason into play. – In the evening dined with Mr J.M. Forbes[151] at Milton Hill, & met Mr Emmerson[152] the writer, Mr Wendell Philips,[153] Mr Ashburner,[154] etc.

June 5 – Had a long conversation with Captain Swift[155] the Trustee for the English shareholders in the Illinois Canal. – Called on Doctor Warren[156] who showed me Spurzheims

[151] John Murray Forbes was one of the incorporators of the Illinois Central Railroad and a chief promoter of the Michigan Central. In these capacities he effected western railroad extensions to and beyond Chicago; and constructed additional connecting railroads in Iowa and Missouri, part of which system became known as the Chicago, Burlington & Quincy Lines. One of the nation's foremost financiers, he was also active in public affairs. DAB. See also Gates, *The Illinois Central Railroad*, pp. 49, 87.

[152] Ralph Waldo Emerson, fifty-six at this time, had been famous in England for many years.

[153] Effective as an orator, Phillips was one of the country's leading abolitionists. After the Civil War he agitated in behalf of other reforms such as prohibition, improvement in penal methods, woman suffrage, and the strengthening of labor. DAB.

[154] See *infra*.

[155] Formerly a soldier and civil engineer, William H. Swift had been successively president of two eastern railroads and was, at this time, president of the board of trustees of the Illinois and Michigan Canal. He entertained considerable hostility to the Illinois Central; and his unfavorable accounts of it seriously prejudiced the Baring Brothers (to whom he became financial adviser) and others against it. See Gates, *The Illinois Central Railroad*, pp. 72 and n., 163, etc., and DAB. See *infra*.

[156] Jonathan M. Warren, attending physician to the Massachusetts general hospital, was the son of John Collins Warren, the famous surgeon who was also known as a natural historian, having collected several rare specimens. (See *Apple-*

skull which he preserves in a glass case, & which presents a very fine phrenological development. A very wet day. - - Learn from the newspapers the sudden death of my friend Joseph Sturge,[157]- a man of great earnestness in the pursuit of some of the highest objects to which humanity can aspire. He was the champion of the slave, the devoted friend of peace, the unwearied advocate of temperance, & the opponent of all monopoly whether commercial political or religious. - His energy was so untiring that he never seemed to stop to examine the difficulties or the magnitude of any undertaking which commended itself to his conscientiousness. - He was ready at a moments notice, if prompted by a sense of duty, to embark on a voyage to the Antipodes to minister to the necessities of the needy or oppressed, or to plead their cause in the courts or camps of the rulers of the nations. - In contemplating his activity & courage I have often thought that a few thousand such men would effect a moral revolution in the world. - I have not met three men equal to him in their attributes. -

June 6. Met Mr Haven & Mr Healey[158] to discuss Illinois Central Railway affairs, & met Sir George Bonham,[159] Mr Homer, etc. - Called on Mr S. Ashburner.[160]- Accompanied Mr. J.M. Forbes[161] to the Country & called on Mr Quincy[162]

---

tons' Cyclopædia.) This was apparently the Warren who had been a fellow passenger with Cobden on his first trip to America, and whom Cobden had seen when he visited Boston at that time. See also *infra.*

[157] Sturge, the English anti-slavery and peace crusader, closely associated with Cobden in humanitarian projects, was one of his best friends. Cobden's letters to Sturge over twenty years are in the British Museum as Add. MSS. 43722. In this collection is the fine letter of condolence which Cobden wrote to Mrs. Sturge upon his return to London from America, July 1, 1859. *Ibid* 43722, Bdl. 2, Part 7.

[158] Possibly John P. Healy, lawyer, who had served several terms in the Massachusetts legislature, and at this time was solicitor of Boston. *Appletons' Cyclopædia.*

[159] Bonham had been a colonial governor, first, of Prince of Wales Island, Singapore and Malacca, and then of Hongkong, where he also superintended British trade to China. DNB.

[160] See just above and below.   [161] Mentioned just above and also below.

[162] Relatively unsuccessful as a politician, Josiah Quincy is best known for his municipal reforms in the Boston mayoralty and for signal achievements in his administration as president of Harvard University. DAB.

an old gentleman aged 87 who was born the same year as Lord Lyndhurst – He shewed me the gorget worn by Washington at the defeat of Braddock. – In remarking upon the portraits of Washington he described them as "idealised" likenesses & said that none of them satisfied him – His family had occupied the same house for upwards of 200 years. – Afterwards called on Mr Adams[163] the son of John Quincy Adams, & grandson of John Adams who occupies the same house in which lived the first president of his name. Several family portraits. – The house of wood. – At dinner at Mr Forbes[164] met Senator Wilson[165] who was originally a shoemaker & is still a young man, – Mr George Sumner,[166] Mr Quincy Jr,[167] Mr Adams (Member of Congress) Mr Hale[168] the Speaker of the Assembly of Mass. a young man, Captn Swift,[169] Mr S.G. Ward[170] – Mr Forbes drove me home at night to Mr Bradfords. –

June 7 – Called on Mr S. Ashburner,[171] then to Doctor War-

[163] Charles Francis Adams at this time was a member of the House of Representatives. Two years later he became United States minister to England. When he arrived there during the crucial opening days of the Civil War, Cobden was the only person active in public life that he had met. Throughout the critical years which were to follow Cobden effectively supported Adams and the cause of the North. *Ibid.* and references in Add. MSS. 43652.

[164] See just above.

[165] See *infra*. Within two years of this time, Wilson was to become chairman of the committee on military affairs of the Senate, rendering significant service in this capacity at the beginning of the Civil War. He was elected Vice-President of the United States in 1872. DAB.

[166] Cobden had known George Sumner (the brother of Charles Sumner, Cobden's personal friend) when he was in London ten years earlier. (Add. MSS. 43659, Part 3, Cobden to Sturge, June 21, 1849.) George was a political economist working for improved social institutions and writing extensively on related subjects. *Appletons' Cyclopædia.*

[167] Probably Edmund Quincy, second son of Josiah Quincy. Quincy, though a patrician, was an abolitionist of the extreme Garrisonian following. He was editor of or contributor to several of the leading anti-slavery journals, and had a literary reputation as well in biography and fiction. DAB.

[168] Journalist and political figure, Charles Hale was the youngest person to hold the position of speaker of the Massachusetts assembly; he was twenty-eight at this time, 1859, the year he was chosen as speaker. *Ibid.*

[169] See just above.

[170] Referred to on p. 201.

[171] See just above.

ren[172] who took us to see the skeleton of a Mastodon found near the Hudson river, a huge animal which must have thrown the elephant into the shade. There was also the fossil remains of a marine serpent 60 feet long, & which judging from the vertebrae must have been as big in circumference as an ox. – Then to see some schools where the young "ladies" displayed great skill in mental arithmetic. – The two sexes are not blended to the same extent in Boston as in the schools of the West. – Called on General Sumner.[173] – Boston with a population of 180,000 has 60,000 Irish. – In West Roxbury near Boston containing about 20,000, nearly half the popul[n]. are Irish. – Saw a patent brick manufactory where a mixture of 13 parts of sand to one of lime is subjected to a heavy pressure in a mould (by a steam engine) with a hole through the centre & the bricks thus formed are left for a few days to dry in the air. –

June 8 – Went with Mr Bradford to Plymouth, 40 miles, to see the scene of the first landing of the Pilgrim Fathers. – The country through which we passed was uneven & rocky & generally covered with a growth of scrubby trees. – Visited Mr R.B. Hall[174] who took us to see a museum of curiosities & relics connected with the history of the first settlement of this continent. Stood on the rock where the Pilgrims are said to have landed, & which has been irreverently styled the New England "blarney stone." – The chief objects of interest are chairs & other furniture from the *Mayflower* the vessel in which the first settlers arrived. – Like the pieces of the "true cross" which are every where to be seen by the devout believers in those relics, these memorials of the Pilgrims seem capable of indefinite multiplication to meet the demands of the faithful. – After a drive round the neighbor-

---

[172] See *supra*.

[173] Probably William H. Sumner who from 1818 to 1835 had served as adjutant-general of Massachusetts, with the rank of brigadier-general. *Appletons' Cyclopædia*.

[174] See *supra*, p. 145 and n.

hood & a visit to the old cemetery, I went to see the archives at the building where the registry for the transfer of real estate is kept. Saw the original book for recording the earliest transactions of the first settlers. – One entry records that Miles Standish purchased 8/13[ths] part of "the" *red cow*. – Was told by the registrars that for three or four dollars, & in a few hours, the transfer of a large estate can be effected – Mr Hall narrated that Mr Henry Wilson[175] the present Senator from Massachusetts to Washington is the son of a dissolute man named Johnson, that he left home, changed his name, threw himself on his own resources, worked with his hands as a shoemaker, & afterwards employed a number of workpeople, took to politics, rose from step to step, & is now the colleague of Charles Sumner as member of the most august assembly in America The account given me of the present governor of this State, Mr Banks,[176] still more extraordinary He is the son of very poor parents & in early life obtained employment in a machine shop connected with a factory in which his present wife was working as a spinner, that he eked out his resources by following the calling of dancing master & play actor, till he was enabled to improve his education & place himself in a lawyers office, that he turned his mind to politics, became a member of the State legislature, & thence was elected to Congress where he became Speaker (his wife & he conducting themselves with dignity) & is now governor of Massachusetts with the prospect of being elected President of the United States. Mr Hall also gave me the anecdote of Mr   [177] Senator who in speaking in the Senate at Washington pointed to the pillars which supported the building etc said his father had helped with his own hands to fashion them. –

[175] See *supra* and n. Wilson's original name was not "Johnson" but "Colbath." DAB.

[176] As governor, Nathaniel P. Banks gave Massachusetts a progressive administration. In January of 1861 he replaced McClellan as vice-president of the Illinois Central Railroad; he served but a few months before he was commissioned major-general in the northern army. *Ibid.*

[177] Cobden left this space blank.

June 9. Visited a free grammar school, being the superior branch of the common school system, where the master pointed out the son of a plasterer & the son of the richest wholesale dealer in the city Mr Bigbee both preparing themselves for Harvard College. – Then to the Cambridge University, or Harvard College, founded in the beginning of the 17th Century where about 700 young men are finishing their education. – Was shewn over the establishment by the President Walker[178] who is a unitarian clergyman. – The young men attend various places of worship on Sundays, but all attend the daily prayers (including the Catholics) of the College. Was shewn a gallery of pictures containing original portraits of Adams, Washington & other heroes of the Revolution. – The President gave some anecdotes of the manner in which Adams & other contemporaries disparaged the character of Washington quoting an instance in which Jno Adams spoke of Washington as a mere "block of wood." –

June 10 – Parted with my good friends Mr & Mrs Bradford[179] & left Boston at ½ p 7 a.m. for Ogdensburg on the St Lawrence river passing through the manufacturing districts of New England comprising Lowell, Manchester, Lawrence etc where the factory system has been planted under great disadvantages from the dearness of coal & iron. – There is however a great facility afforded by the water power of the Merrimack river, & the skill & intelligence of the working people whose hours of labor are longer than in England enable the capitalists to compete with those in Lancashire The country over which I passed today was generally hilly & clothed with forests reminding me of the scenery of the roots of the Pyrenees. – The road passed through parts of Massachusetts Vermont, New Hampshire, & New York. Vermont with its green mountains where horses & cattle are raised, presents some beautiful scenes. – The numerous lakes bosomed in the wooded hollows gave a great charm to the

[178] James Walker was president of Harvard from 1853 to 1860. *Ibid.*
[179] See *supra*, pp. 143, 201, and *passim.*

scene. – Vermont offers a singular contrast to the other New England States in the absence of the large stones which are strewed over their surface. – In passing over the corner of New York State the railroad skirts the shore of Lake Champlain containing innumerable islets which are the characteristics of the Lake & river scenery of the region of the Upper St Lawrence. – At Ogdensburg (June 11th) I left the territory of the United States, & crossed the St Lawrence to Prescott where I took the British Mail Steamer to Montreal. –

OBSERVATIONS

Was struck with the prevalence of wooden houses in the old-settled States of New England where they are almost as general as at the West. Even the Villa residences of the rich merchants in the neighborhood of Boston are generally of wood. – They are prettily & often elegantly designed in point of architectural taste, & I am told are more warm in the winter than stone. – Slates instead of "shingles" are however being generally used for roofing. –

Comparing class with class the people of the United States are raised to a much higher level than in any other country. – Writers & travellers fall into a great unfairness in comparing the middle & upper classes with whom alone the tourists & the book-writing class associate in Europe with the *whole people* whom they meet at the table d'hotes & in the railway cars in the United States. – There are no second or third class railway carriages. The American mechanic or day laborer puts on his broad cloth coat & steps into the same car as that which the richest merchant or the governor of the State occupies, & where his manners are quite as sedate & orderly as are those of what we in England should call his "betters." – I have as a rule travelled with 40 or 50 persons of these mixed classes at a time whilst in the U.S. & have never met with one instance of a rude or boisterous remark. – Every one takes his seat without the intervention of policemen or

conductors depositing his little travelling bag which is a sort
of small institution on a side rack, & carrying it off with him
at the end of his journey. – Nobody expects the porter to
assist him in carrying his bag or calling a cab. – At Cincinnati the governor of the State Mr Chase who is talked of as
a candidate for the Presidency carried off his bag like the
rest to the hotel. – Persons who leave their seats at a station
& return to them will always find any one who has by mistake occupied their places ready to vacate them. –

A great decency is observable among the people. – I did not
in all my travels see an individual obeying the call of nature
in any corner however secluded Was told by a person to
whom I mentioned this that it would not be permitted by
the police. –

The Americans seem to be careful of their horses & kind to
dumb animals. Their cart & carriage horses seem to be well
broken & to be left standing alone at doors of houses in the
streets with less fear of accidents than in Europe. Horse
cloths & Macintosh covers are thrown over them, in wet &
cold weather It was suggested to me that perhaps this care
of their cattle arose from the fact of people more frequently
driving their own horses here than in Engl^d

The substantial privileges accorded to women, in the U.
States strike the attention of foreigners. – It is highly honorable to the *men* of America & places them, in a most important point of view, in the front rank of civilized nations. –
But the women appear to me to take the courtesies & privileges accorded to them too much as a right, & the manner in
which they look for such concessions & attentions as are here
yielded to them gives them a confident bearing which de-
tracts from that air of timidity & feebleness which constitutes
their title to the generosity of the rougher sex. – Some of the
periodical papers have begun to notice the *exactions* of the
ladies when travelling etc If they lose their privileges it

will be from not sufficiently appreciating the principle on which they are conceded.

The Americans are a truthful people, otherwise their political institutions could not be maintained. – They would not utter deliberate falsehoods. – But their "fast" habits & their confidence in the future lead them into hasty & exaggerated statements, & make them often very inexact in their conversation when matters of fact are involved. They are not so outspoken as the English. – It seems as if the higher level at which every man is placed here than in other countries, by the general assent & claim of the Americans, inspires a greater mutual respect among the people which restrains them from that plainspoken style with which Englishmen call each others conduct in question. – I have observed that one meets with little of that banter in America which characterises the familiar intercourse of all classes in England.[180]

June 11th 1859 – Left Prescott on the Saint Lawrence at 11 a.m. for Montreal. The scenery of this river is very fine. Frequently the Steamer is winding among innumerable little islands, some of them not larger than the island opposite to the castle of Chillon on the Geneva lake, & all of them clothed in wood down to the waters edge. – Before reaching Montreal we passed over the famous rapids where the water of the river dashes down inclines for miles, the water surging & foaming like breakers on a rocky shore. – One shudders for the first time as the vessel darts among the rocks which the boiling & eddying river here & there discloses to view, but a glance at the cool & steady eyes of the four men who have charge of the wheel is sufficient to assure the passengers of their safety. – Passed a mouth of the Ottowa which empties itself into the St Lawrence. As we approached Montreal the huge structure the tubular bridge

[180] The small (6″ x 4″), plum-colored, leather booklet, known as Add. MSS. 43808 A, is concluded at this point. On the last four numbered folios in the booklet are lists of people and addresses. The diary is resumed on nine loose folios of quarto-size, Add. MSS. 43808 B.

was visible stretching across the river, – a splendid monument of engineering skill & of wasted capital. – At the dinner table today observed that the great majority drank beer or wine, thus reminding me that I am on British territory. – The aspect of my fellow passengers presented a more fleshy appearance, & their movements were slower than those I had been accustomed to on the American side. – Reached my friends house (Hon John Young)[181] at 7 p.m.

June 12 – Sunday. – Looked in at the Cathedral, a vast building capable of holding nearly 10,000 persons & which was nearly full of devout Roman Catholics. – In Lower Canada the ancient ecclesiastical buildings & endowments were at the Conquest left in the hands of the French population, & the income of the Catholic church is consequently very great. – The large & handsome edifices thus left to the old church seems to have imparted a spirit of rivalry to other sects, for nowhere on the American continent have I seen more solid structures devoted to religious worship than here. – The general appearance of Montreal is that of a wealthy & old community, & which gave occasion to a remark by an American traveller that "it looked like a town that had been paid for." – In the evening Sir Wm Logan[182] the geologist of the Province an intelligent & enthusiastic man dined with us. He observed that Canada was almost every where auriferous, but that the labor of seeking for gold would not probably produce more than 2/6 a day. – – Mr Holmes an old merchant & Bank Director was also present. – He spoke in strong terms of condemnation against the man-

---

[181] See *supra*, p. 181, and *infra*. In the fifties Young had represented Montreal in the Legislative Assembly of Canada, serving for a short time as commissioner of public works for Canada. He had formerly been chairman of the board of harbor commissioners for the port of Montreal; and had organized a Free Trade Association which published the *Canadian Economist*. He wrote extensively on Canadian trade and commerce. Later, he was to represent Montreal in the Canadian House of Commons. *The Dictionary of Canadian Biography*.

[182] Logan was director of the Canadian Geological Survey from 1843 to 1870. "He revolutionized the current conceptions of Canadian geology," and was honored widely for his contribution. *Ibid.*

agement of the Grand Trunk railway, & censured Tho[s] Baring & George Glyn for having misled the public as to the prospects of the Company. – (Mr Holmes was himself formerly a Director & had a dispute with the party at present in power) – Mr Young & Mr Holmes agreed that the shareholders would never receive a farthing for their investment. –

June 13 – Visited the Geological Museum & was favored with much information genially imparted by Sir William Logan. – The coal fields of the United States larger than the whole surface of Great Britain & Ireland. – Illinois is almost wholly underlaid with coal. – At dinner today at Mr Youngs met Mr Ross[183] the Engineer of the great tubular bridge, Mr Dorrien[184] said to be one of the best speakers in French & English, Mr M[c]Ghie[185] an Irish orator, Mr Renaud, Mr Kay etc. –

June 14. – At breakfast Mr Hart[186] observed, in alluding to the honesty of the Country population, that he owned some property in a village where such a thing as a lock or bolt on a door was unknown. – Was accompanied by Mr Ross the chief engineer to inspect the Victoria tubular bridge which is to be a mile & a quarter in length across the Saint Lawrence. – – Mr R. says that the idea of this form of bridge originated in an accident at the launch of an iron ship witnessed by Robert Stephenson when the vessel was suspended by its two extremities for some time without causing any fracture or strain to the iron of which it was composed. – The

---

[183] Referred to below.

[184] The jurist, Sir Antoine Aimé Dorion, was at this time Montreal's representative in the Legislative Assembly of Canada. He was later to hold office in various administrations and to serve for many years as chief justice of the court of Queen's Bench, Quebec. *Ibid.*

[185] Thomas D'Arcy McGee in 1858 had become the representative of Montreal West in the Legislative Assembly of Canada, and was to continue an important figure in Canadian political affairs over the following decade. He was one of the "Fathers of Confederation," and has been called "the chief apostle of Canadian national unity." One of Canada's most effective orators, McGee also was an author of some merit. *Ibid.*

[186] See just below.

iron of which one of the tubes is made would, if melted into a solid mass of 22 inches square, & suspended in the place of the tube, break from its own weight. – This bridge is to cost a million & a quarter sterling. – Alas for the poor shareholders! –

June 15. Called on Mr Rose[187]– met Sir F. Head[188] the Governor of the Province – Drove round the suburbs of the City. – Dined with Mr Theodore Hart (who is a holder of Ill. Cent Stock & is recommending the investment to his friends) & met Mr Cramp, Mr Halton etc. A very sultry day. –

June 16 – At 6 p.m. left Montreal by the steamer for Quebec, about 150 miles. – The country generally flat on the banks of the Saint Lawrence until we came to about 20 miles from Quebec where it rose into irregular mountain ridges. – The principal passengers on board were government employés. – Several officers of the British army came on board accompanied by their friends. – I have seen more *government* military officers since I have been in Canada than I did in all my travels in the States. I have not met with a sensible man who does not regard the British army posted in Canada as a piece of useless folly. – It is useless in time of peace & would be powerless in case of war with the United States. – The defense & security of Canada must depend wholly on the people. – Rose at 5 o'clock to see the scenery as we approached Quebec. –

June 17. – The "Platform" view of the scenery around Quebec presents a scene of great beauty. – The river broken into two branches by the island of Orleans & the country in the distance rising into mountainous ranges, with the whole

[187] Probably Sir John Rose, Montreal's representative in the Legislative Assembly of Canada, and, at this time, minister of public works. Later he was to serve for a short period as minister of finance for Canada. *Ibid.*

[188] Sir Francis B. Head had been an unsuccessful lieutenant-governor of Upper Canada from 1835 to 1838. (*Ibid.*) He was better known as an author of popular books. *Appletons' Cyclopædia.*

scene dotted with houses & churches many of their roofs
covered with glittering tin tiles, – altogether the view surpasses any thing I remember to have seen in City scenery
in America. – Went upon the Citadel, but although the view
was more distant I did not think it equal to that from the
Platform. – It will leave an impression like that of Constantinople. – Mr Noad called with Colonel Rhodes an English
gentleman living here on his estate; & who with Mons Dubord a French Canadian, member of the Assembly or Pro-
vincial Parliament, accompanied me to see the falls of the
Montmorency about 4 miles from Quebec. – One of the
striking peculiarities of the Lower Canadian landscape is
the great number of farm houses & cottages, generally white,
which every where meet the eye, forming straggling lines of
buildings along the course of the river & the main roads On
going to the falls of the Montmorency today we seemed to
pass through almost a continues row of houses. – The
"Fall" is more than 60 feet greater in depth than Niagara, &
would in Europe be an unrivalled spectacle – But although
a grand sight when seen from the platform immediately
above it yet the eye which has recently rested on Niagara is
apt to draw comparisons which throw it into insignificance. –
At lunch at the falls Mr Dubord the French Canadian was
very merry & amusing, & after a few glasses of Champagne
he played a game of banter very successfully with his English companions. I gathered from their conversation that the
politics of Canada are not without their future difficulties &
dangers owing to the differences between Upper & Lower
Canada. – But Mr Dubord observed that the feeling between
the two races is more cordial than it was 20 years ago. –
I have heard a different opinion from others. On returning
from the falls of the Montmorenci we visited the battle
field on the heights of Abraham where a poor monument
has been erected to mark the spot where Wolfe fell. – The
road by which the English army reached the high ground
was pointed out to me – It was merely a somewhat steep

ascent quite accessible by horses & even wheeled carriages & presented none of those dangers or difficulties which the views presented to us by painters & engravers would lead the visitor to expect. It is thus that I have generally found the actual inspection of scenes of battle or heroic achievements to fail to realize my anticipations. – Proceeded along the bank of the river to call on Sir Edm[d] Head[189] the Governor General who had come from Upper Canada on his way to a fishing excursion. – By the way his reception here with a royal salute as he stepped on shore accompanied by Secretaries & aides-de-camp contrasted a good deal with what I saw in Ohio when Governor Chase stepped from the railway car with me at Cincinnati unnoticed, & walked in his travelling "duster" his carpet-bag in his hand, to the hotel where he merged unnoticed in the body of strangers & travellers who at the same time reached that destination. – The governor Head walked with me through the grounds of his residence which overhang the river & afford several views of the vast rafts of lumber which lie there & constitute in the labor of sawing, squaring, stacking, & loading, the staple industry of Quebec. – Passed several merchants villas prettily situated on the bank of the river. –

June 18. – Took my departure from the continent of America at 11 o'clk this morning. Mr Noad & Mr Forsyth[190] offering me kind attentions at parting. – The view of Quebec from the "Indian" screw propeller as we descended the Saint Lawrence was very striking & confirmed me in the first impression I formed that with the sole exception of Constantinople I had hardly ever seen a finer spectacle than this city & the surrounding scenery present. As we descended the river the same feature which I had remarked on its banks higher up presented itself – in the continuous line of white washed houses which formed almost a street for nearly the whole

---

[189] See *supra*, p. 149 and n.
[190] Probably James Bell Forsyth, merchant and author. See *Dictionary of Canadian Biography*.

space through which we passed during the day. – In the evening the pilot left us & carried a number of letters from the passengers.

June 19 Sunday – Had two services on board – morning & evening – the first by an Episcopal clergyman, & the second by one of the Presbyterian denomination. – Both banks of the river were still visible, but owing to the great breadth of the St Lawrence as we descended, the scenery was but indistinctly seen. – The views on each side from Quebec for more than a hundred miles are magnificent, the banks rising gradually from the water to a back ground of high rugged hills the slopes of which were studded with houses & farms. – Am told the farms are moderate in size & that the farmers are generally prosperous, – retaining with their name of "habitans" many of the primitive habits of their French ancestry before the revolution. – Find that we have about 60 cabin passengers, less than the usual compliment.

June 20. Still we see land occasionally on both sides of the river. – Though we are accustomed to regard Quebec as at the lower part of the St Lawrence it is really 700 miles above the point where we first see land at the entrance of what is called the Gulf of St Lawrence. – The route from Quebec to Liverpool besides saving upwards of 300 miles in actual distance avoids more than 700 miles of ocean navigation. – Although the weather is fine & we are generally within sight of land several of the passengers are sea-sick. –

June 21 – This morning we pass the Straits of Belleisle & soon afterwards leave behind us the island of that name. – We soon lose sight of the Coast of Labrador & enter on the wide ocean to behold no more land until we reach the shores of Ireland. – Here we saw several whales spouting. – Shortly after breakfast we find ourselves approaching several icebergs, the objects of special dread to mariners. – During the whole day we were surrounded with huge floating masses of ice & snow, varying in size from mountains upwards of a mile in circumference to small scattered fragments just vanishing in the water of the ocean. – The temperature sunk to the coldness of winter. – Every bodys anxious attention was directed to these terrible visitors. – Some of the icebergs were in shape like castles, others resembled cathedrals, or ruins, or clusters of houses. – As we threaded our way among them they assumed all sorts of shapes – "that's a lion" – "that, a swan" – "thats a slice of the chalky South Downs" – "thats a great wedding cake," were the exclamations of the passengers. – Fortunately it was a fine day, & there was no fog which is generally the dreaded accompaniment of these visitors – happily too it was a complete calm, & it was the longest day when the night is only three hours long. – Towards evening the icebergs were left behind, but we approached a still more unmanageable difficulty. – The whole ocean became covered as far as we could see with drift ice which formed a field so thick that the Captain was obliged to let off the Steam & allow the vessel to drift with the entangled mass. – At the same time a dense fog prevented any look out being kept, & in order to warn any ship that might possibly be near of our proximity the steam whistle occasionally broke the silence of our solitude. – The Captain has not been in bed any night since our departure, & he is keeping most anxious & vigilant watch tonight. – He is fortunately a young man & can bear the fatigues of his post. – Give me young men when there is work to do.

June 22. – As the sun gathered strength to day the fog was dispelled & we found ourselves in the midst of a vast field of floating ice through which the Captain tried to thread his way putting on a little steam & going only at the rate of 4 or 5 miles an hour. – Sometimes when the obstruction ahead became quite impenetrable the ship was laid to. – The Captain was always at his post, & there were two "look outs" at the bows besides a man up aloft to give the signal of danger when we approached a mass of ice of more than usual dimensions. – In spite of these precautions we now & then bumped against the ice with a force which made the vessel tremble. – Whilst thus imprisoned, & steering in all directions trying all points of the compass for an escape we found ourselves about 2 oc'lk p.m. emerging into the open ocean, & for nearly two hours we made our usual course at the ordinary speed. – But our difficulties were not yet at an end for in about two hours we found ourselves locked in another field of ice through which the ship struggled till the evening when we again emerged into clear water; & the long heavy swell of the Atlantic ocean now was for the first time experienced. – During the last three nights the Captain of our ship (Smith) has not taken off his clothes or been for hardly an hour below deck. – We now had favorable winds, but the weather was rough & cold & what the sailors call "dirty"; the ship rolled a good deal which added to the discomfort of the cold & rain sent nearly all the passengers sick to their births. – I was as usual one of the greatest sufferers, & for several days could hardly crawl on deck. – No incidents occurred to break the usual monotony of a sea-voyage excepting that in a heavy lurch of the sea one of the passengers was thrown down & broke one of his toes. The surgeon belonging to the ship was disabled by sickness but there happened to be one of the profession among the passengers who attended to the case. –

June 28. At 11 o'clock to day the high land of the western coast of Ireland was descried, – being our first introduction to the Eastern hemisphere. Our last view of the coast of Labrador was on the 21st at about 10 a.m., consequently we have taken seven days to make the passage between the two continents. – In the course of the day we passed through the "northern passage" as it is called where vessels from America go round the north of Ireland in their way to Liverpool. – Passed near the *Giants Causeway* during a shower of rain which partially obscured the view. – Some of the passengers requested me to draw up an address expressive of our approval of the conduct of the Captain during our difficulties in the ice which I did accordingly, and it was presented to him after dinner. – It was signed by the whole of the Cabin passengers. – We only saw two ships during the whole voyage. –

On Board the "Indian" Steamer from Quebec
to Liverpool, June 29 - 1859.

———————

The undersigned, passengers by the Steamer "Indian"
from Quebec to Liverpool, having experienced in their passage unusual obstructions from ice, which called for the
display of much prudence & energy in the management of
the vessel, have pleasure in recording their appreciation of
the judicious & able conduct of their Captain, and their
thanks for his patient & unwearied exertions, and for the
total disregard of personal sacrifices which he has shewn in
the performance of his arduous duties. – In congratulating
Captain Smith on the successful termination of his first
voyage in command of the "Indian," they beg to express
their hearty wishes for the prosperity of his future professional career. –[191]

[191] This is the statement of appreciation (drawn up by Cobden) which was
presented to the captain of the ship.

SELECTIVE BIBLIOGRAPHY

NOTE ON THE PRINCIPAL SOURCE

The Cobden Papers in the British Museum constitute the main body of source material. The many hundreds of Cobden letters are catalogued as Additional Manuscripts 43647—43678, inclusive. The American diaries are listed as 43807 and 43808. Those of primary importance in connection with this particular project are Additional Manuscripts 43647 to 43664 and 43676 to 43678, inclusive, which contain, principally, the major correspondence with Bright, Sturge, Ashworth, Combe, Hargreaves, Richard, Robertson, Baines, Villiers, Gilpin, Parkes, Tait, Dufour, Fitzmayer, Rawson, Slagg, and Sumner.

There are also important Cobden letters in the Sturge Papers, Additional Manuscripts 43722, and several individual Cobden letters concerning America in the Gladstone Papers, LI, Additional Manuscripts 44136. (It may be noted here that the relatively few Cobden letters in the Peel Papers – Additional Manuscripts 40594 and 40600, in the Hill Papers – Additional Manuscripts 31978, and in the Ireland Papers – Additional Manuscripts 33515, yielded nothing for the purposes of this book.)

OTHER WRITINGS

Of the many works examined, only those which were of the most direct use in preparing the introduction and notes are here recorded.

COBDEN

In the preparation of that part of the introduction dealing mainly with Cobden's life and activities, works in the British Museum, in the Cobden Library at Dunford House (Midhurst, Sussex), and at the Princeton University Library were explored. Primary sources consisted for the most part of Cobden's speeches, pamphlets, and correspondence; the letters, memoirs, diaries, and writings of friends who knew him personally (such as John Bright, Charles Sumner, etc.); and official records. Of the many other materials, the following were of particular service:

Axon, W. E. A. *Cobden as a Citizen, a Chapter in Manchester History*, London, 1907.

Bowen, Ian. *Cobden*. London, 1935.

Brett, J. *Facts and Fallacies of Free Trade*.

Bright, John. *Speeches of the Right Hon. John Bright, M. P., Delivered in Bradford, on the Occasion of the Inauguration of the Cobden Memorial*. London, 1877.

Cunningham, William. *Richard Cobden and Adam Smith, Two Lectures*. London, 1904.

Dawson, William Harbutt. *Richard Cobden and Foreign Policy*. London, 1926.

Dunham, Arthur Louis. *The Anglo-French Treaty of Commerce of 1860 and the Progress of the Industrial Revolution in France*. Ann Arbor, 1930.

Halévy, Elie. *The Age of Peel and Cobden*. London, 1947.

Hall, Newman. *Richard Cobden M. P.* London, 1865.

Hirst, Francis, W. *Richard Cobden and John Morley*. Swindon, 1941.

———. *The Repeal of the Corn Laws*. Issued by The Cobden Club, Dunford House, Midhurst, 1946.

Hobart, Lord. *The Mission of Richard Cobden*. London, 1867.

Hobson, John A. *Richard Cobden The International Man*. London, 1918.

Leroy-Beaulieu, Paul. "Richard Cobden: His Work and the Outcome of His Ideas" in *Richard Cobden and the Jubilee of Free Trade*. London, 1896.

Maccoby, S. *English Radicalism, 1832-1852*. London, 1935.

———. *English Radicalism, 1853-1886*. London, 1938.

Mallet, Charles. *Richard Cobden*. London, 1929.

Mallet, Louis. *The Political Opinions of Richard Cobden*. London, 1869.

McGilchrist, John. *Richard Cobden, The Apostle of Free Trade, His Political Career and Public Services. A Biography*. London, 1865.

Morley, John. *The Life of Richard Cobden*, two volumes. London, 1881.

Nevill, Ralph, editor. *The Reminiscences of Lady Dorothy Nevill*. London, 1906.

Platt-Higgins, Frederick. *The Rise and Decline of the Free Trade Movement*. London, 1905.

Schwabe, Mrs. Salis. *Reminiscences of Richard Cobden*. London, 1895.

Villiers, Brougham, and Chesson, Wilfrid Hugh. *Anglo-American Relations, 1861-1865.* London, 1919.
Watkin, Edward W. *Alderman Cobden of Manchester. Letters and Reminiscences of Richard Cobden, with Portraits, Illustrations, Facsimiles, and Index.* London, 1891.

TRAVEL

Various travel accounts of the period, such as those of Dickens, Kemble, Martineau, Maury, Trollope, Goldwin Smith, and many others, are of interest in connection with Cobden's diaries. Of the other books in the field, frequently in the nature of surveys or samplings of travel records, there are several excellent ones dealing more specifically with such matters as travel conditions of the time, social, economic, and political life in America, reactions of British travelers, and the English attitude toward America throughout this period of the nineteenth century. Of these the most helpful have been:

Albion, Robert Greenhalgh. *Square-Riggers on Schedule.* Princeton, 1938.
Berger, Max. *British Traveller in America, 1836-1860. Columbia University Studies in History, Economics, and Public Law.* 502, New York, 1943.
Commager, Henry Steele, editor. *America in Perspective: The United States through Foreign Eyes.* New York, 1947.
Mesick, Jane Louise. *The English Traveller in America, 1785-1835, Columbia University Studies in English and Comparative Literature.* New York, 1922.
Nevins, Allan, editor. *American Social History as Recorded by British Travellers.* New York, 1923.
———, editor. *America Through British Eyes* (second and revised edition of above study). New York, 1948.
Riegel, Robert E. *Young America, 1830-1840.* Norman, Oklahoma, 1949.

Files of several newspapers in 1859 were consulted, notably the *New-York Daily Tribune* and the *New York Herald.* They contained little.

ILLINOIS CENTRAL RAILROAD

Various short studies and long surveys of economic conditions in Britain and America at the time have been used. Indispensable have been the books dealing specifically with the Illinois Central Railroad, notably the work by Gates.

Brownson, Howard Gray. *History of the Illinois Central Railroad to 1870, Studies in the Social Sciences,* IV, Nos. 3, 4, University of Illinois. Urbana, 1915.

Corliss, Carlton J. *Main Line of Mid-America, The Story of the Illinois Central.* New York, 1950.

Gates, Paul Wallace. *The Illinois Central Railroad and Its Colonization Work. Harvard Economic Studies,* XLII, Cambridge, 1934.

BIOGRAPHICAL DATA

Apart from individual biographies, the following biographical sources have yielded the best information on persons identified in the notes:

Appletons' Cyclopædia of American Biography.

Barrett, Walter. *The Old Merchants of New York City.* New York, First Series, 1862; Second Series, 1863; Third Series, 1865; Fourth Series, 1866.

Beach, Moses Vale. *The Wealth and Biography of the Wealthy Citizens of The City of New York.* New York, 1855.

Dictionary of American Biography.

Dictionary of Canadian Biography.

Dictionary of National Biography.

The Encyclopædia Britannica, 13th Edition.

Lamb's Biographical Dictionary of the United States.

Meredith, Roy. *Mr. Lincoln's Contemporaries.* New York, 1951.

The National Cyclopædia of American Biography.

Parton, James. *Famous Americans of Recent Times.* Boston, 1867.

Preston, Wheeler. *American Biographies.* New York, 1940.

INDEX

𝒜

Academy of Arts (Philadelphia), 69, 175

Adams, Charles Francis, 64, 204 and n

Adams, John, 204, 207

Additional Manuscripts, Cobden papers in, ix-x, 24-25; see also Bibliography

Albany, in 1835, 11, 13, 14 and n, 21, 111-112, 121n, 132; in 1859, 59, 61, 63, 64, 65, 69, 72, 148, 167-169, 194

American Philosophical Society, 69, 173 and n

Anderson, 161, 191, 192

Anglo-French Commercial Treaty of 1860, 8, 57

Appleton Publishing Company, 69, 147

arbitration, Cobden's work in behalf of, 7, 10, 34

armament, Cobden's attitude toward, 7, 9, 10, 17, 31, 32, 33, 80, 85, 213

Armstrong, Governor, 119

Arnold, Isaac N., 65, 161 and n, 162, 192

Ashburner, Miss and Misses, 167, 198

Ashburner, S., 202, 203, 204

Ashworth, Henry, 23 and n, 41 and n, 68

Astor, William Backhouse, 63, 148 and n, 171, 172

Athenaeum, of Manchester, 5

Athenaeum Club (New York), 69, 164

Athenaeum Library (Boston), 118-119

Auburn, state prison of, 16, 109-110, 110n

ℬ

Bache, Franklin, 173 and n

Bacon, 65, 198-199

Bailey, Gamaliel, 146 and n

Baines, 27 and n

Baltimore, 11, 14n, 21, 23n, 92-93, 132, 177

Bancroft, George, 25, 63, 148 and n, 166 and n, 171

Banks, Nathaniel P., 206 and n

banks, 101, 164, 195, 196

Barlow, Samuel L. M., 147 and n

Barney, Hiram, 164 and n

Beecher, Henry Ward, 194-195, 194n

Bellows, Henry W., 165 and n, 198

Bennett, Gordon, 30

Bissell, William H., 189 and n

boat transportation, 17, 62, 128-131, 215-220; in America, in 1835, 18-19, 91, 92, 98, 99, 102-104, 119, 121, 123, 125, 126, 127; in 1859, 59, 62, 152, 153-154, 155, 157-159, 168, 169, 208, 210-211

Bonaparte, Jerome, 63, 171 and n

Bonham, Sir George, 203 and n

Boston, in 1835, 11, 13, 14 and n., 21, 107n, 113-116, 118-119, 132; in 1859, 59, 61-62, 63, 64, 69, 70, 143-144, 200, 201-205, 207, 208

Boutwell, George S., 64, 201 and n

Bradford, S. D., 63, 64, 143-144, 201, 204, 205, 207

Brainard, Daniel, 162 and n

Bright, John, 5, 29, 47, 57, 63, 64, 65; see many footnotes in Introduction III, IV

Britannia, 86-87, 86n, 87-88, 126, 128-131

Brown, George, 14, 92 and n

Brown, James, 1835, 14n, 50, 63

Brown, James, 1859, 171 and n

Brownsville, 14, 95-96, 97-98

Bryant, William Cullen, 63, 147 and n

Buchanan, James, 25, 61, 63, 64, 68, 74-75, 144, 145, 146 and n, 177-178, 177n, 179, 180

Buffalo, 11, 21, 104, 132, 193

Burch, J. H., 49, 63, 65, 161 and n, 162, 163, 188, 190, 192

Burns, William B., 50, 155 and n

Burnside, Ambrose, 49 and n, 50-51, 65, 191 and n, 192

Burtsell, 13, 120 and n, 122, 125, 127, 128

Byron, 111, 149

INDEX

C

Caird, Sir James, 46, 51
Cairo, 52, 53, 55, 58, 61, 150-152, 154, 155, 157, 185
Canada, 106, 108, 143, 149-150, 188, 216; comparison with America, 80, 104, 108, 149-150, 211, 215; country, 210, 213-216; fortification of, 9, 80, 213
Canada, 143
Canadian Legislative Assembly, 67, 149
Canandaigua, 109
Carey, Henry C., 173 and n
Cass, Lewis, 35, 64, 146 and n
Cassidy, William, 14, 111 and n
Catskill Mountains, 13, 121 and n, 122-125, 124n
Centralia, 52, 61, 151, 155, 160, 186
Century Club (New York), 69, 166
changes in United States, between 1835 and 1859, 59, 62, 70-71, 73, 74, 149, 169
Chase, Salmon P., 78-79, 181 and n, 209, 215
Cheever, George B., 164 and n
Chicago, 52, 53, 59, 61, 63, 65, 69, 74, 150, 160-163, 188, 190-193
Chouteau, Pierre, 49, 160 and n, 170n
Church, 1835, 14, 104, 107
Church, 1859, 62, 183, 195
Church, Frederick E., 148 and n
churches, Cobden's visit to, 115, 144, 163, 165, 166, 168-169, 173, 180, 185, 190, 194-195, 197-198; see also religion
Cincinnati, 61, 62, 65, 78, 180, 181, 182-183, 209, 215
Cisco, 196
Clark, Judge, 157
Cobden, Frederick, 39, 115 and n
Cobden, Henry, 11, 13, 88, 89, 103, 107, 127 and n, 128
Cobden, Richard, activities, influenced by things American, 17, 24, 26-34, 37, 121
admiration of things American, 20-21, 26, 27, 28-31, 33 and n, 66, 69, 71, 70-74, 120, 188 (attitude toward America, 24-37, 38, 57, 68-69, 70-74, 81, 152, as a trav-

eler, vii-viii; faith in America, 22, 23, 24, 26, 31-34, 68-69, 69n, 73-74, 150), see also changes in United States, 1835-1859; democracy in United States; economic conditions, in United States; education; Europe, comparisons of United States with; government of United States; people; progress or strength of United States; religion; schools; social conditions, in United States; travel, by Americans; women, treatment of
American attitude toward, 20, 62-66, 68, 98, 99; see also honor accorded to
author of, character sketches of fellow-passengers, 15, 134-139; pamphlets, 4, 7, 11 and n
characterization of, 4, 10, 14, 15, 16, 66, 67, 69-70, 81, 101, 104-105, 109, 149
disapproval of America, 35-36, 67, 145, 200
early years of, 4
entertainment of, in 1859, 63-66, 144-145, 146, 147, 148, 156, 160, 162, 163, 164, 165, 166, 167, 168, 169, 170, 171-172, 173, 176, 177, 180, 182, 183, 184, 188, 189, 190, 191, 192, 193, 196, 197, 198, 201, 202, 203, 204, 205, 211, 212, 213
estimate of, 3-4, 9-10, 69-70
honor accorded to, in America, 62-66, 144-145, 150, 160, 162, 166, 168, 177, 181, 183, 190, 197, 199, 200; see also entertainment of
and the Illinois Central Railroad, 39, 40-41, 41-58; see Illinois Central Railroad
interest of, in America, 25-26, 57n; in Illinois, 1835, 17, 109, 113; in the Irish, 1835, 98, 110, 111, 116, 117, 125, 128; interests of, later, as indicated in 1835 diary, 16-17, in America, 1859, 66-70
life of, 3-10
opposition of, to imperialism, 10, 33, 85, to intervention, 10, 31, 35, 36-37
trips of, to United States, see trip to United States, 1835, 1859